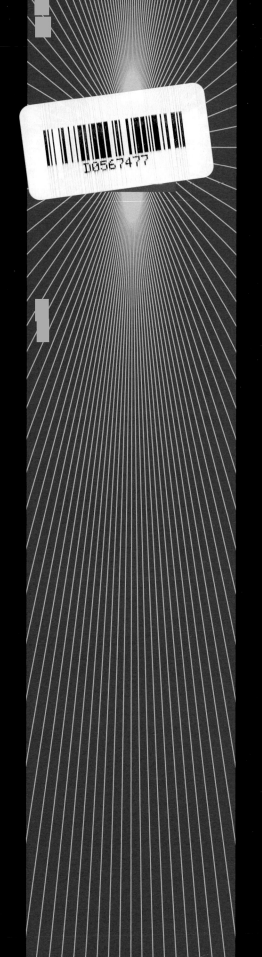

WILDSTORM: MICHAEL CRAY VOLUME 1

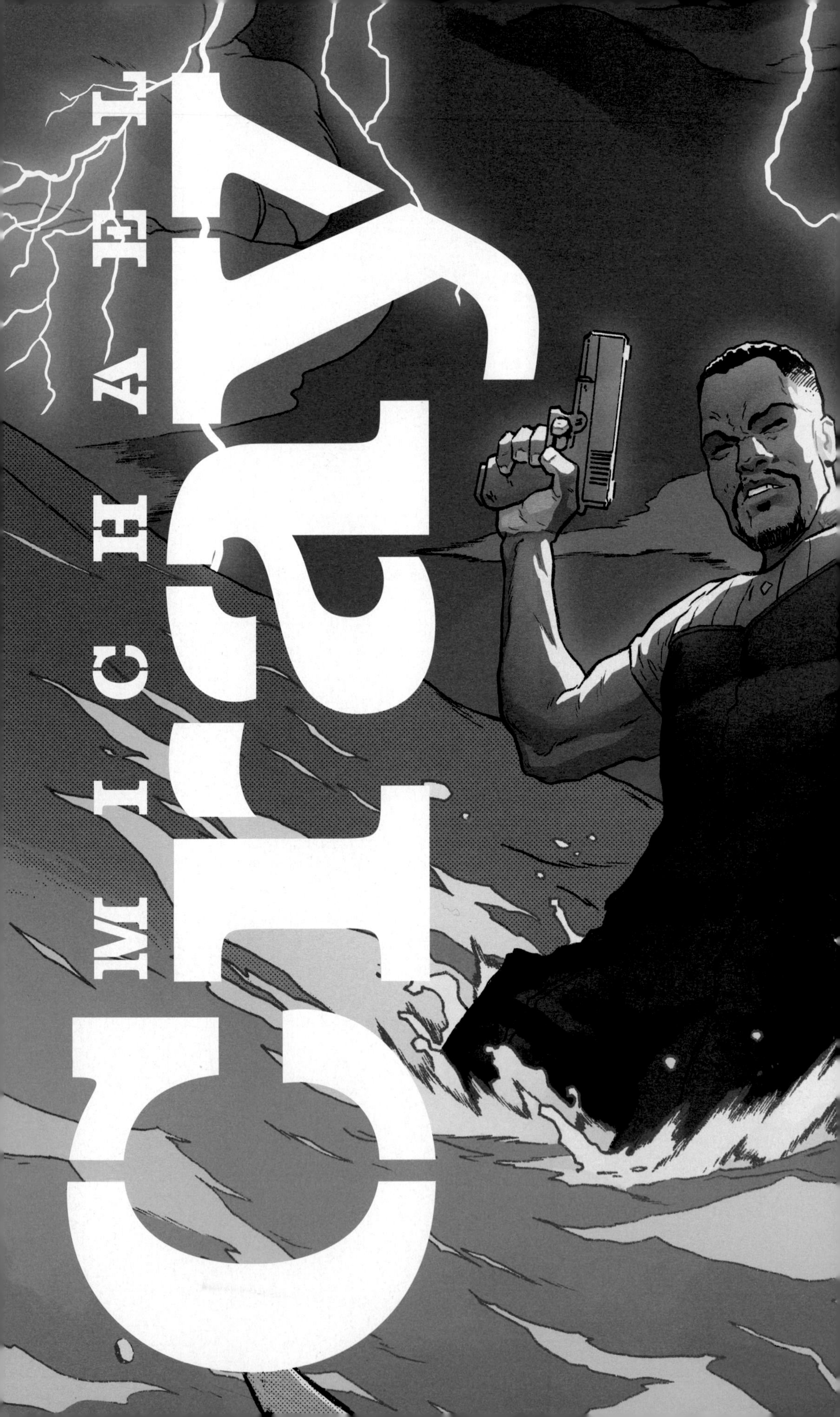
MICHAEL
CRAY

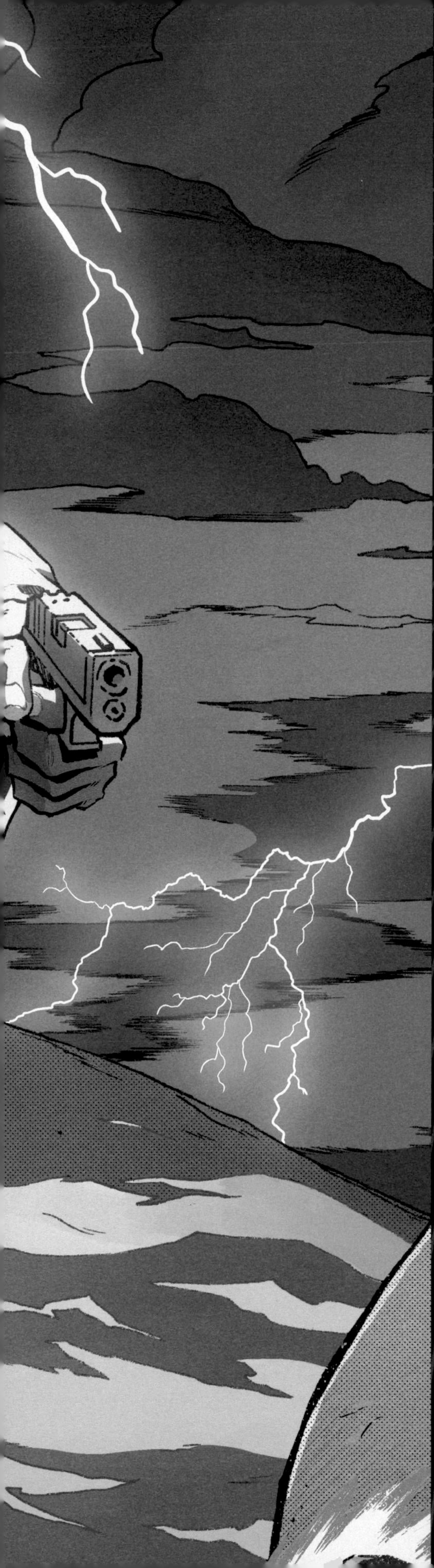

WILDSTORM
MICHAEL CRAY
VOLUME 1

BRYAN HILL
writer

N. STEVEN HARRIS
penciller

LARRY HAMA
breakdowns
[issues #4-6]

DEXTER VINES
ANDY OWENS
inkers

DEARBHLA KELLY
STEVE BUCCELLATO
colorists

SIMON BOWLAND
letterer

KHARY RANDOLPH
and **EMILIO LOPEZ**
collection cover
artists

Based on a story by
WARREN ELLIS

MICHAEL CRAY
created by
JIM LEE and
BRANDON CHOI

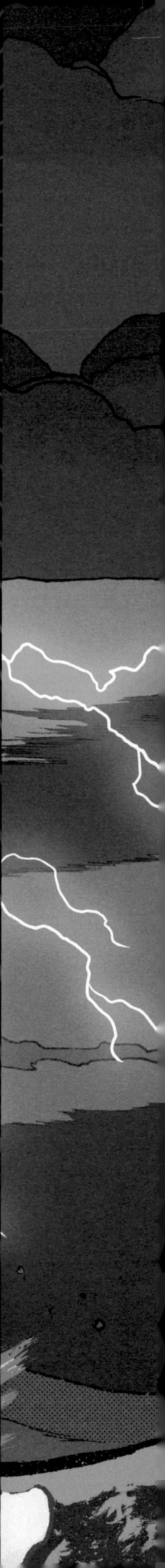

MARIE JAVINS	Editor – Original Series
DIEGO LOPEZ, ROB LEVIN	Assistant Editors – Original Series
JEB WOODARD	Group Editor – Collected Editions
STEVE COOK	Design Director – Books and Publication Design
BOB HARRAS	Senior VP – Editor-in-Chief, DC Comics
PAT McCALLUM	Executive Editor, DC Comics
DIANE NELSON	President
DAN DiDIO	Publisher
JIM LEE	Publisher
GEOFF JOHNS	President & Chief Creative Officer
AMIT DESAI	Executive VP – Business & Marketing Strategy, Direct to Consumer & Global Franchise Management
SAM ADES	Senior VP & General Manager, Digital Services
BOBBIE CHASE	VP & Executive Editor, Young Reader & Talent Development
MARK CHIARELLO	Senior VP – Art, Design & Collected Editions
JOHN CUNNINGHAM	Senior VP – Sales & Trade Marketing
ANNE DePIES	Senior VP – Business Strategy, Finance & Administration
DON FALLETTI	VP – Manufacturing Operations
LAWRENCE GANEM	VP – Editorial Administration & Talent Relations
ALISON GILL	Senior VP – Manufacturing & Operations
HANK KANALZ	Senior VP – Editorial Strategy & Administration
JAY KOGAN	VP – Legal Affairs
JACK MAHAN	VP – Business Affairs
NICK J. NAPOLITANO	VP – Manufacturing Administration
EDDIE SCANNELL	VP – Consumer Marketing
COURTNEY SIMMONS	Senior VP – Publicity & Communications
JIM (SKI) SOKOLOWSKI	VP – Comic Book Specialty Sales & Trade Marketing
NANCY SPEARS	VP – Mass, Book, Digital Sales & Trade Marketing
MICHELE R. WELLS	VP – Content Strategy

WILDSTORM: MICHAEL CRAY VOLUME 1

DC Comics, 2900 West Alameda Ave., Burbank, CA 91505
Printed by LSC Communications, Kendallville, IN, USA. 6/15/18.
First Printing. ISBN: 978-1-4012-8105-2

Library of Congress Cataloging-in-Publication Data is available.

PEFC Certified

Printed on paper from sustainably managed forests, controlled sources

PEFC/29-31-337   www.pefc.org

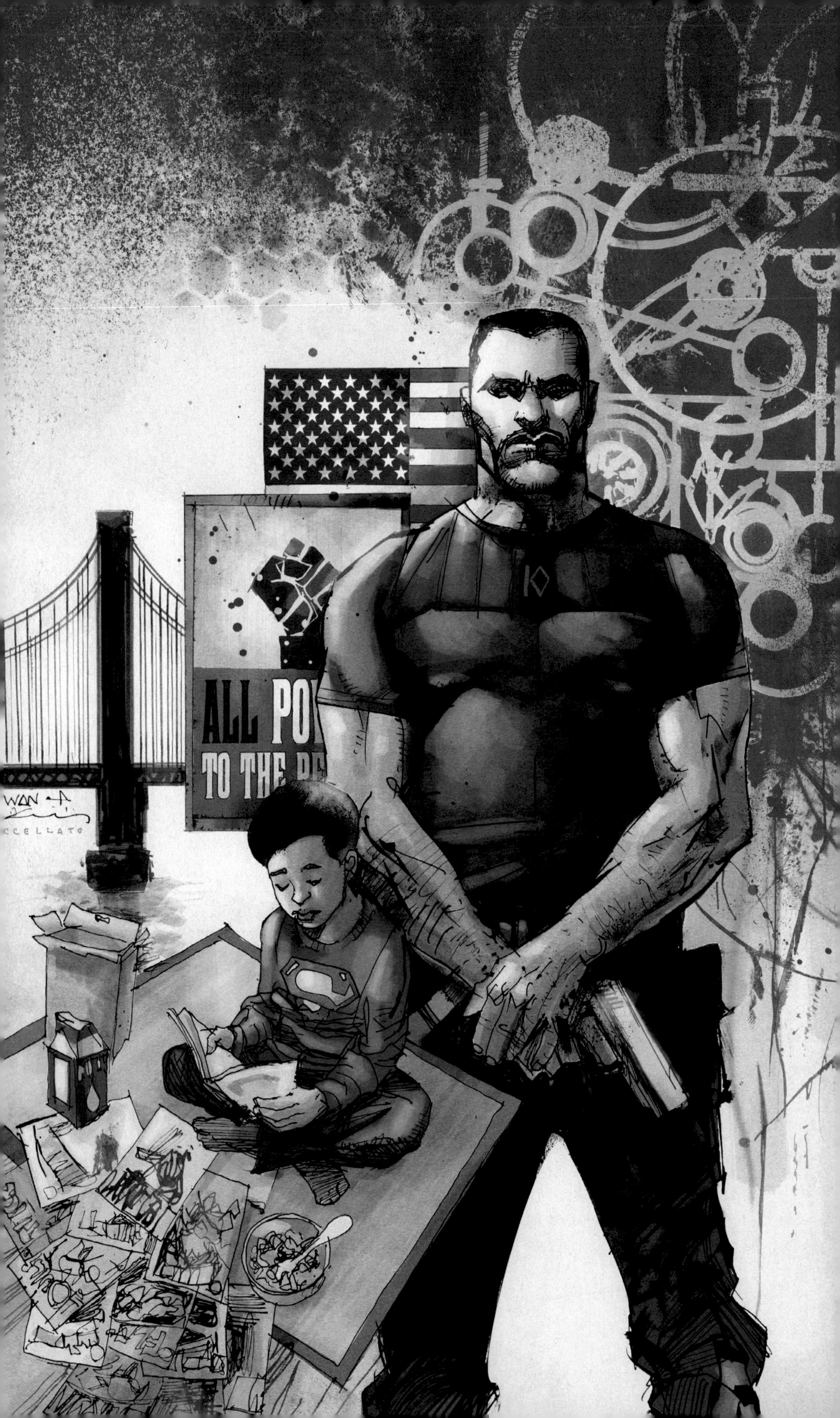
ALL PO
TO THE

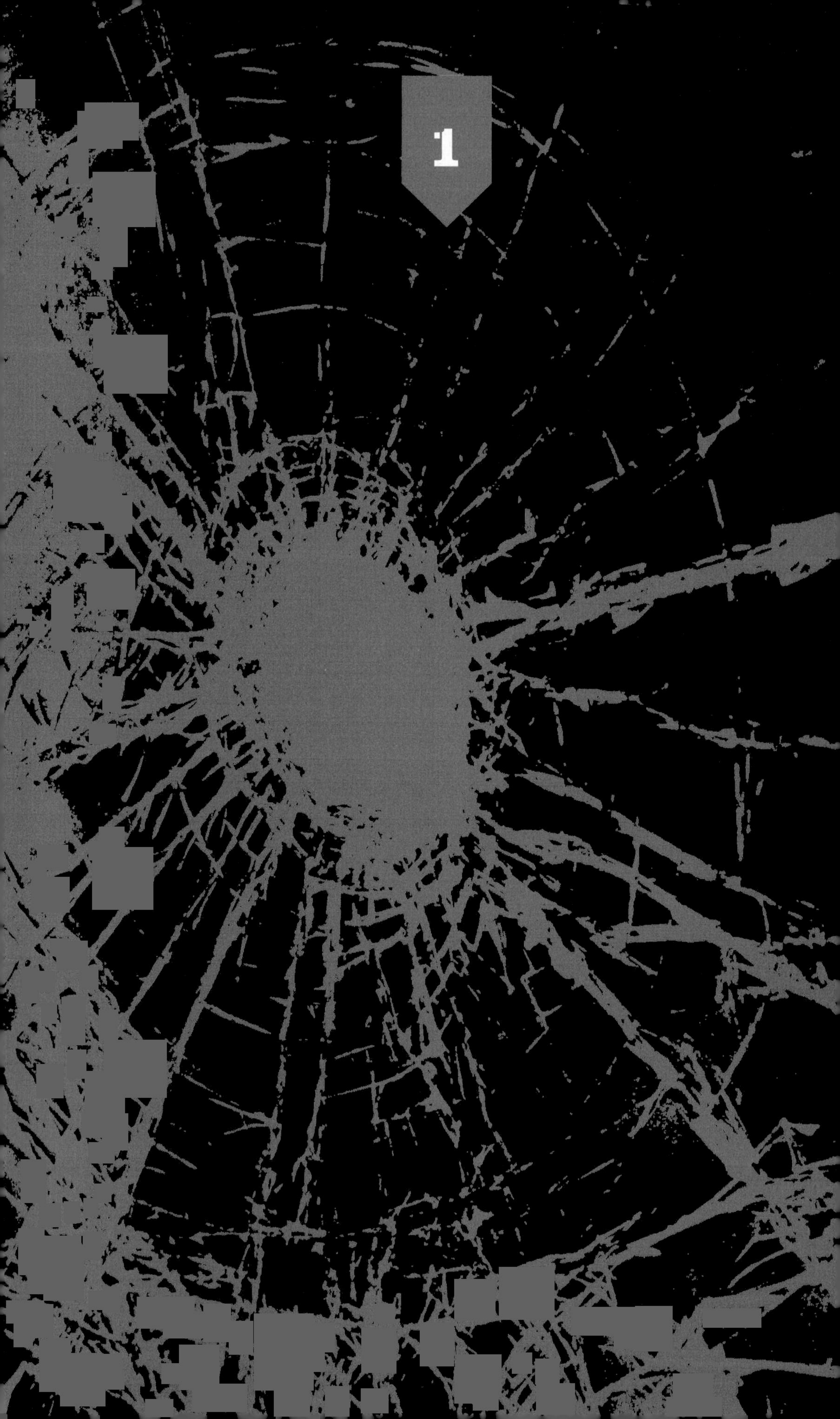
1

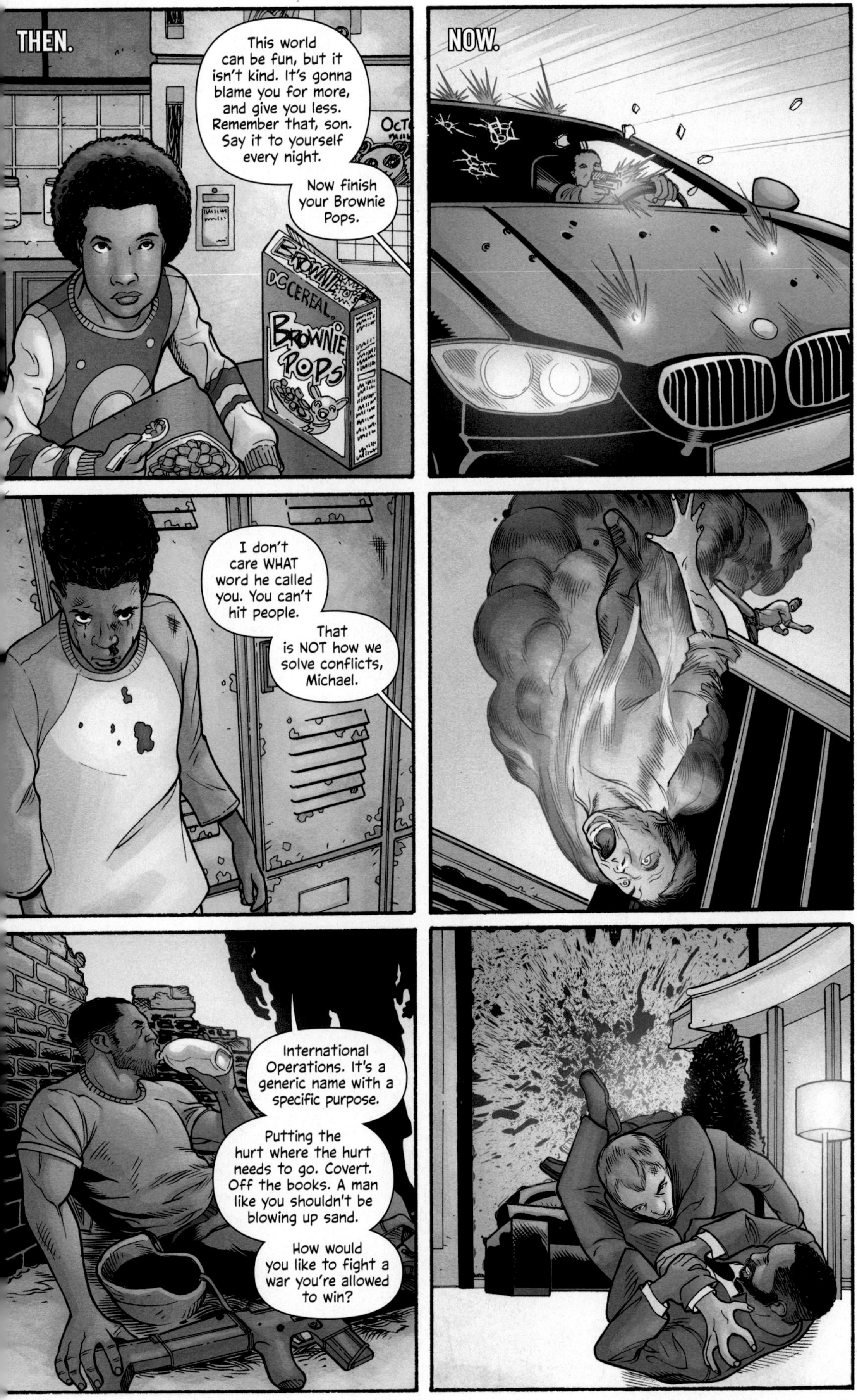
THEN.
This world can be fun, but it isn't kind. It's gonna blame you for more, and give you less. Remember that, son. Say it to yourself every night.
Now finish your Brownie Pops.
DC CEREAL.
BROWNIE POPS
NOW.
I don't care WHAT word he called you. You can't hit people.
That is NOT how we solve conflicts, Michael.
International Operations. It's a generic name with a specific purpose.
Putting the hurt where the hurt needs to go. Covert. Off the books. A man like you shouldn't be blowing up sand.
How would you like to fight a war you're allowed to win?

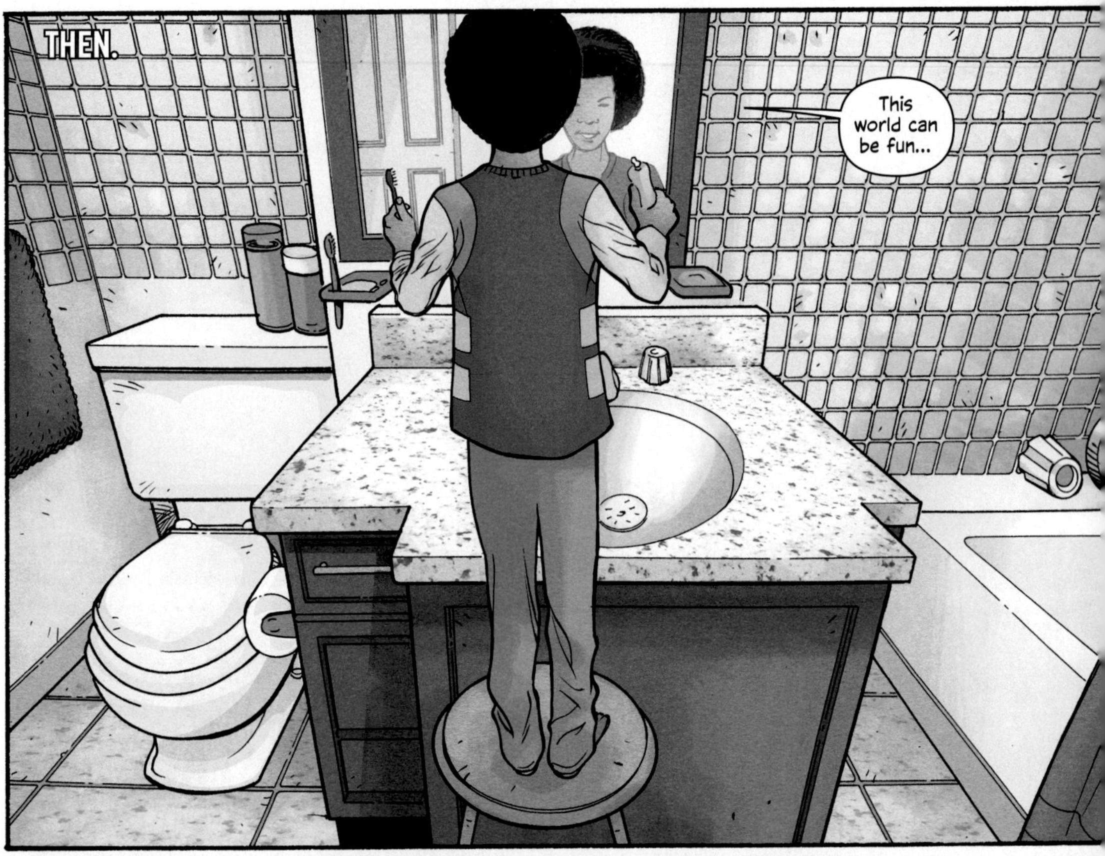
THEN.
This world can be fun...

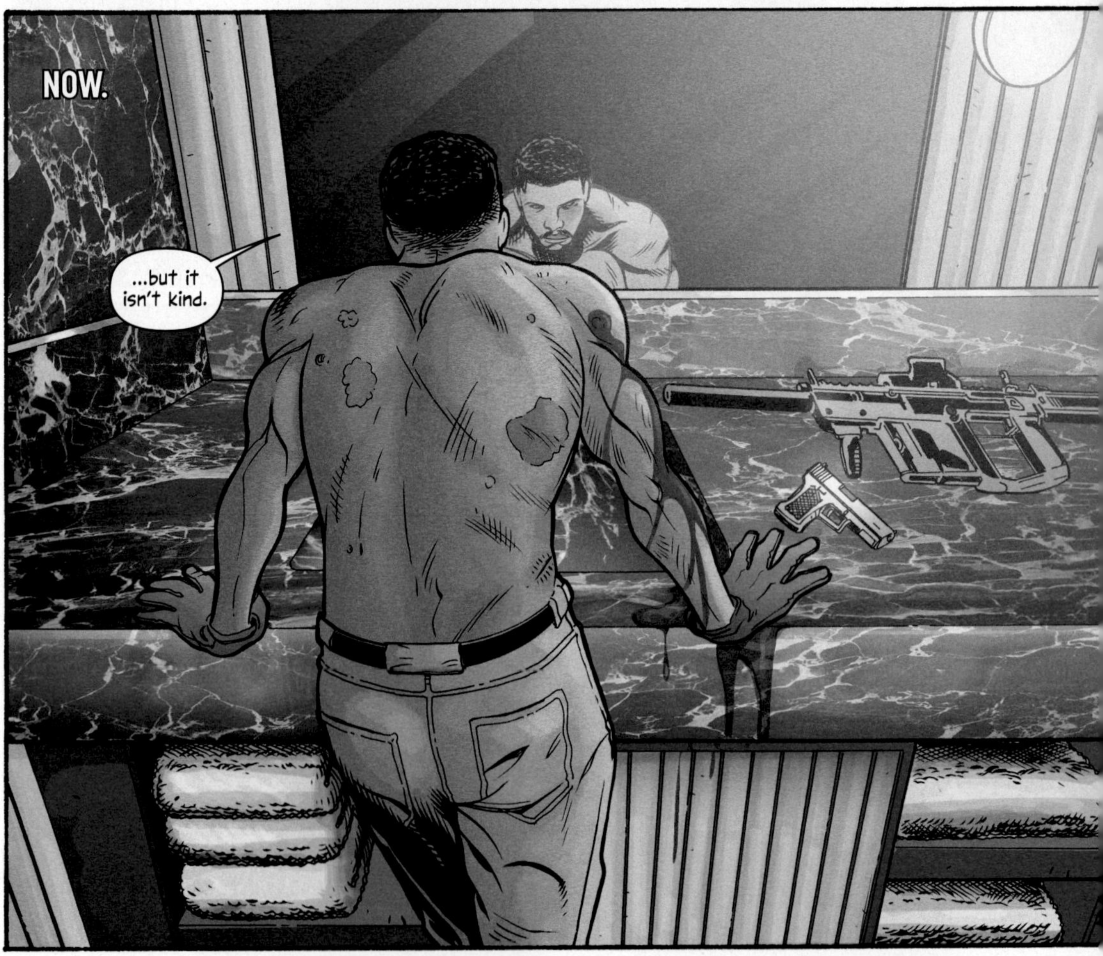
NOW.
...but it isn't kind.

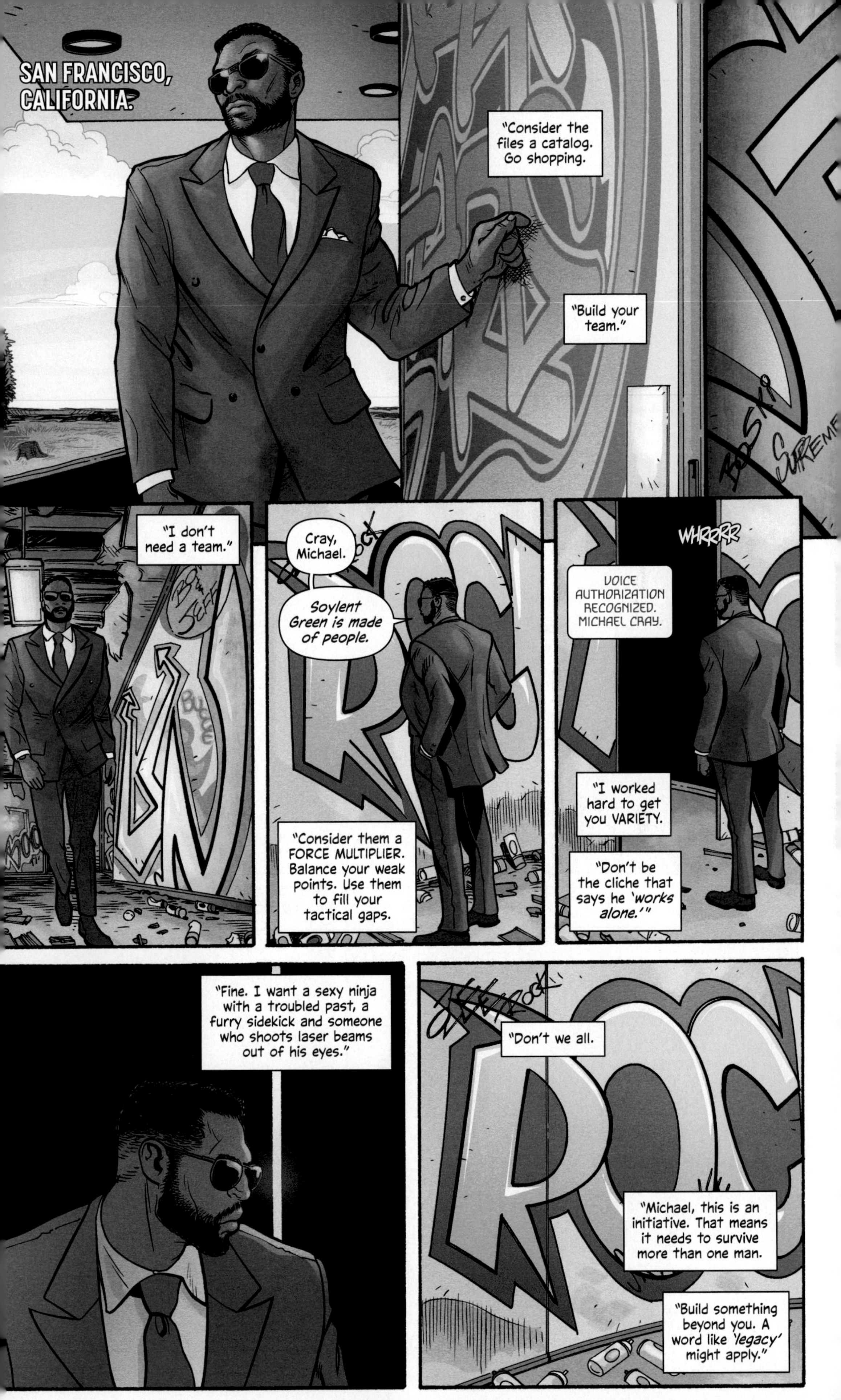

SAN FRANCISCO, CALIFORNIA.
"Consider the files a catalog. Go shopping.
"Build your team."
"I don't need a team."
Cray, Michael.
Soylent Green is made of people.
"Consider them a FORCE MULTIPLIER. Balance your weak points. Use them to fill your tactical gaps.
WHRRRR
VOICE AUTHORIZATION RECOGNIZED. MICHAEL CRAY.
"I worked hard to get you VARIETY.
"Don't be the cliche that says he 'works alone.'"
"Fine. I want a sexy ninja with a troubled past, a furry sidekick and someone who shoots laser beams out of his eyes."
"Don't we all.
"Michael, this is an initiative. That means it needs to survive more than one man.
"Build something beyond you. A word like 'legacy' might apply."

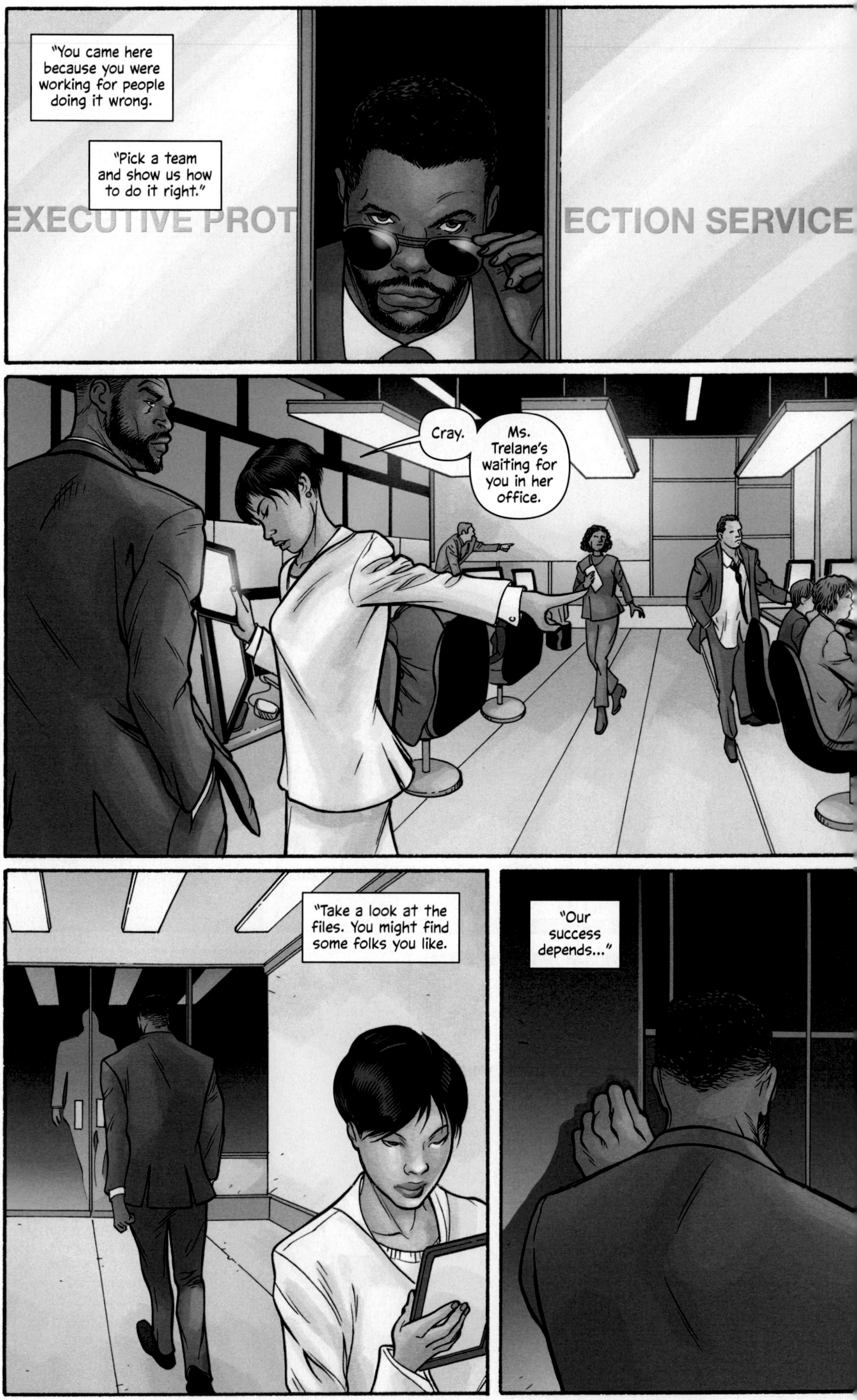
"You came here because you were working for people doing it wrong.
"Pick a team and show us how to do it right."
EXECUTIVE PROTECTION SERVICE
Cray.
Ms. Trelane's waiting for you in her office.
"Take a look at the files. You might find some folks you like.
"Our success depends..."

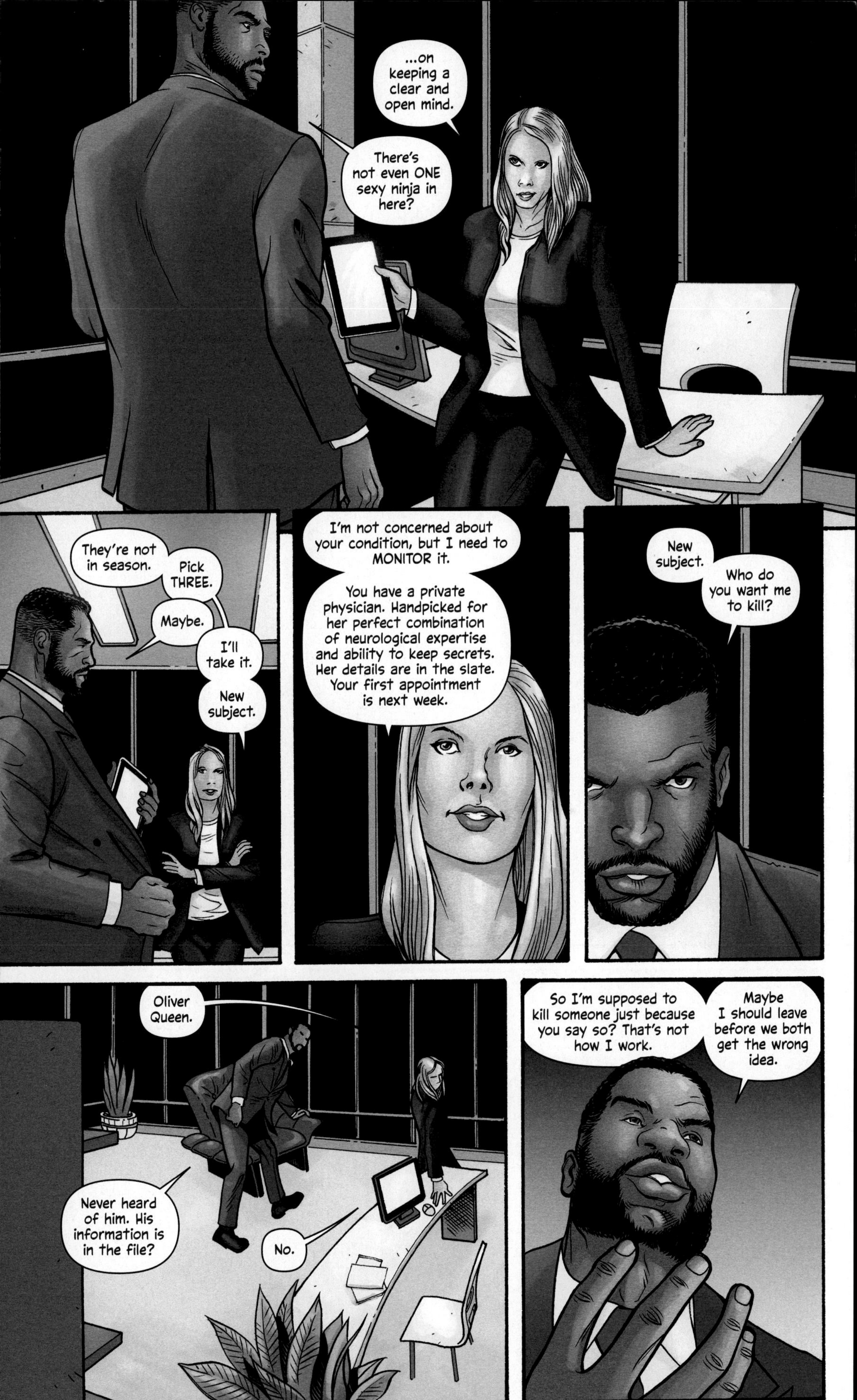
...on keeping a clear and open mind.
There's not even ONE sexy ninja in here?
They're not in season.
Pick THREE.
Maybe.
I'll take it.
New subject.
I'm not concerned about your condition, but I need to MONITOR it.
You have a private physician. Handpicked for her perfect combination of neurological expertise and ability to keep secrets. Her details are in the slate. Your first appointment is next week.
New subject.
Who do you want me to kill?
Oliver Queen.
Never heard of him. His information is in the file?
No.
So I'm supposed to kill someone just because you say so? That's not how I work.
Maybe I should leave before we both get the wrong idea.

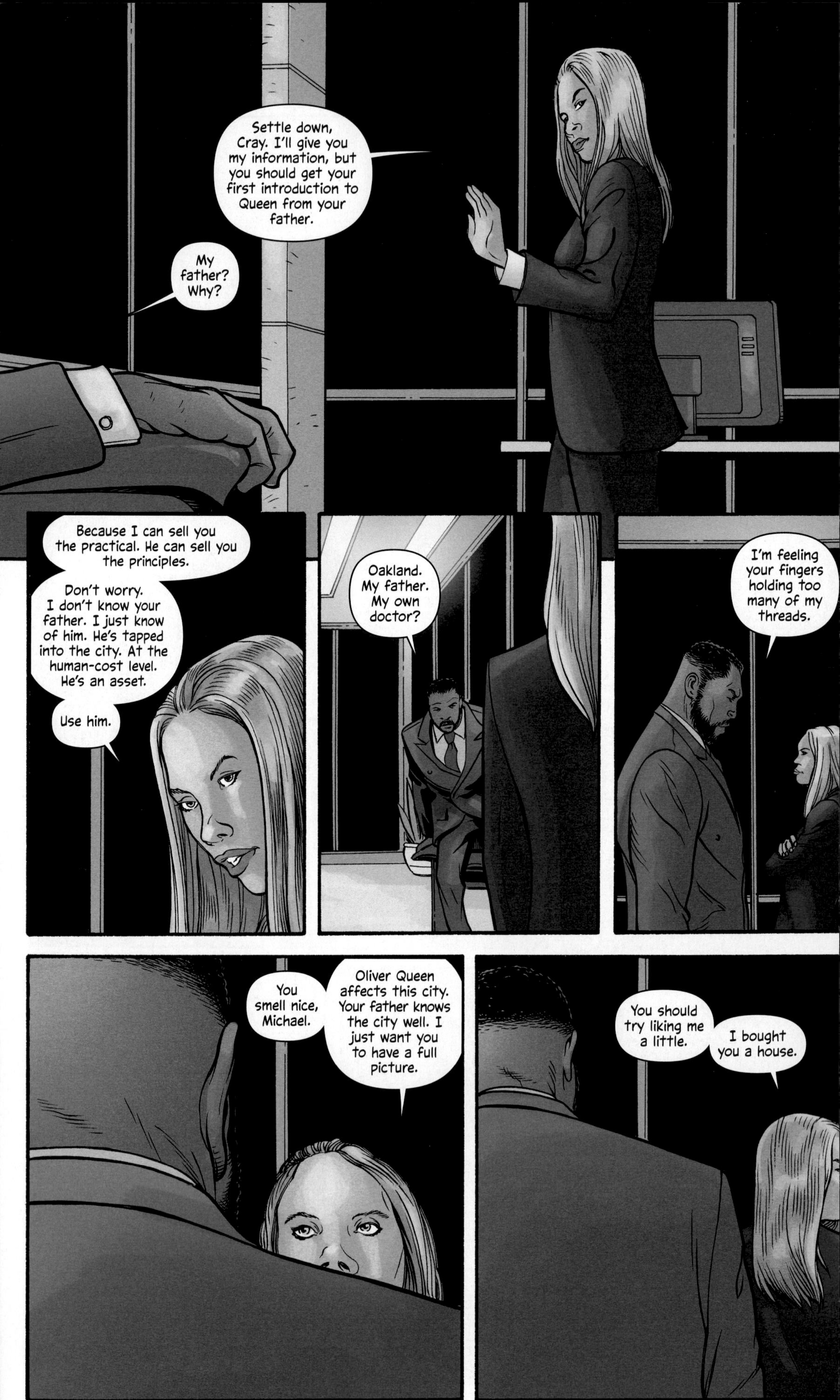
Settle down, Cray. I'll give you my information, but you should get your first introduction to Queen from your father.
My father? Why?
Because I can sell you the practical. He can sell you the principles.
Don't worry. I don't know your father. I just know of him. He's tapped into the city. At the human-cost level. He's an asset.
Use him.
Oakland. My father. My own doctor?
I'm feeling your fingers holding too many of my threads.
You smell nice, Michael.
Oliver Queen affects this city. Your father knows the city well. I just want you to have a full picture.
You should try liking me a little.
I bought you a house.

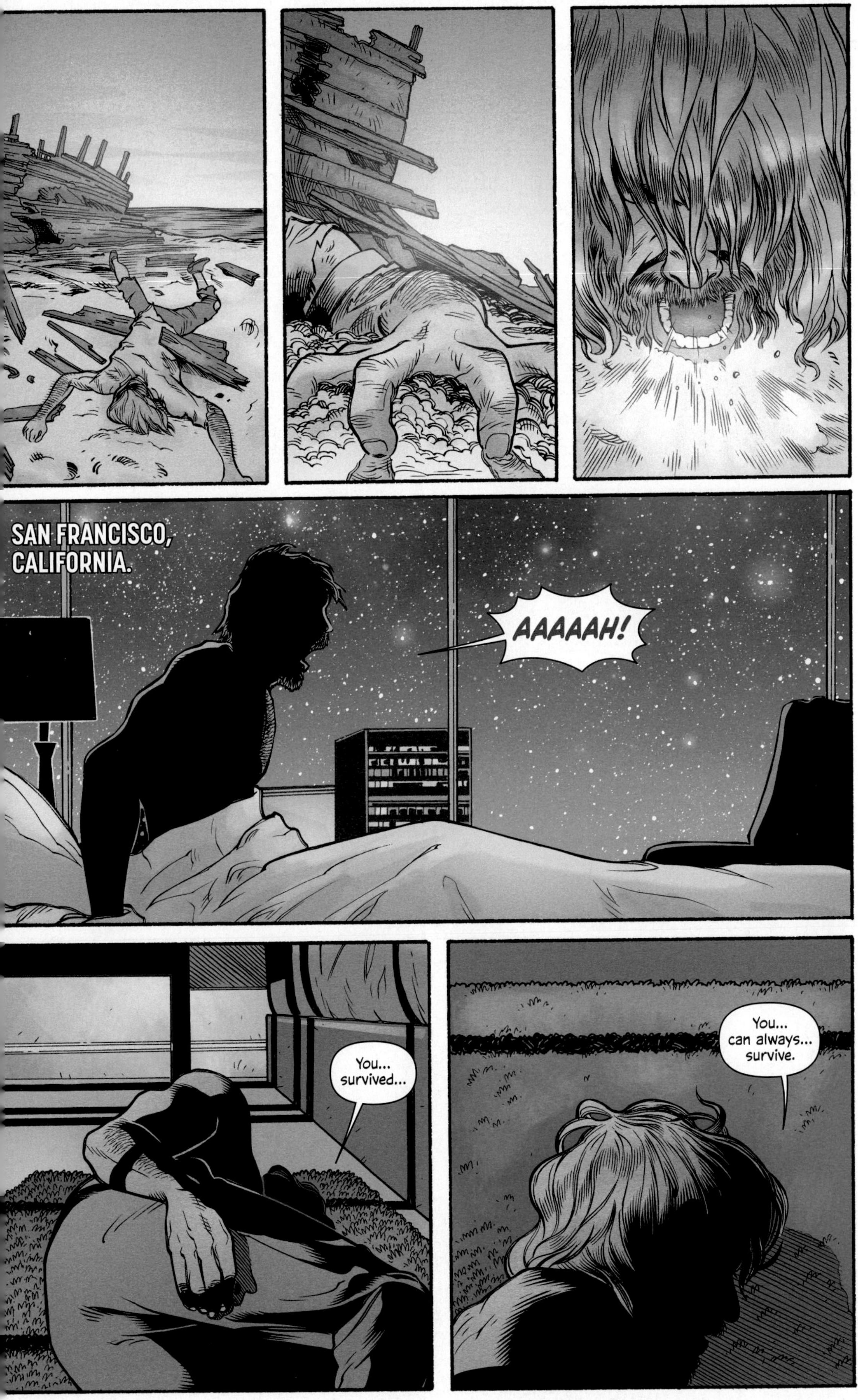
SAN FRANCISCO, CALIFORNIA.
AAAAAH!
You... survived...
You... can always... survive.

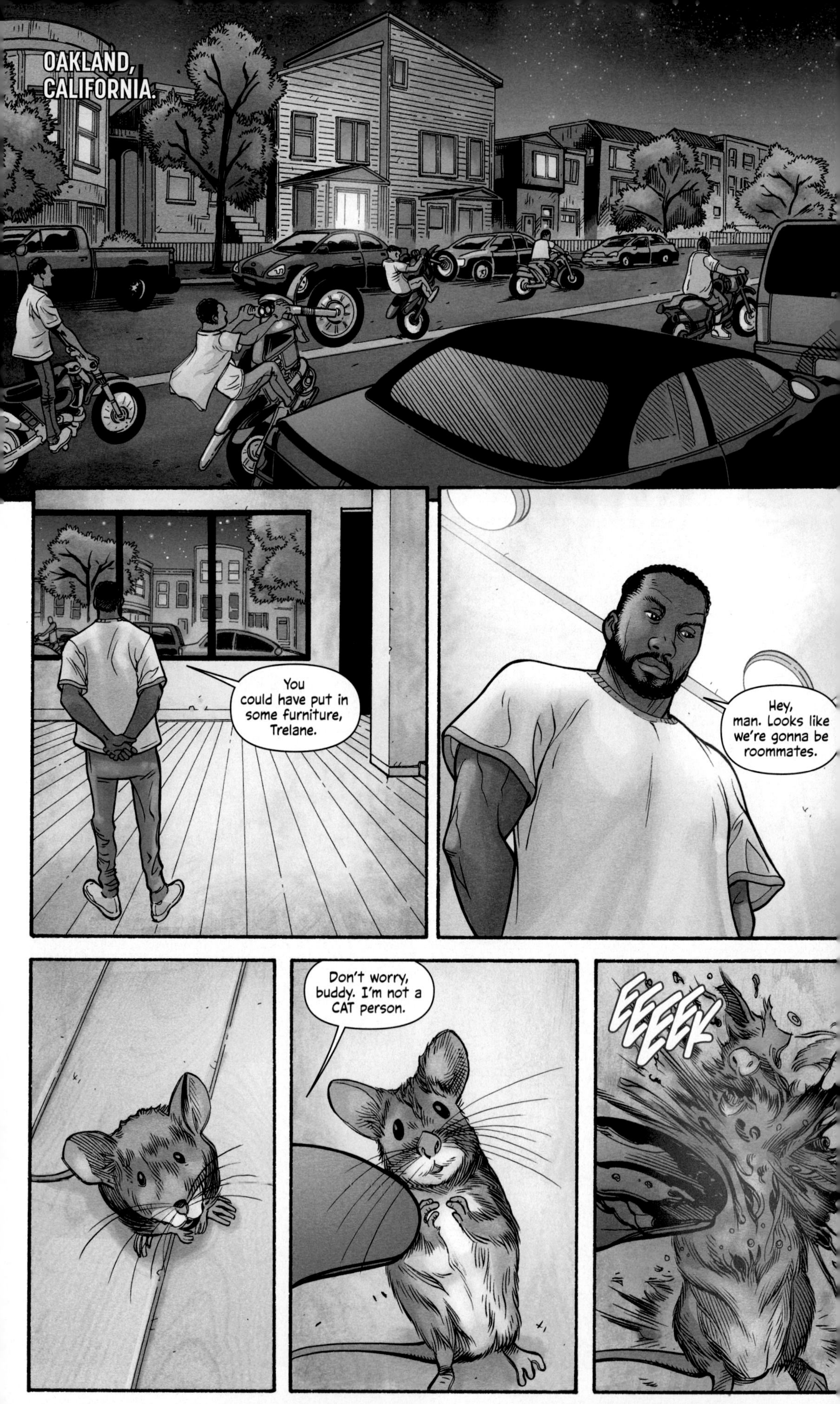
OAKLAND, CALIFORNIA.
You could have put in some furniture, Trelane.
Hey, man. Looks like we're gonna be roommates.
Don't worry, buddy. I'm not a CAT person.
EEEEK

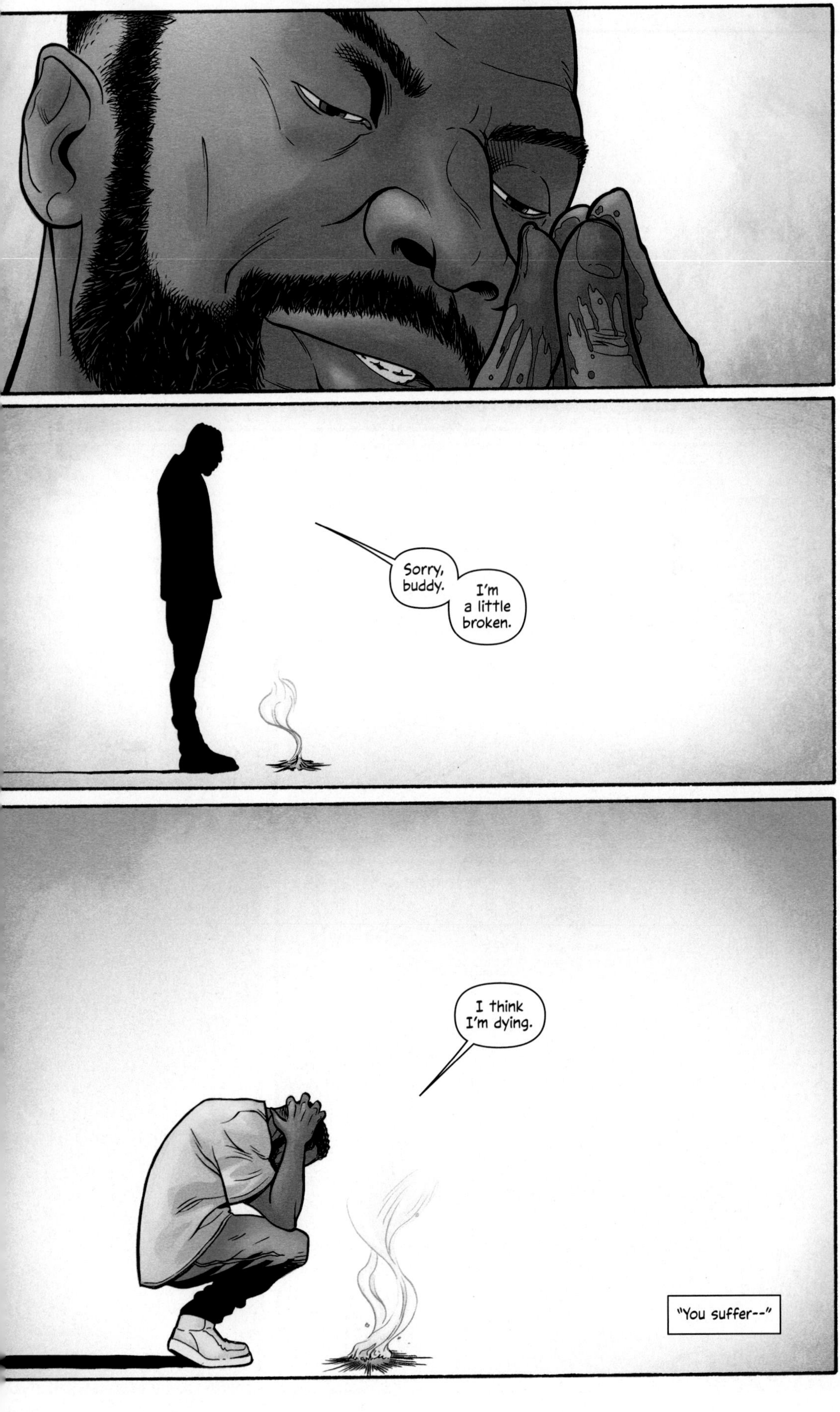
Sorry, buddy.
I'm a little broken.
I think I'm dying.
"You suffer--"

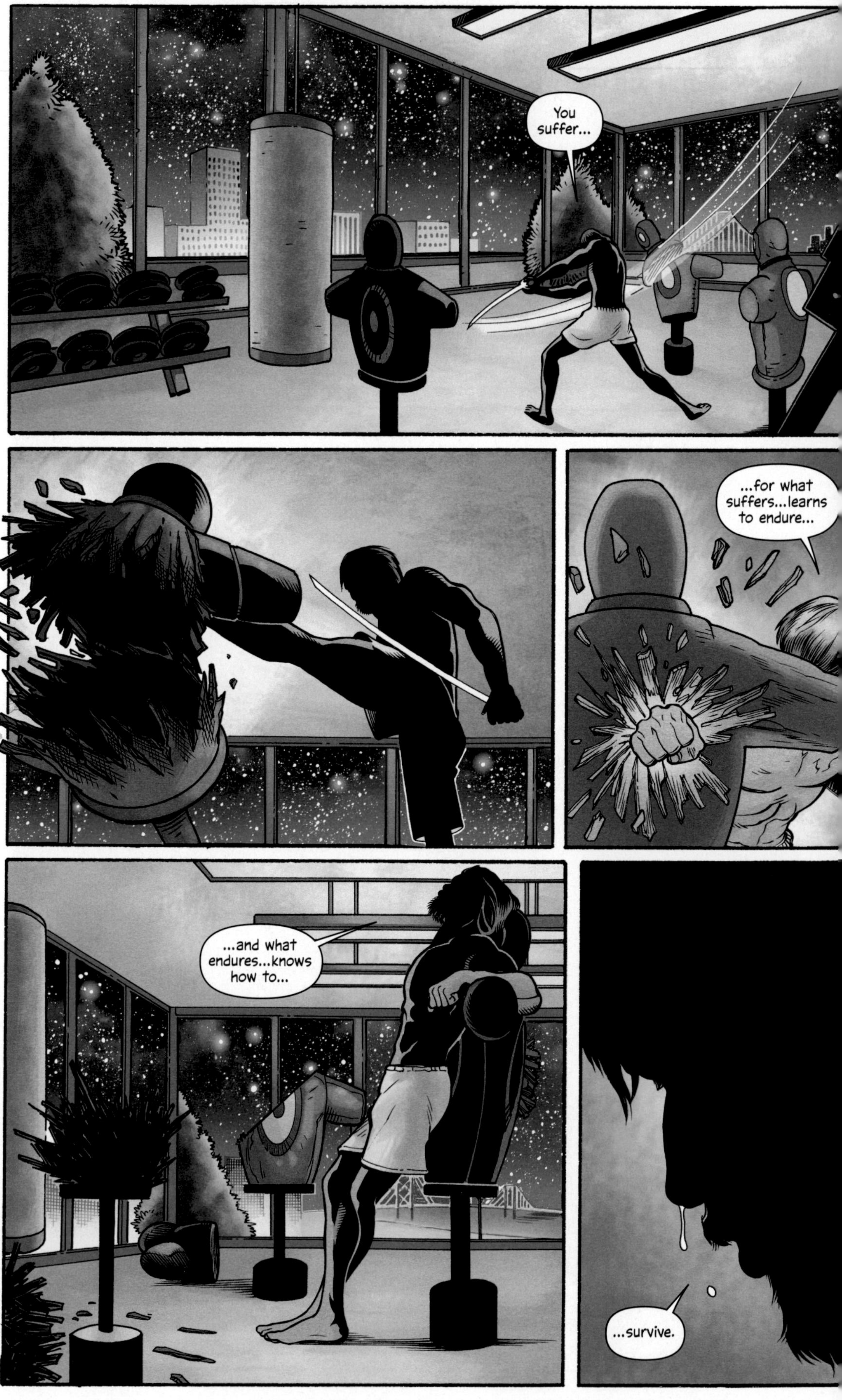
You suffer...
...for what suffers...learns to endure...
...and what endures...knows how to...
...survive.

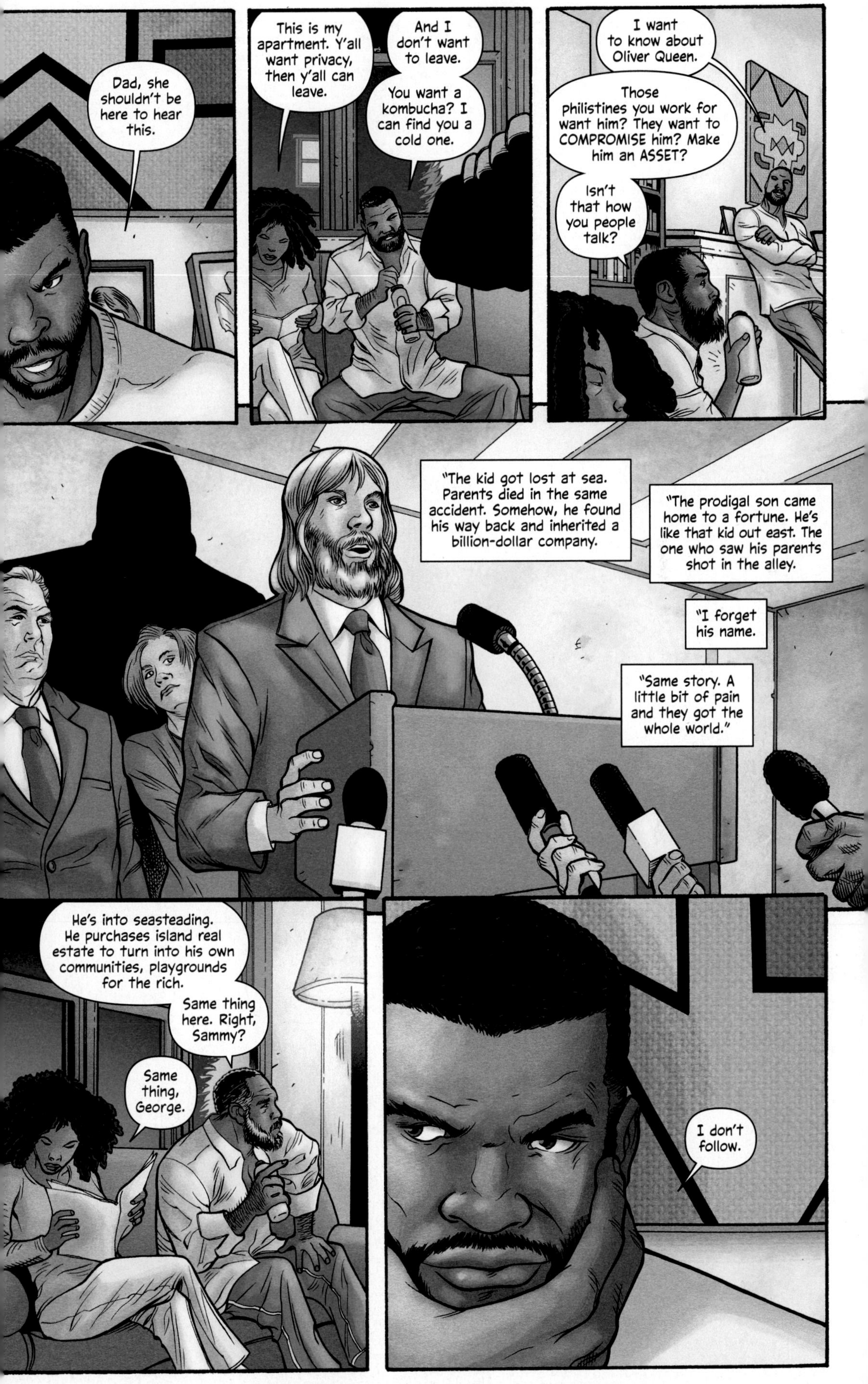
Dad, she shouldn't be here to hear this.
This is my apartment. Y'all want privacy, then y'all can leave.
And I don't want to leave.
You want a kombucha? I can find you a cold one.
I want to know about Oliver Queen.
Those philistines you work for want him? They want to COMPROMISE him? Make him an ASSET?
Isn't that how you people talk?
"The kid got lost at sea. Parents died in the same accident. Somehow, he found his way back and inherited a billion-dollar company.
"The prodigal son came home to a fortune. He's like that kid out east. The one who saw his parents shot in the alley.
"I forget his name.
"Same story. A little bit of pain and they got the whole world."
He's into seasteading. He purchases island real estate to turn into his own communities, playgrounds for the rich.
Same thing here. Right, Sammy?
Same thing, George.
I don't follow.

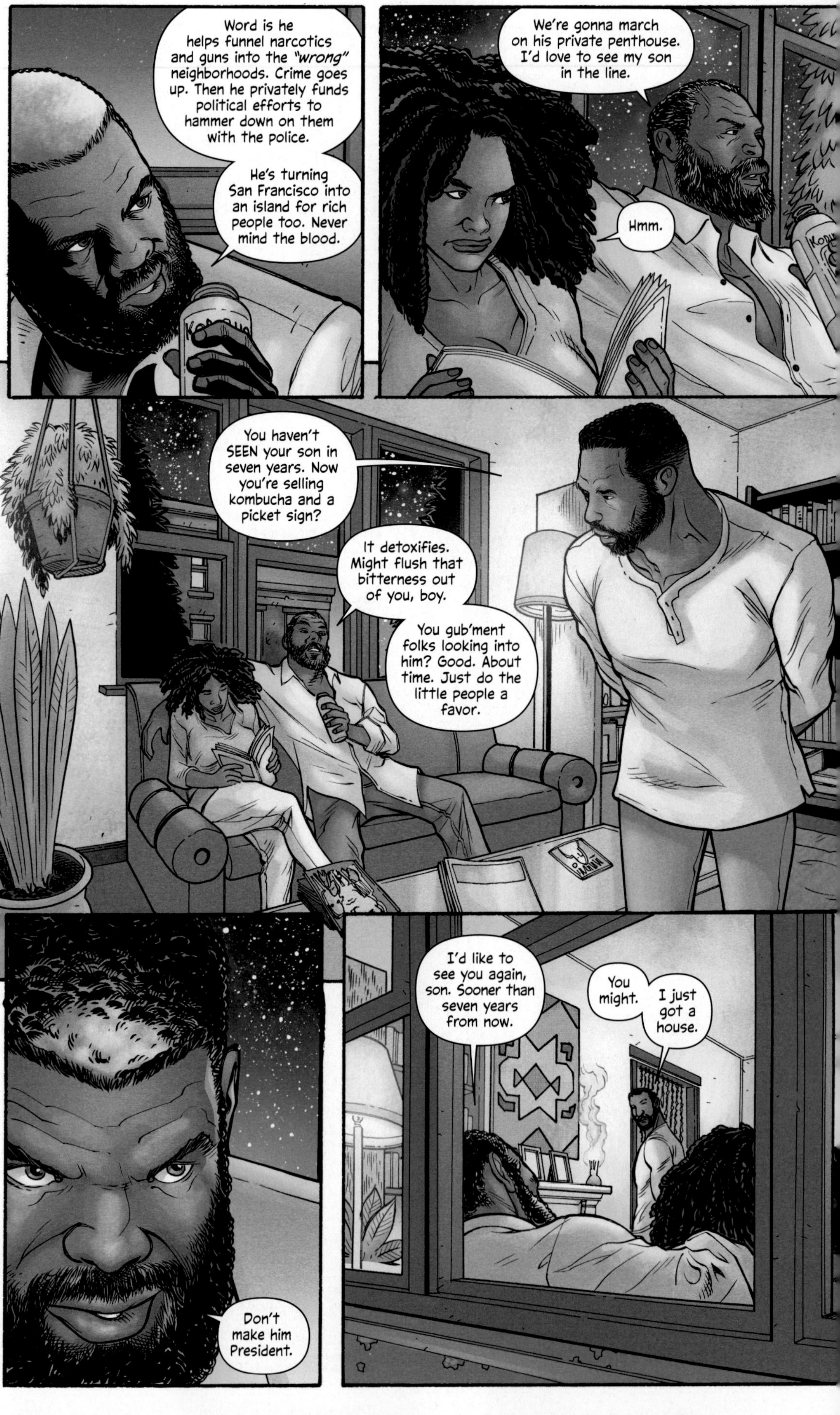
Word is he helps funnel narcotics and guns into the *"wrong"* neighborhoods. Crime goes up. Then he privately funds political efforts to hammer down on them with the police.
He's turning San Francisco into an island for rich people too. Never mind the blood.
We're gonna march on his private penthouse. I'd love to see my son in the line.
Hmm.
You haven't SEEN your son in seven years. Now you're selling kombucha and a picket sign?
It detoxifies. Might flush that bitterness out of you, boy.
You gub'ment folks looking into him? Good. About time. Just do the little people a favor.
Don't make him President.
I'd like to see you again, son. Sooner than seven years from now.
You might.
I just got a house.

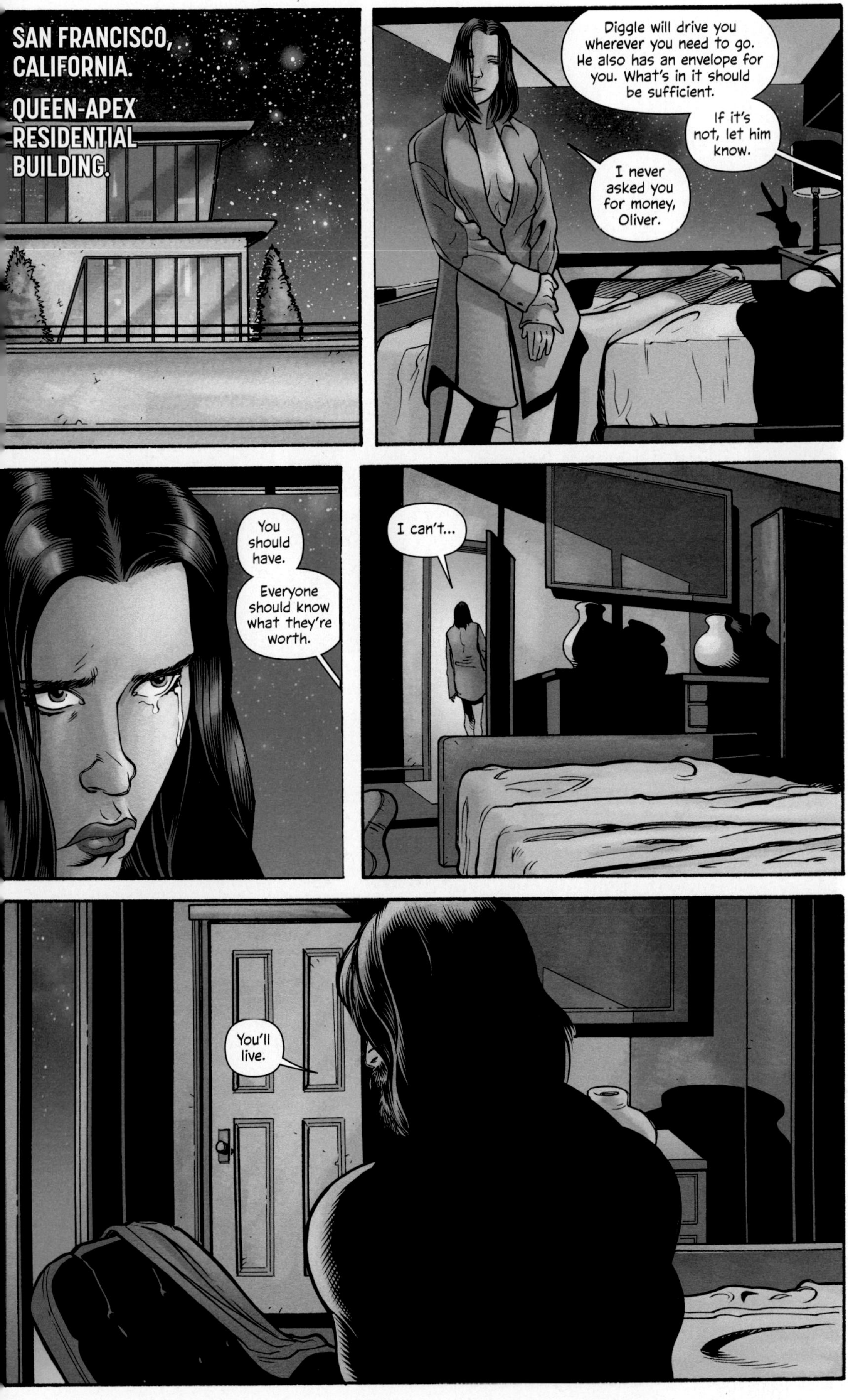

SAN FRANCISCO, CALIFORNIA.
QUEEN-APEX RESIDENTIAL BUILDING.
Diggle will drive you wherever you need to go. He also has an envelope for you. What's in it should be sufficient.
If it's not, let him know.
I never asked you for money, Oliver.
You should have.
Everyone should know what they're worth.
I can't...
You'll live.

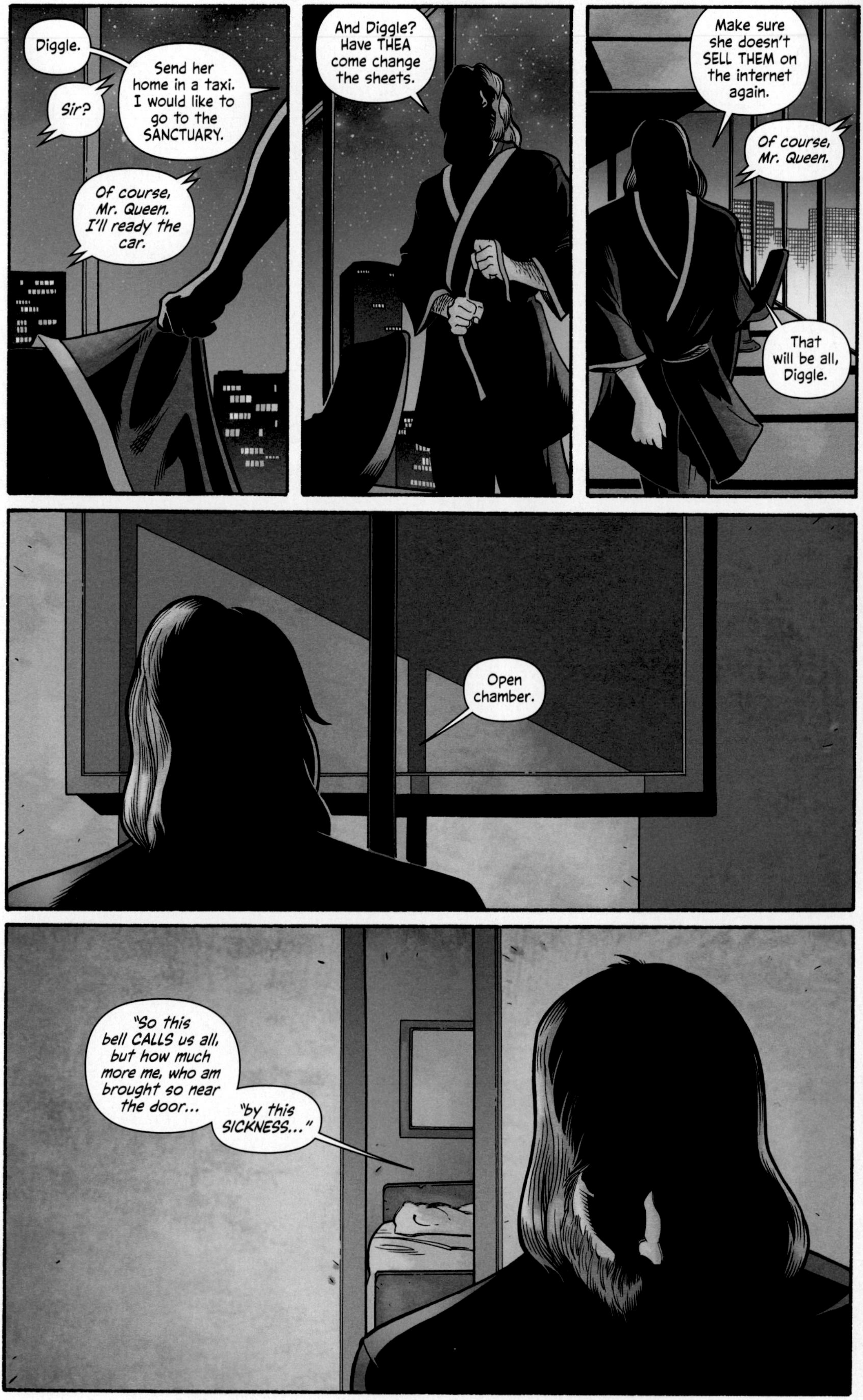
Diggle.
Sir?
Send her home in a taxi. I would like to go to the SANCTUARY.
Of course, Mr. Queen. I'll ready the car.
And Diggle? Have THEA come change the sheets.
Make sure she doesn't SELL THEM on the internet again.
Of course, Mr. Queen.
That will be all, Diggle.
Open chamber.
"So this bell CALLS us all, but how much more me, who am brought so near the door...
"by this SICKNESS..."

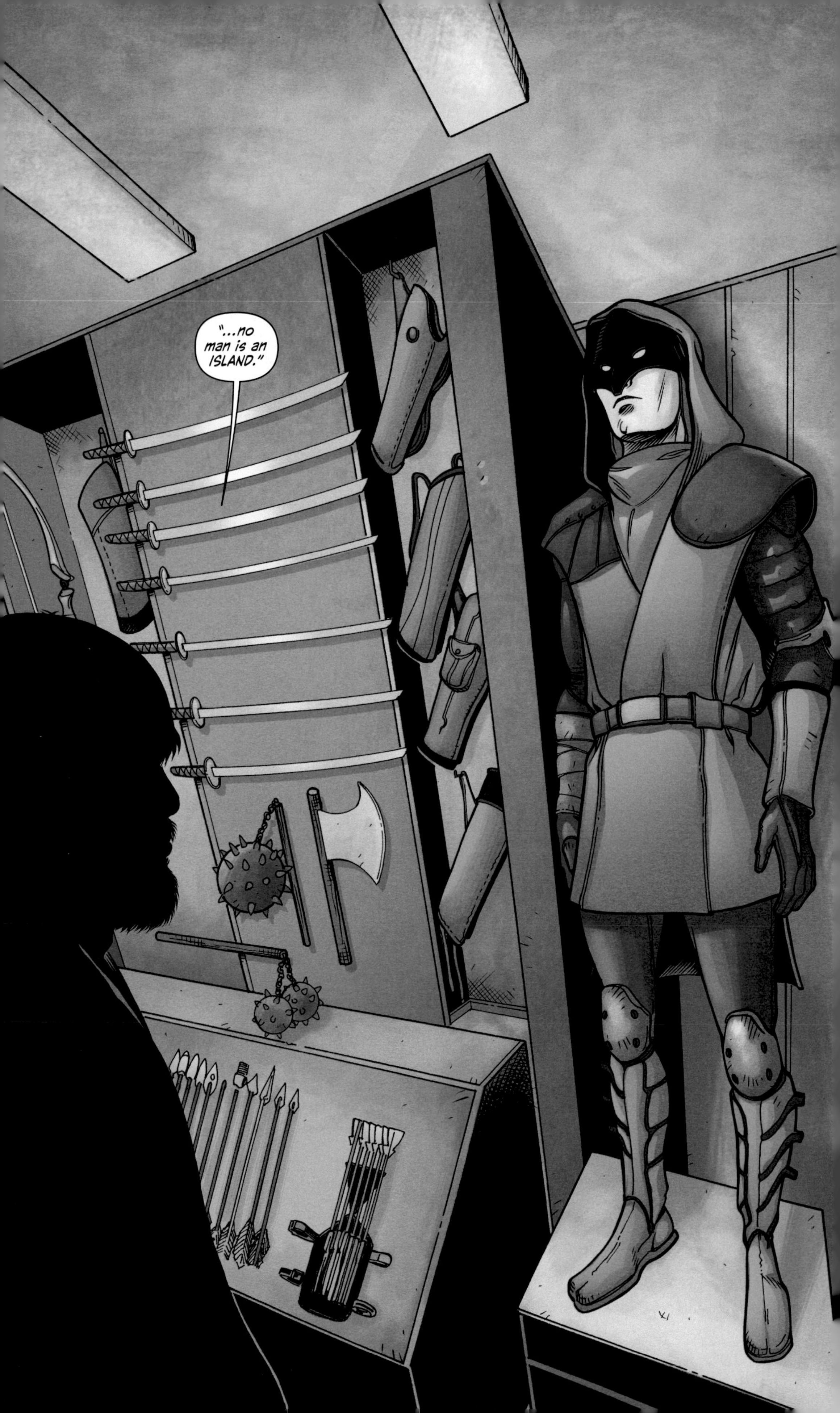
"...no man is an ISLAND."

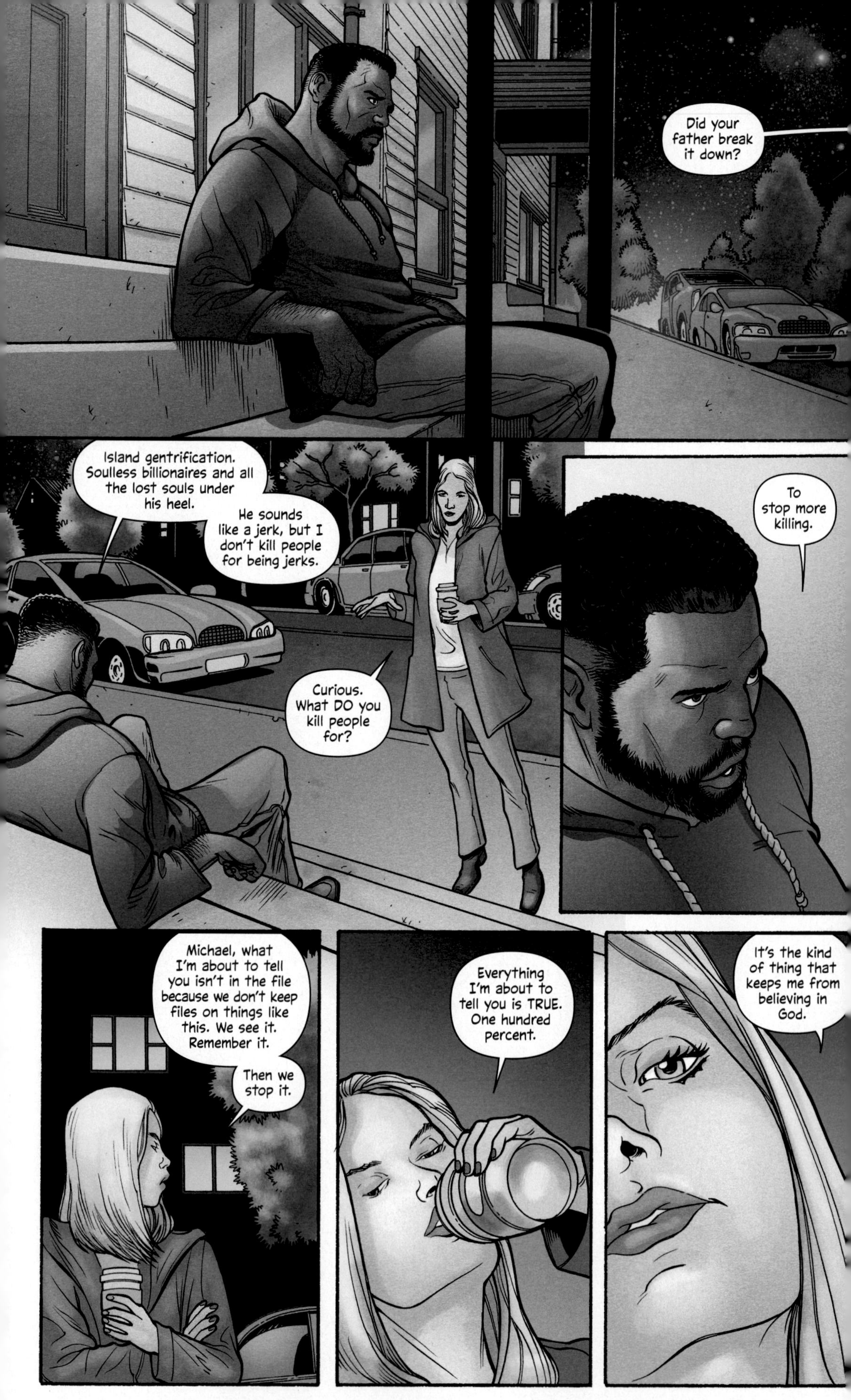
Did your father break it down?
Island gentrification. Soulless billionaires and all the lost souls under his heel.
He sounds like a jerk, but I don't kill people for being jerks.
Curious. What DO you kill people for?
To stop more killing.
Michael, what I'm about to tell you isn't in the file because we don't keep files on things like this. We see it. Remember it.
Then we stop it.
Everything I'm about to tell you is TRUE. One hundred percent.
It's the kind of thing that keeps me from believing in God.

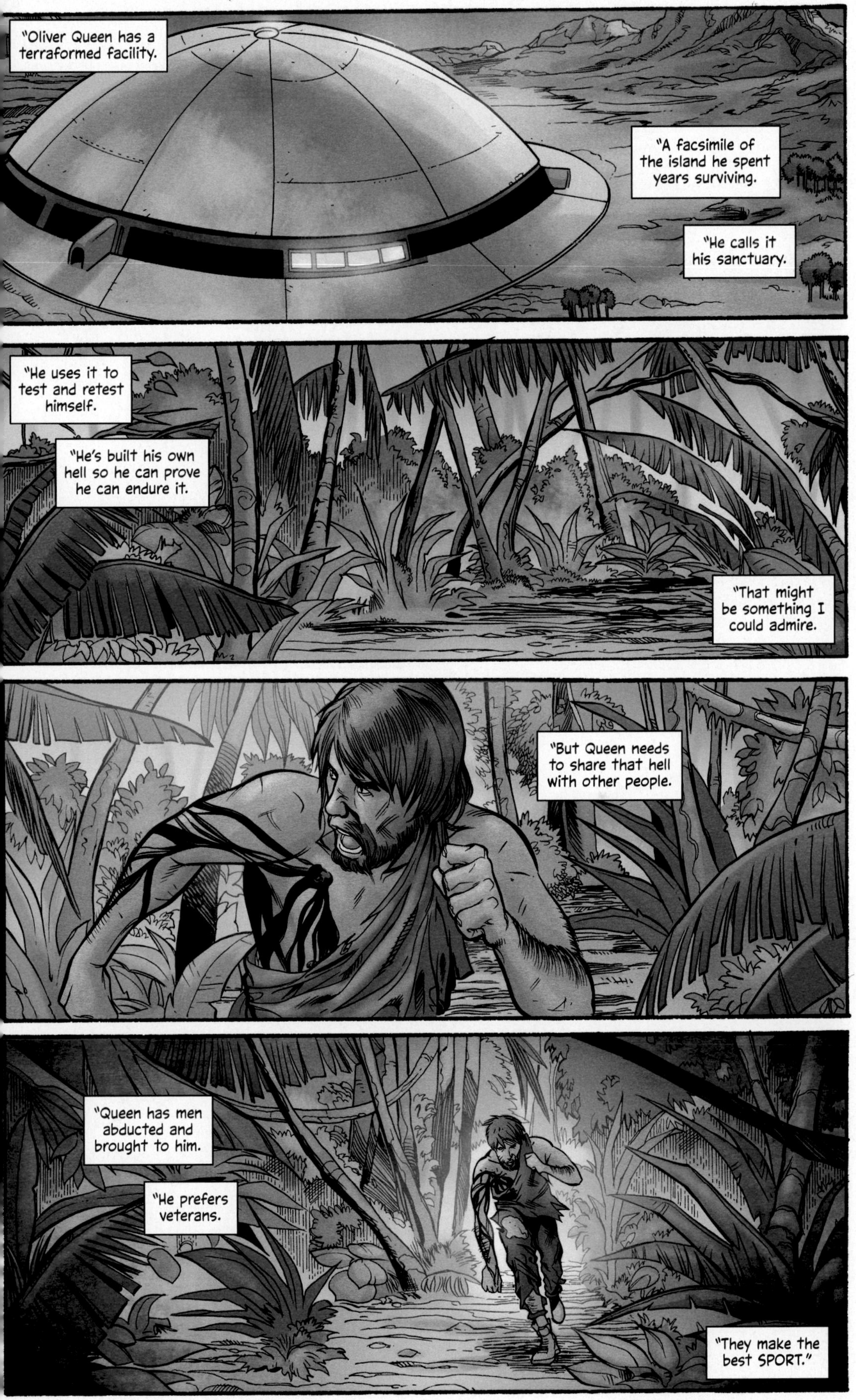
"Oliver Queen has a terraformed facility.
"A facsimile of the island he spent years surviving.
"He calls it his sanctuary.
"He uses it to test and retest himself.
"He's built his own hell so he can prove he can endure it.
"That might be something I could admire.
"But Queen needs to share that hell with other people.
"Queen has men abducted and brought to him.
"He prefers veterans.
"They make the best SPORT."

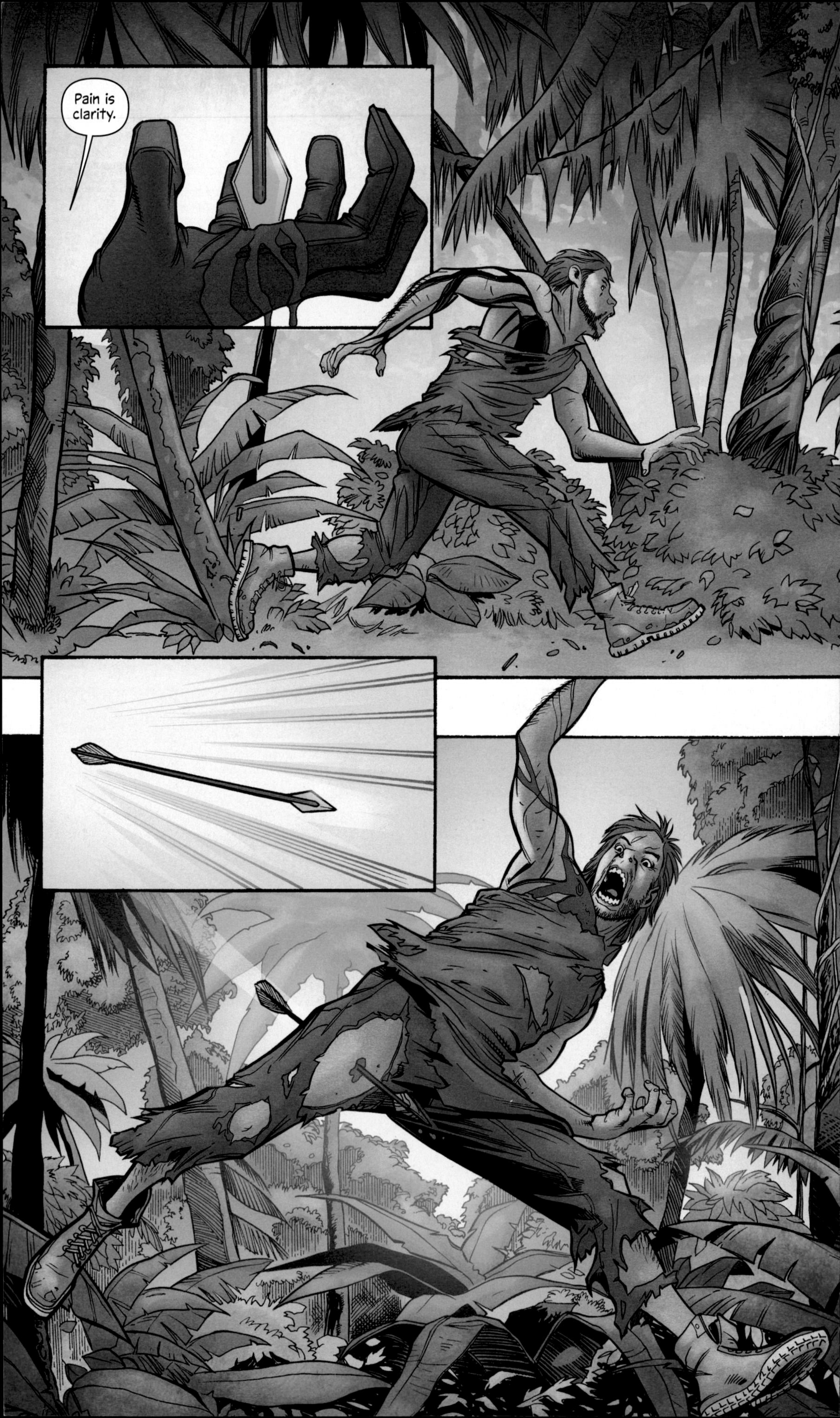
Pain is clarity.

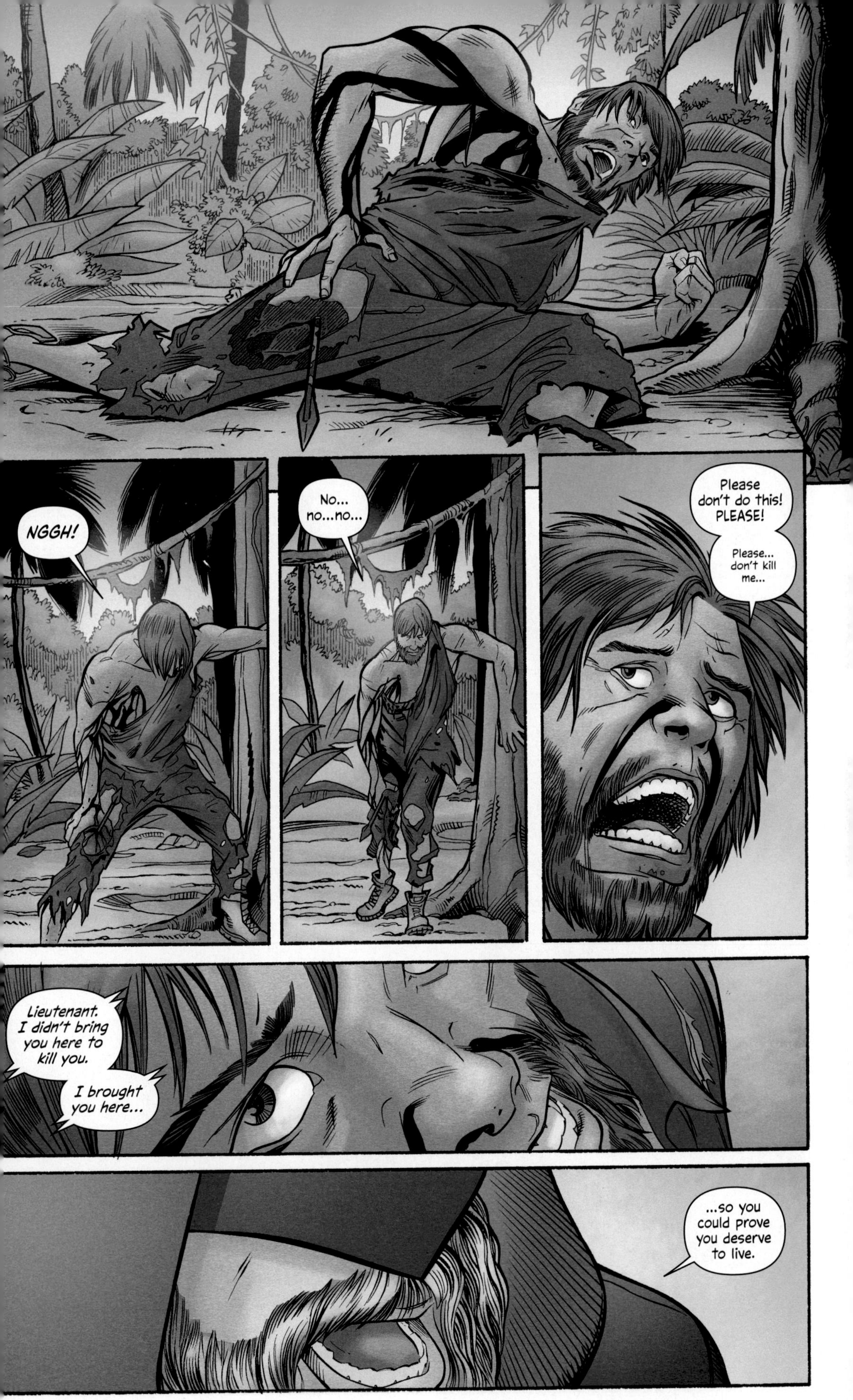
NGGH!
No... no...no...
Please don't do this! PLEASE!
Please... don't kill me...
Lieutenant. I didn't bring you here to kill you.
I brought you here...
...so you could prove you deserve to live.

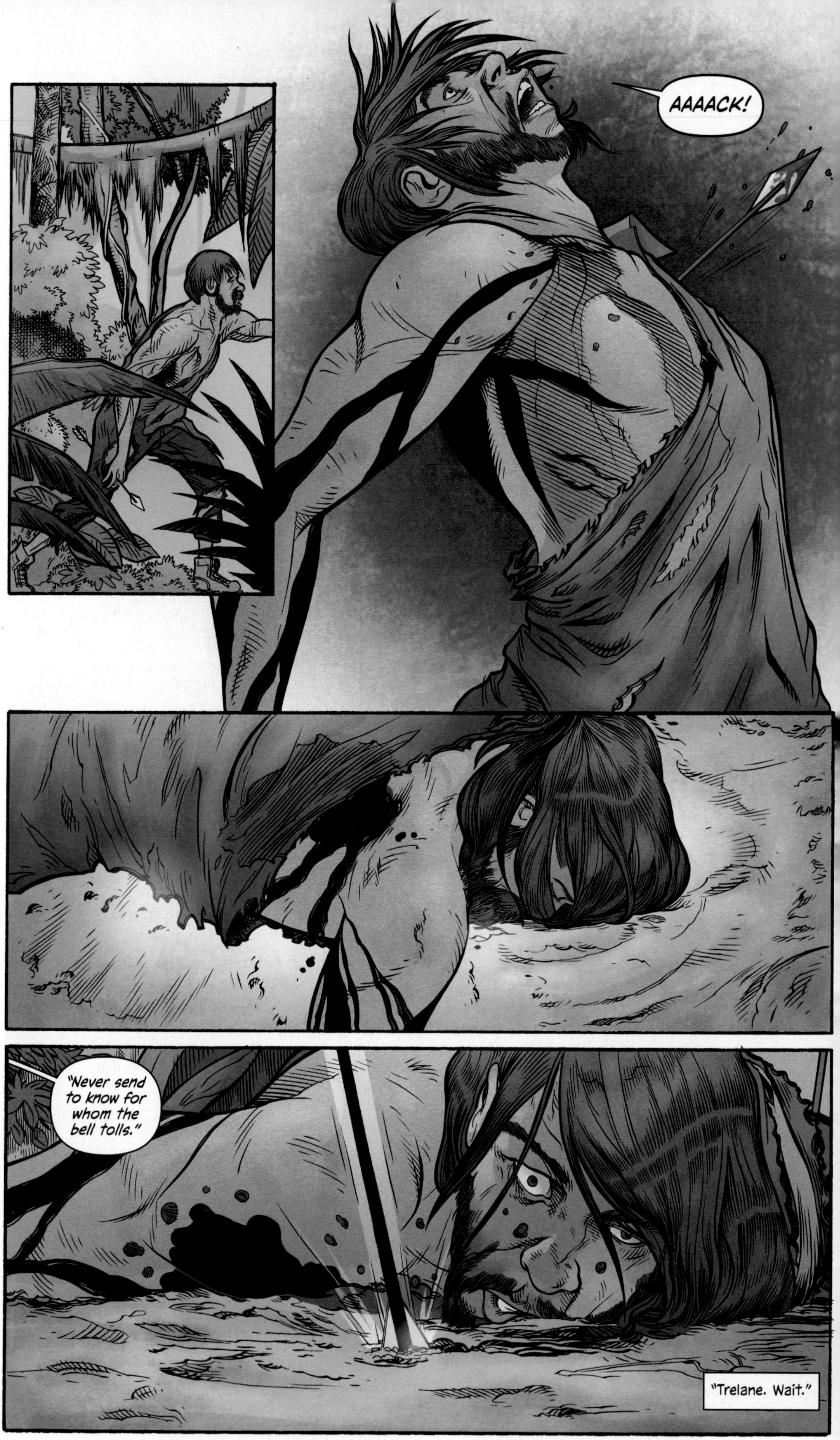
AAAACK!
"Never send to know for whom the bell tolls."
"Trelane. Wait."

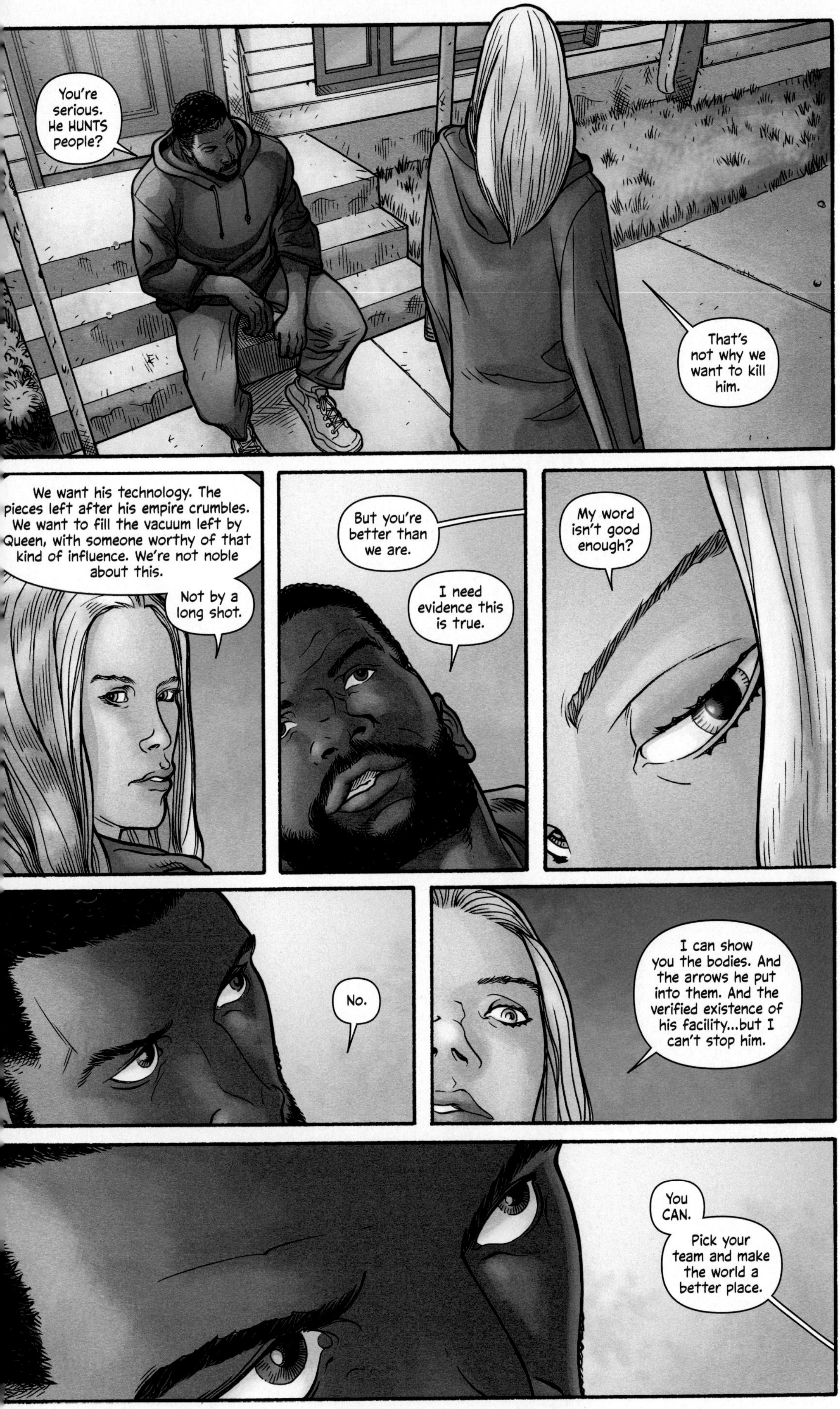

You're serious. He HUNTS people?
That's not why we want to kill him.
We want his technology. The pieces left after his empire crumbles. We want to fill the vacuum left by Queen, with someone worthy of that kind of influence. We're not noble about this.
Not by a long shot.
But you're better than we are.
I need evidence this is true.
My word isn't good enough?
No.
I can show you the bodies. And the arrows he put into them. And the verified existence of his facility...but I can't stop him.
You CAN.
Pick your team and make the world a better place.

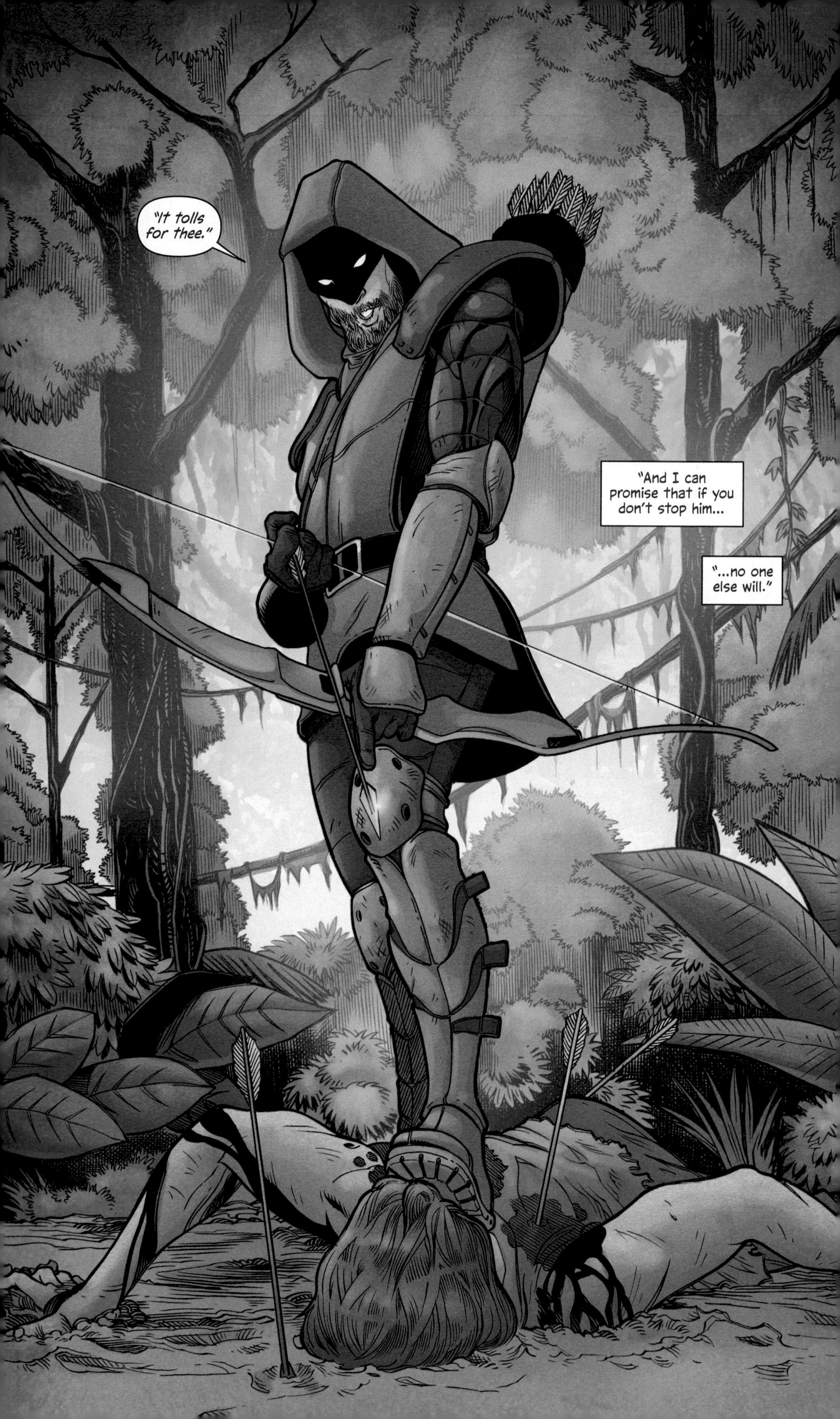
"It tolls for thee."
"And I can promise that if you don't stop him...
"...no one else will."

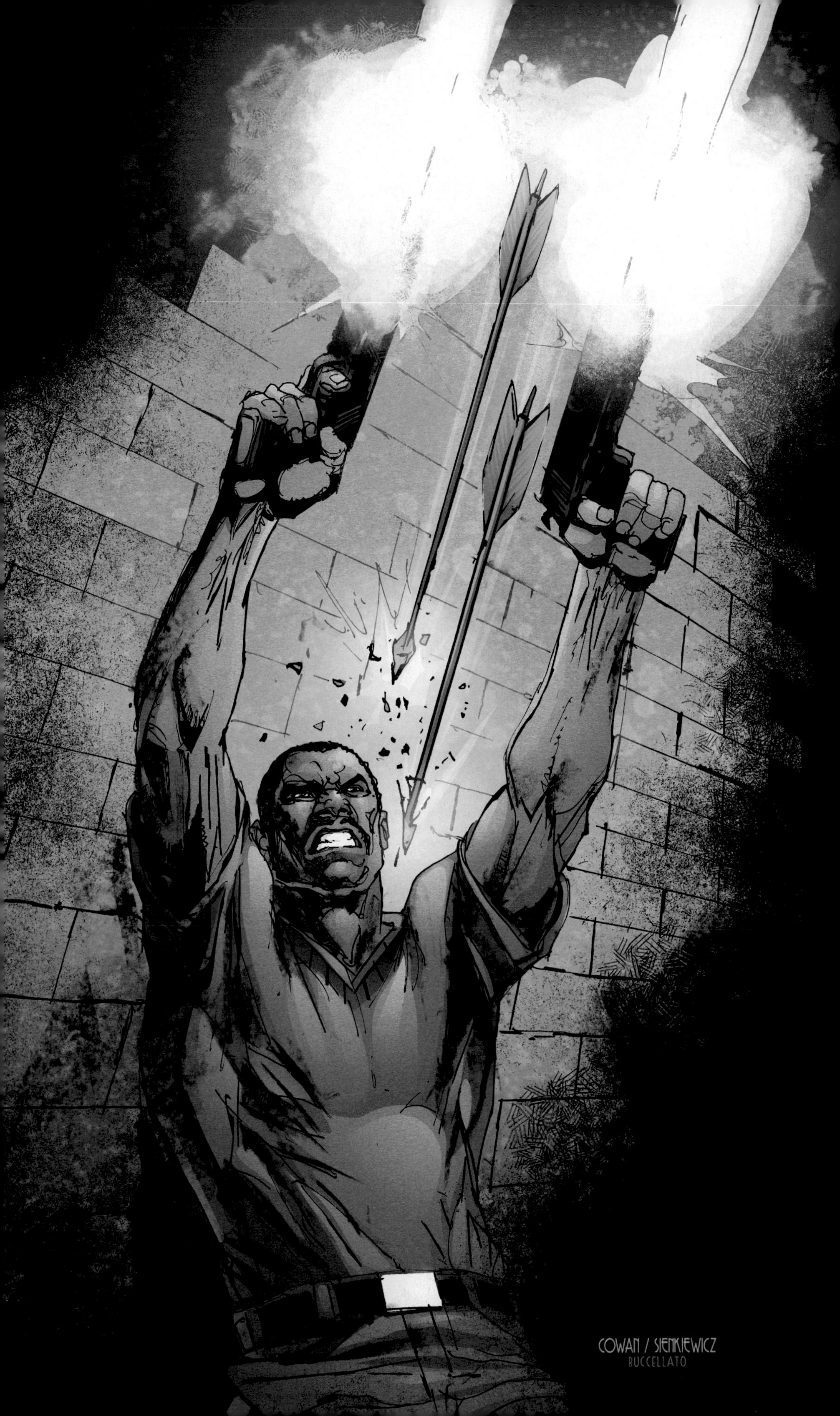
COWAN / SIENKIEWICZ
BUCCELLATO

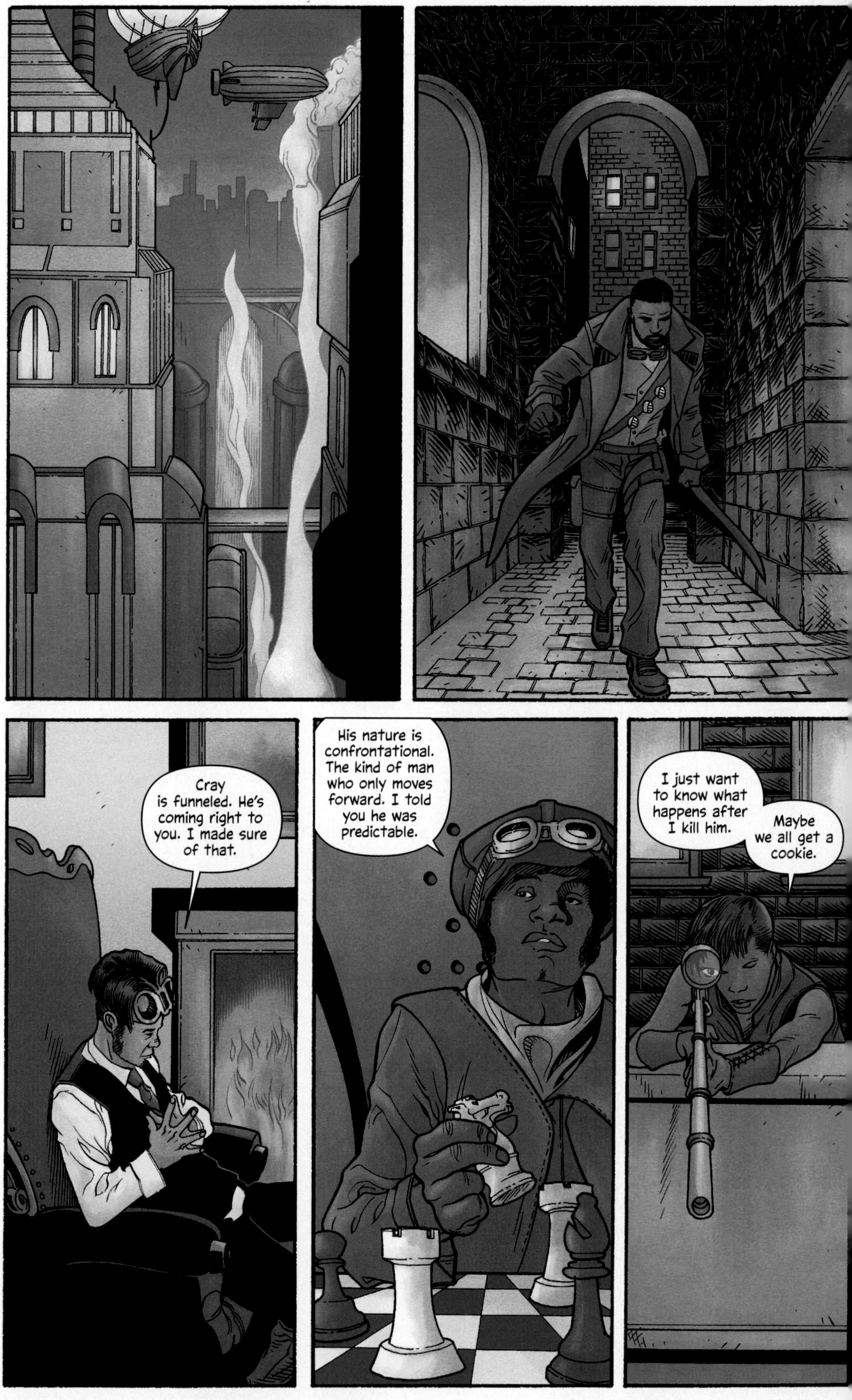
Cray is funneled. He's coming right to you. I made sure of that.
His nature is confrontational. The kind of man who only moves forward. I told you he was predictable.
I just want to know what happens after I kill him.
Maybe we all get a cookie.

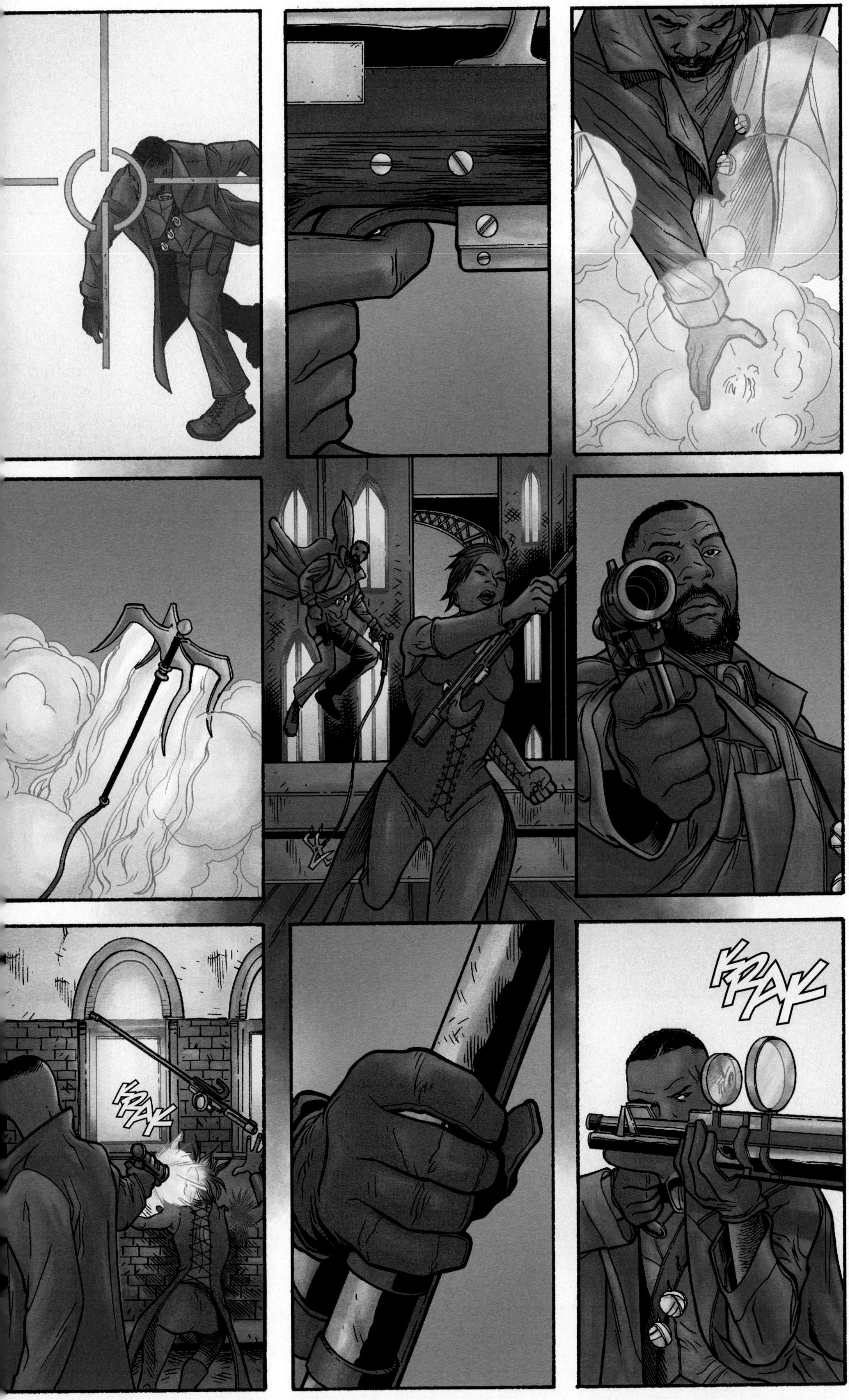
KRAK
KRAK

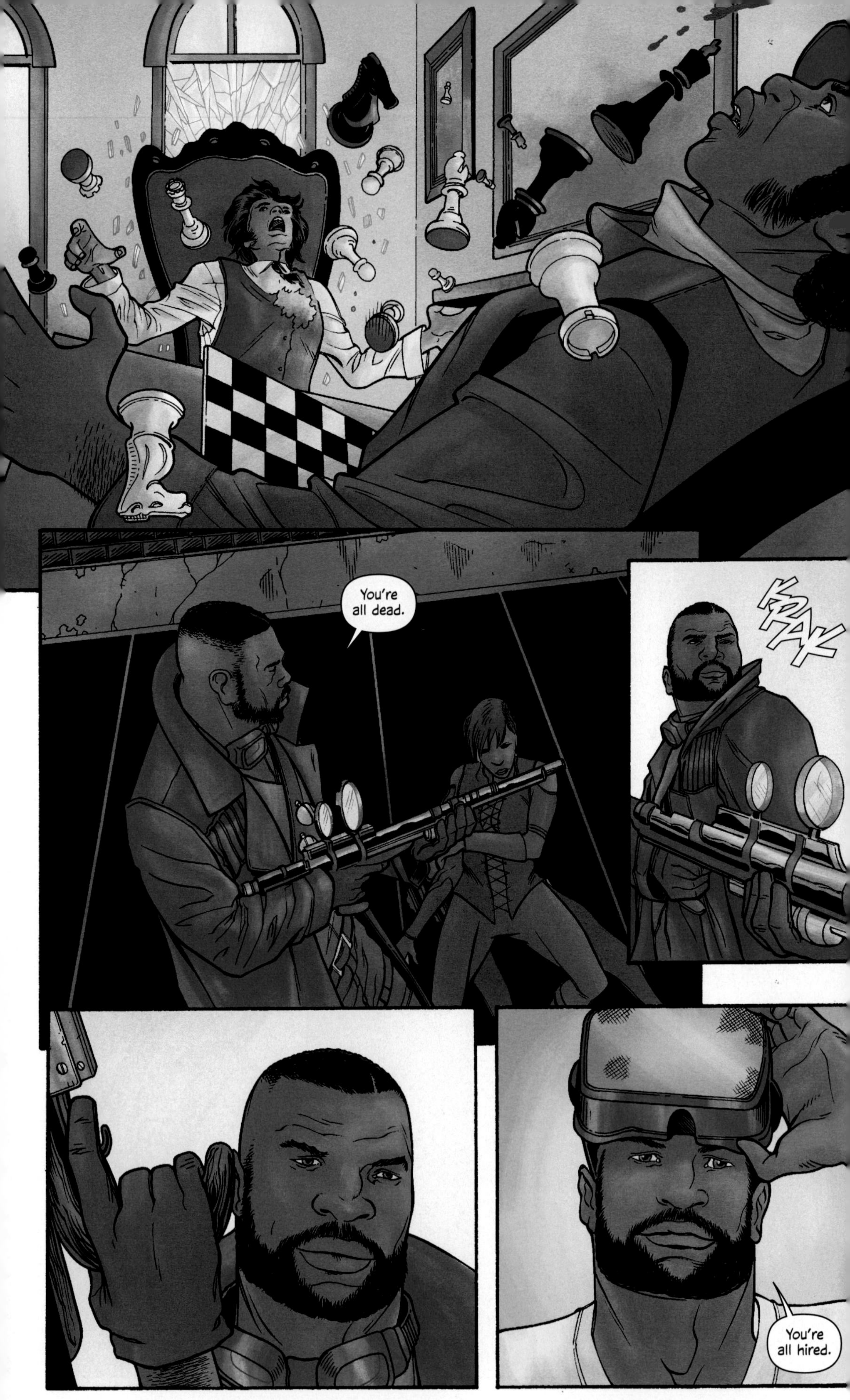
You're all dead.
KRAK
You're all hired.

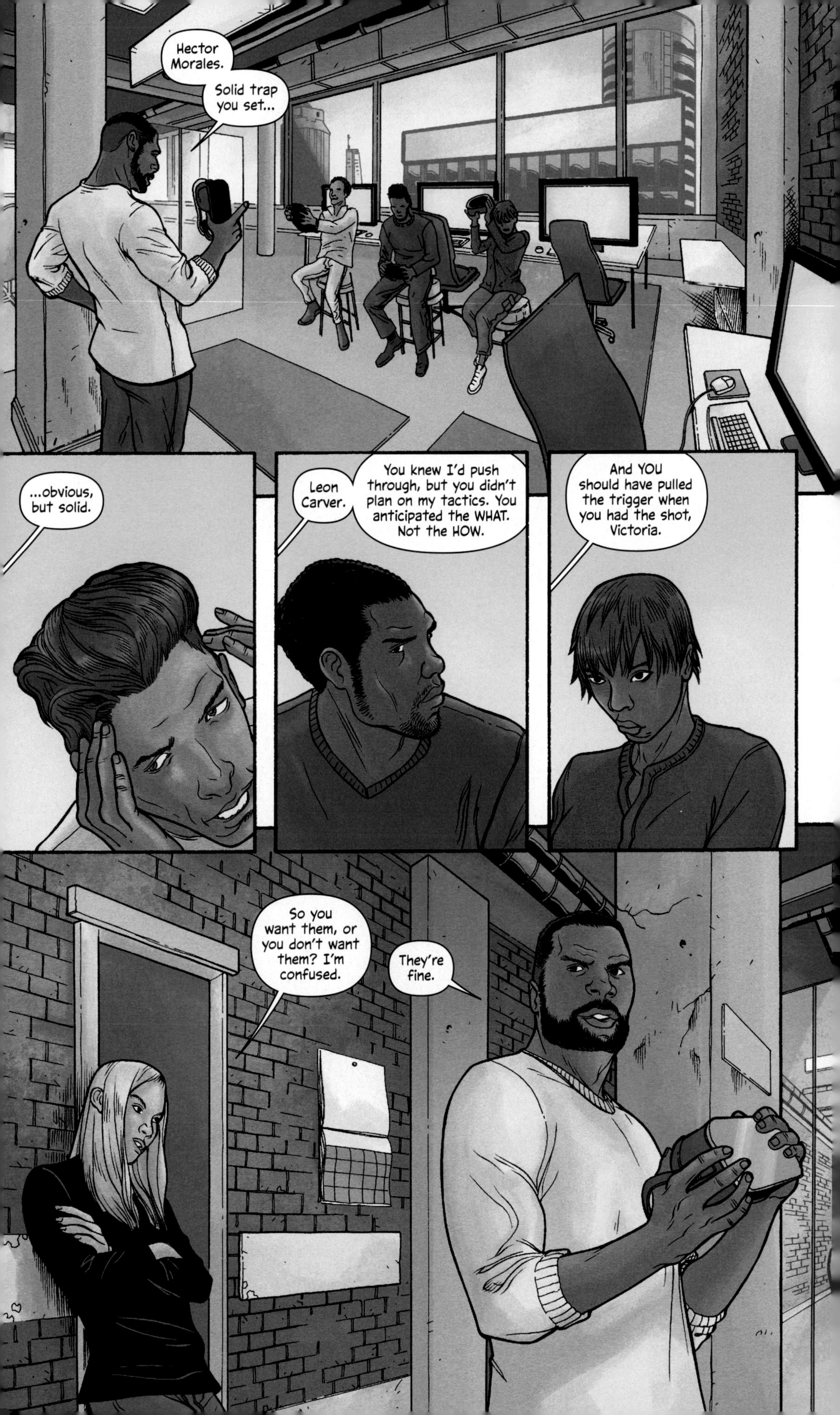

Hector Morales.
Solid trap you set...
...obvious, but solid.
Leon Carver.
You knew I'd push through, but you didn't plan on my tactics. You anticipated the WHAT. Not the HOW.
And YOU should have pulled the trigger when you had the shot, Victoria.
So you want them, or you don't want them? I'm confused.
They're fine.

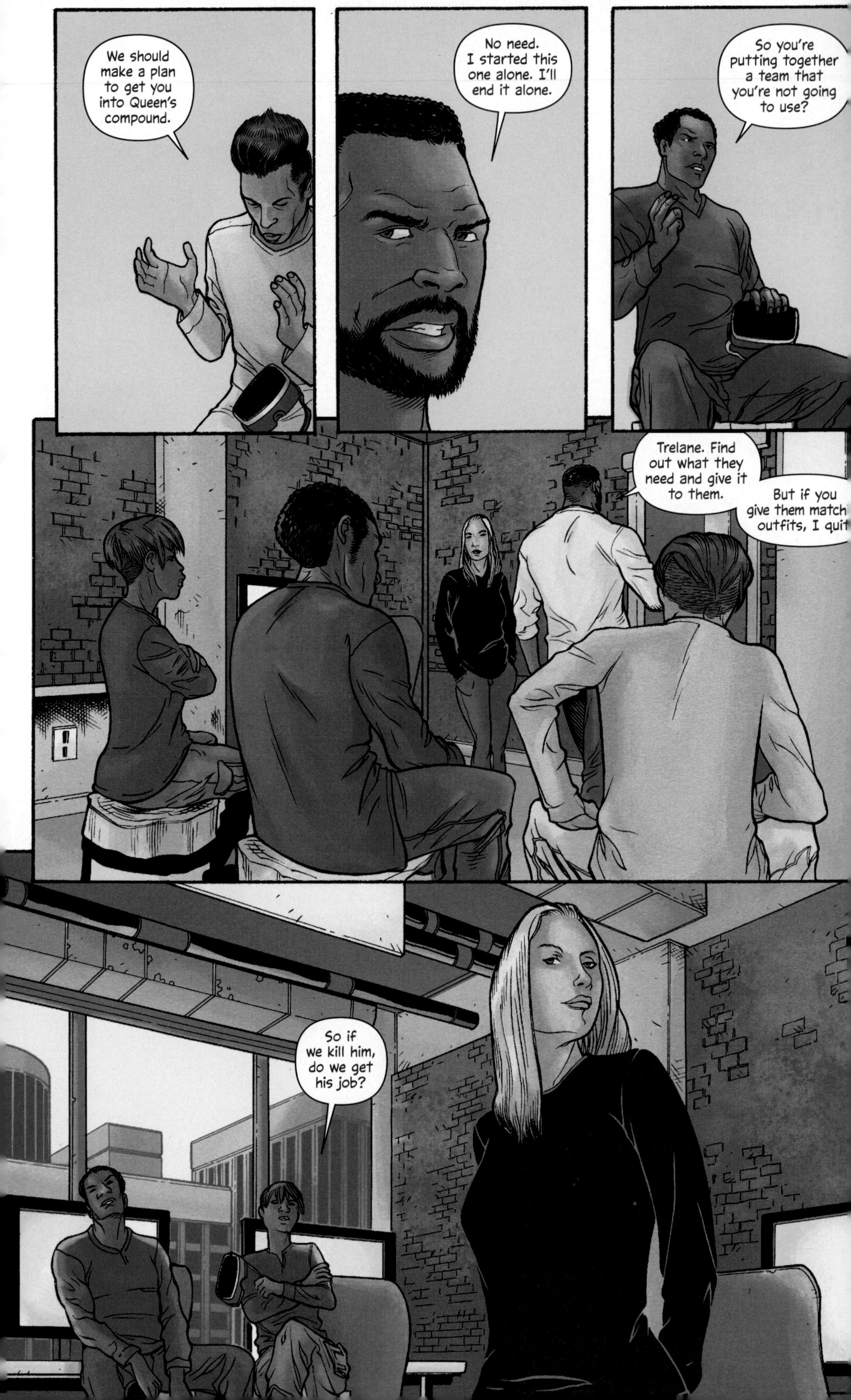
We should make a plan to get you into Queen's compound.
No need. I started this one alone. I'll end it alone.
So you're putting together a team that you're not going to use?
Trelane. Find out what they need and give it to them.
But if you give them match outfits, I quit
So if we kill him, do we get his job?

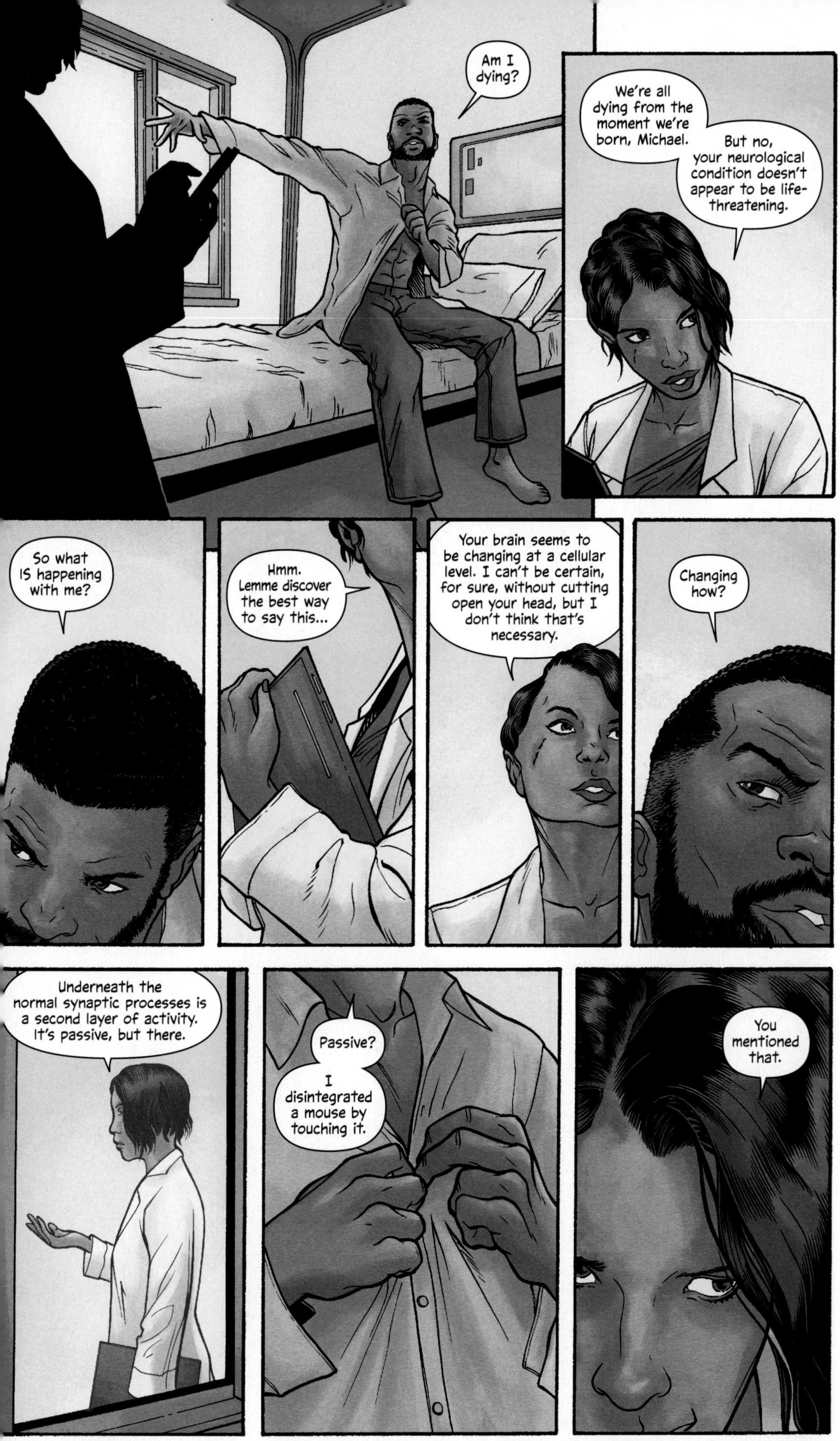

Am I dying?
We're all dying from the moment we're born, Michael.
But no, your neurological condition doesn't appear to be life-threatening.
So what IS happening with me?
Hmm. Lemme discover the best way to say this...
Your brain seems to be changing at a cellular level. I can't be certain, for sure, without cutting open your head, but I don't think that's necessary.
Changing how?
Underneath the normal synaptic processes is a second layer of activity. It's passive, but there.
Passive?
I disintegrated a mouse by touching it.
You mentioned that.

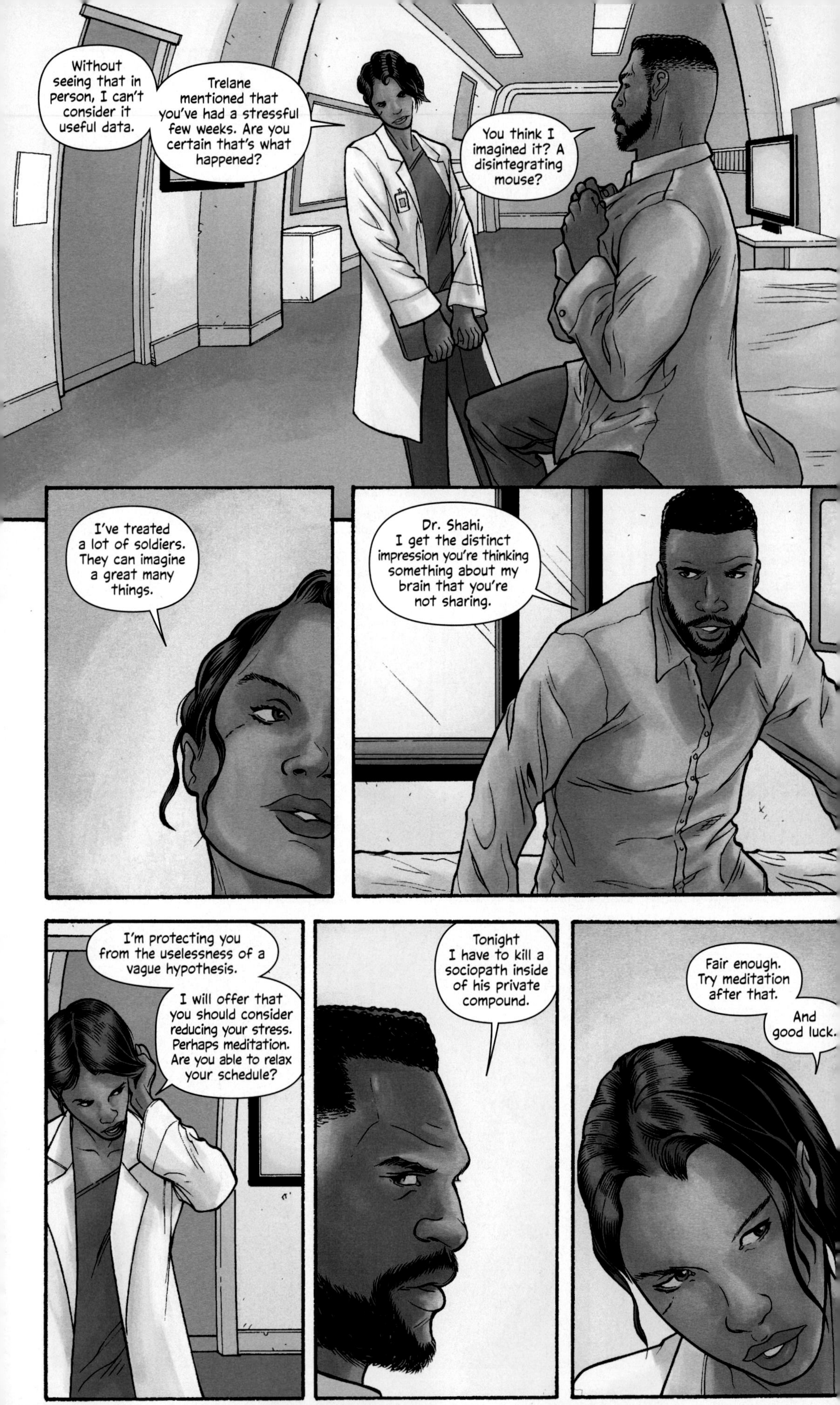
Without seeing that in person, I can't consider it useful data.
Trelane mentioned that you've had a stressful few weeks. Are you certain that's what happened?
You think I imagined it? A disintegrating mouse?
I've treated a lot of soldiers. They can imagine a great many things.
Dr. Shahi, I get the distinct impression you're thinking something about my brain that you're not sharing.
I'm protecting you from the uselessness of a vague hypothesis.
I will offer that you should consider reducing your stress. Perhaps meditation. Are you able to relax your schedule?
Tonight I have to kill a sociopath inside of his private compound.
Fair enough. Try meditation after that.
And good luck.

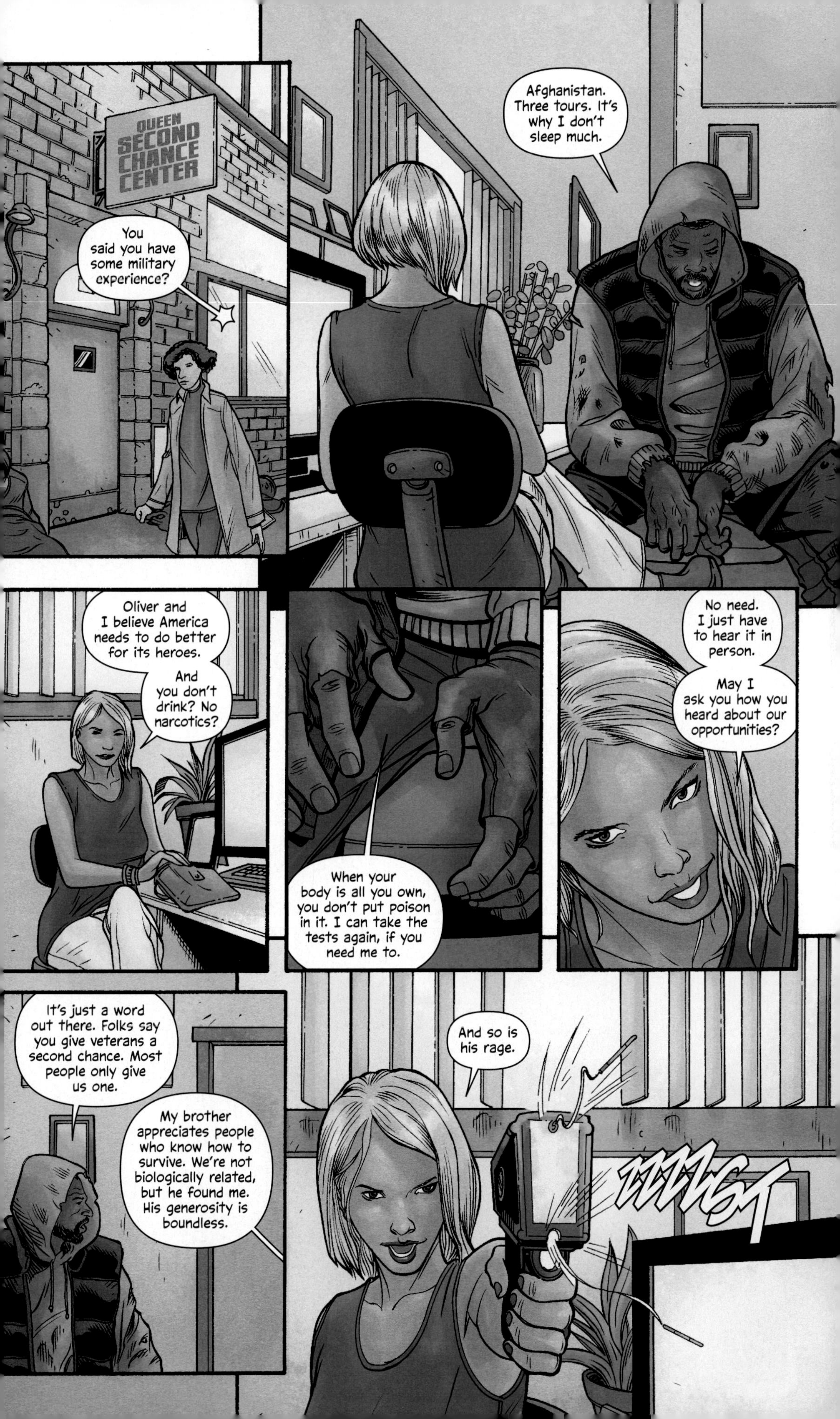
QUEEN SECOND CHANCE CENTER
You said you have some military experience?
Afghanistan. Three tours. It's why I don't sleep much.
Oliver and I believe America needs to do better for its heroes.
And you don't drink? No narcotics?
When your body is all you own, you don't put poison in it. I can take the tests again, if you need me to.
No need. I just have to hear it in person.
May I ask you how you heard about our opportunities?
It's just a word out there. Folks say you give veterans a second chance. Most people only give us one.
My brother appreciates people who know how to survive. We're not biologically related, but he found me. His generosity is boundless.
And so is his rage.
ZZZZST

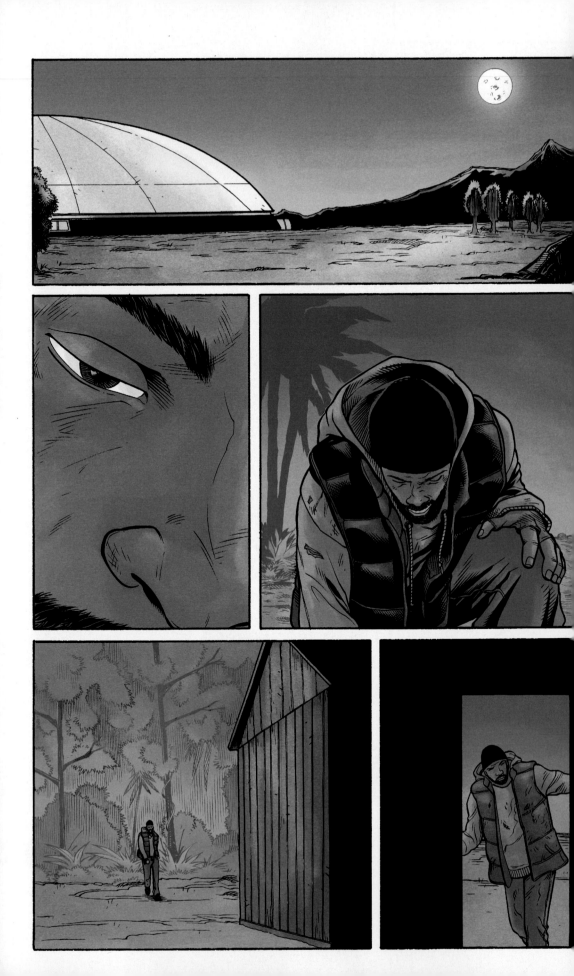

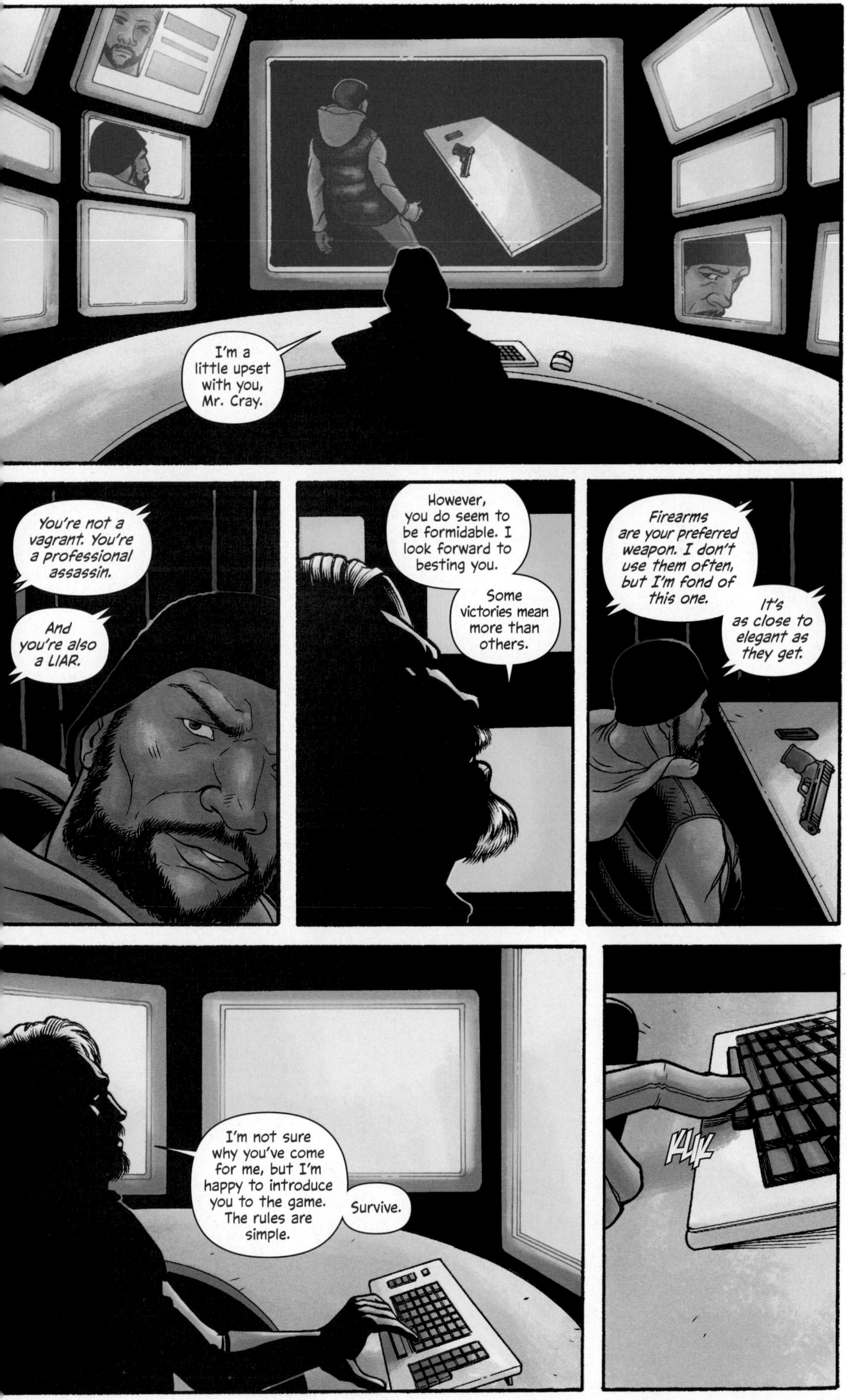
I'm a little upset with you, Mr. Cray.
You're not a vagrant. You're a professional assassin.
And you're also a LIAR.
However, you do seem to be formidable. I look forward to besting you.
Some victories mean more than others.
Firearms are your preferred weapon. I don't use them often, but I'm fond of this one.
It's as close to elegant as they get.
I'm not sure why you've come for me, but I'm happy to introduce you to the game. The rules are simple.
Survive.
KLIK

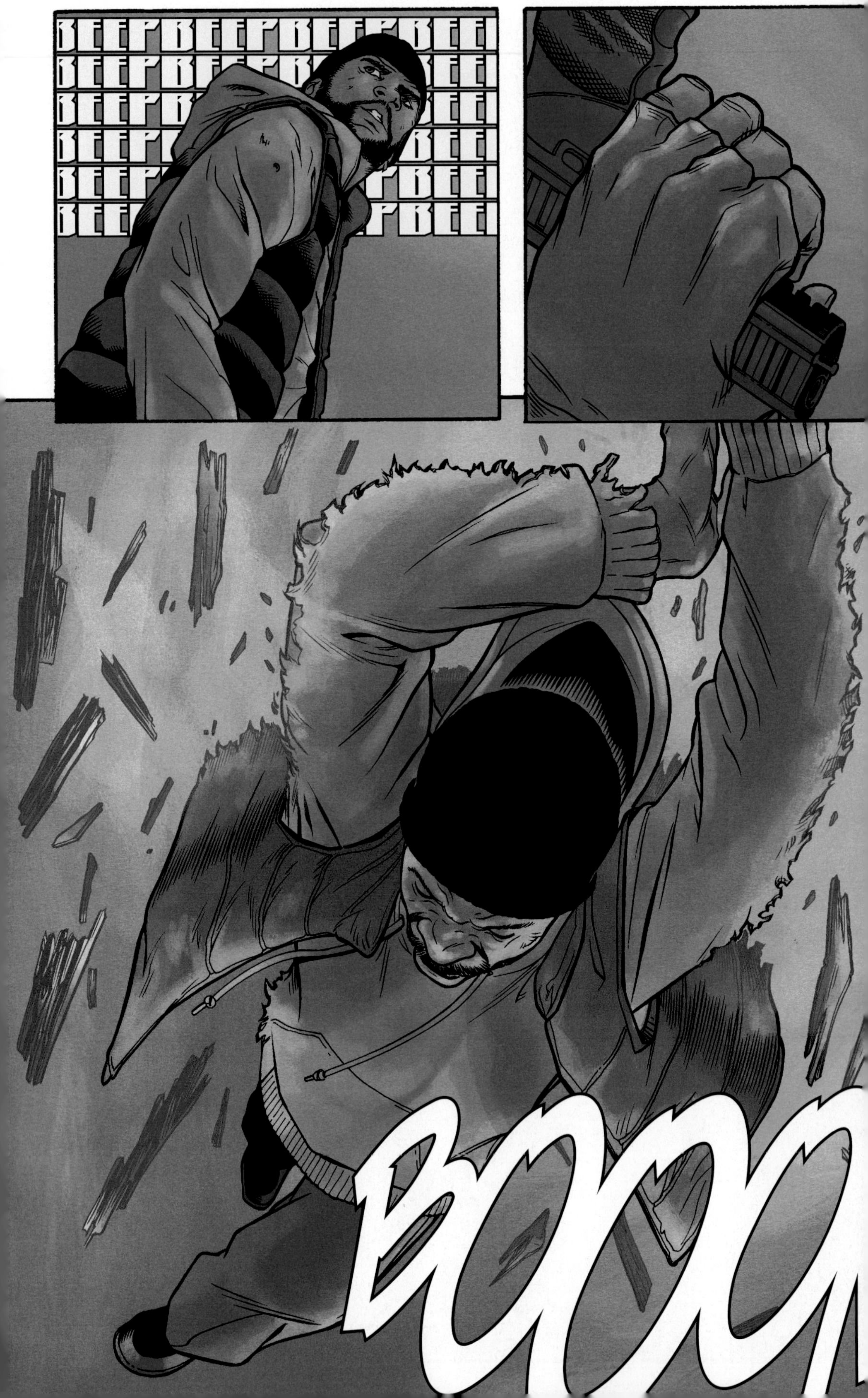
BEEPBEEPBEEPBEE
BOO

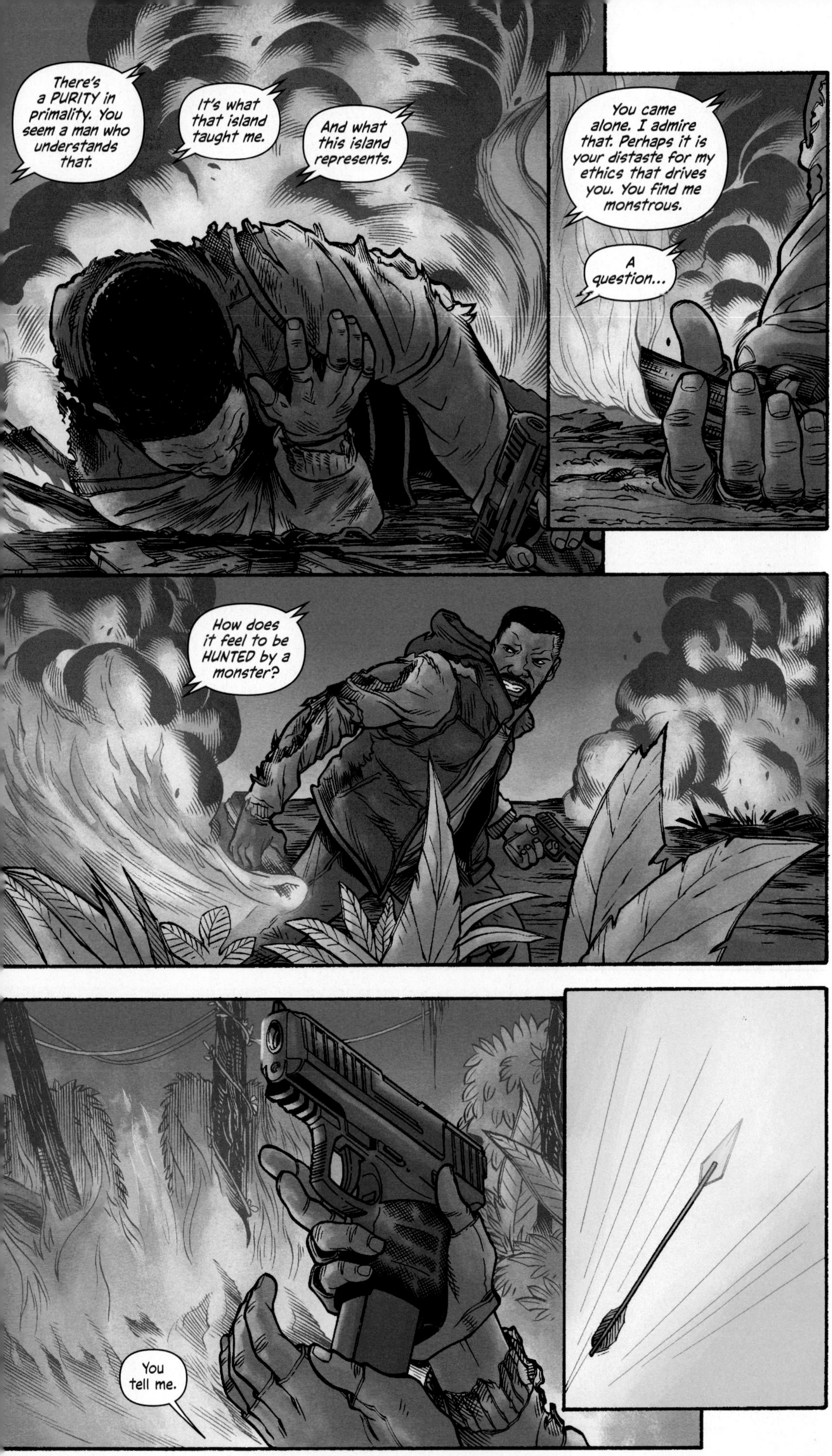
There's a PURITY in primality. You seem a man who understands that.
It's what that island taught me.
And what this island represents.
You came alone. I admire that. Perhaps it is your distaste for my ethics that drives you. You find me monstrous.
A question...
How does it feel to be HUNTED by a monster?
You tell me.

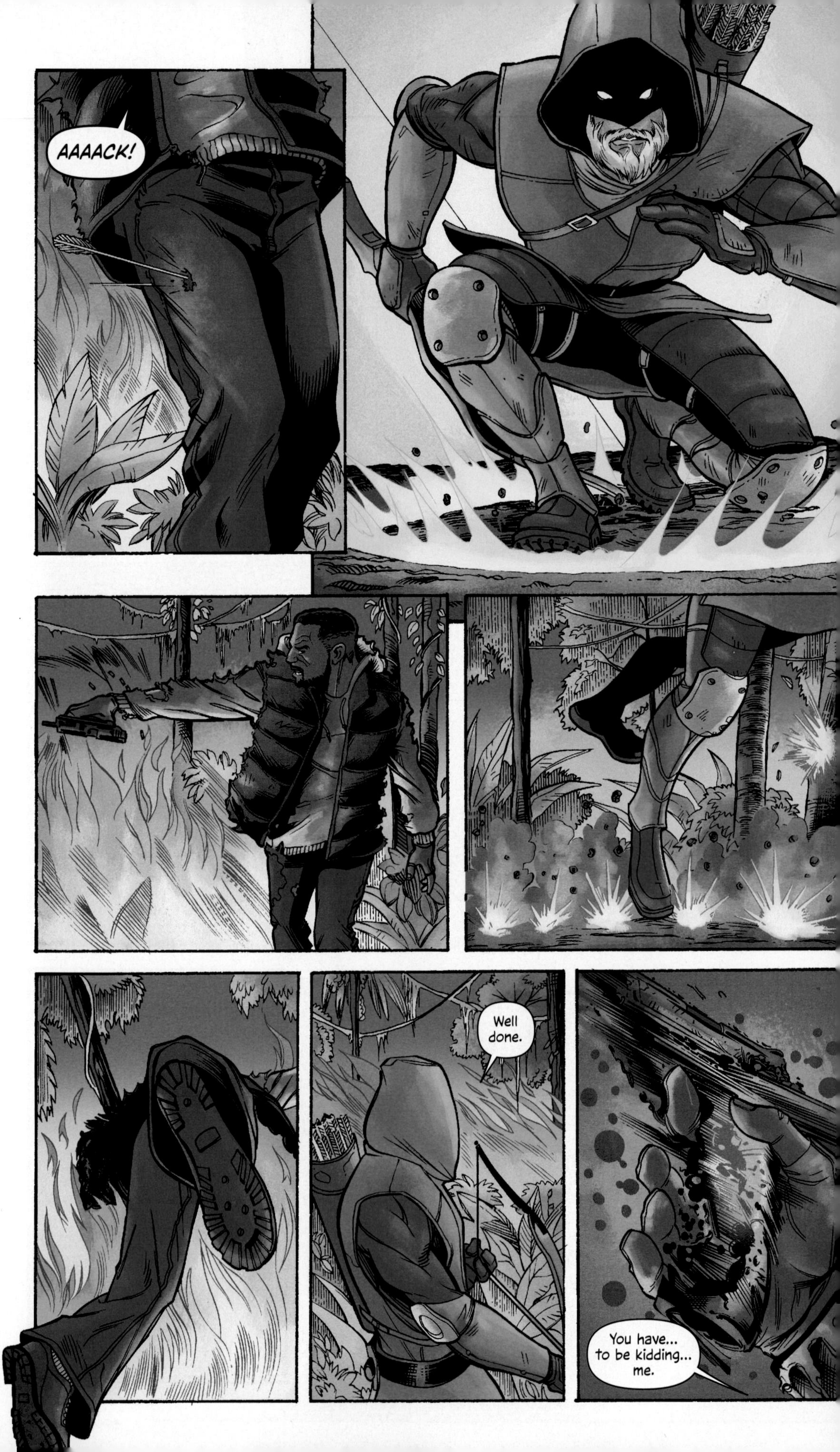
AAAACK!
Well done.
You have... to be kidding... me.

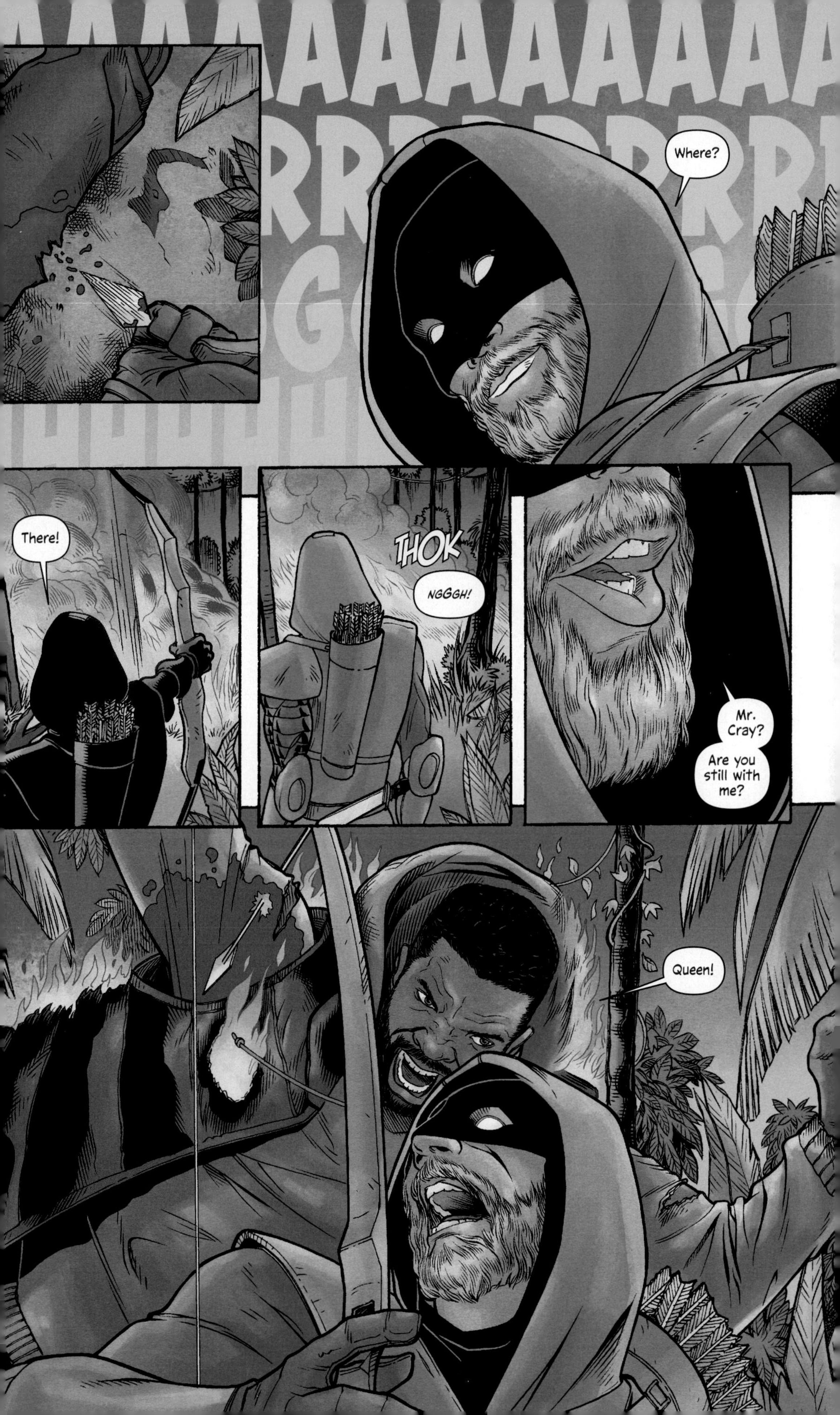
AAAAAAAAAAAAAAA RRRRRRRR GGGGG HHHHH
Where?
There!
THOK
NGGGH!
Mr. Cray?
Are you still with me?
Queen!

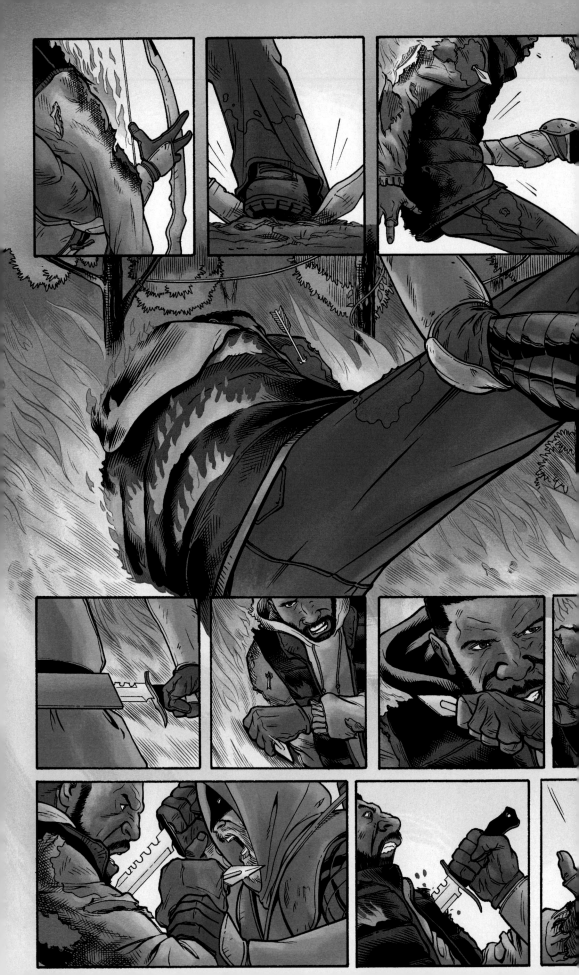

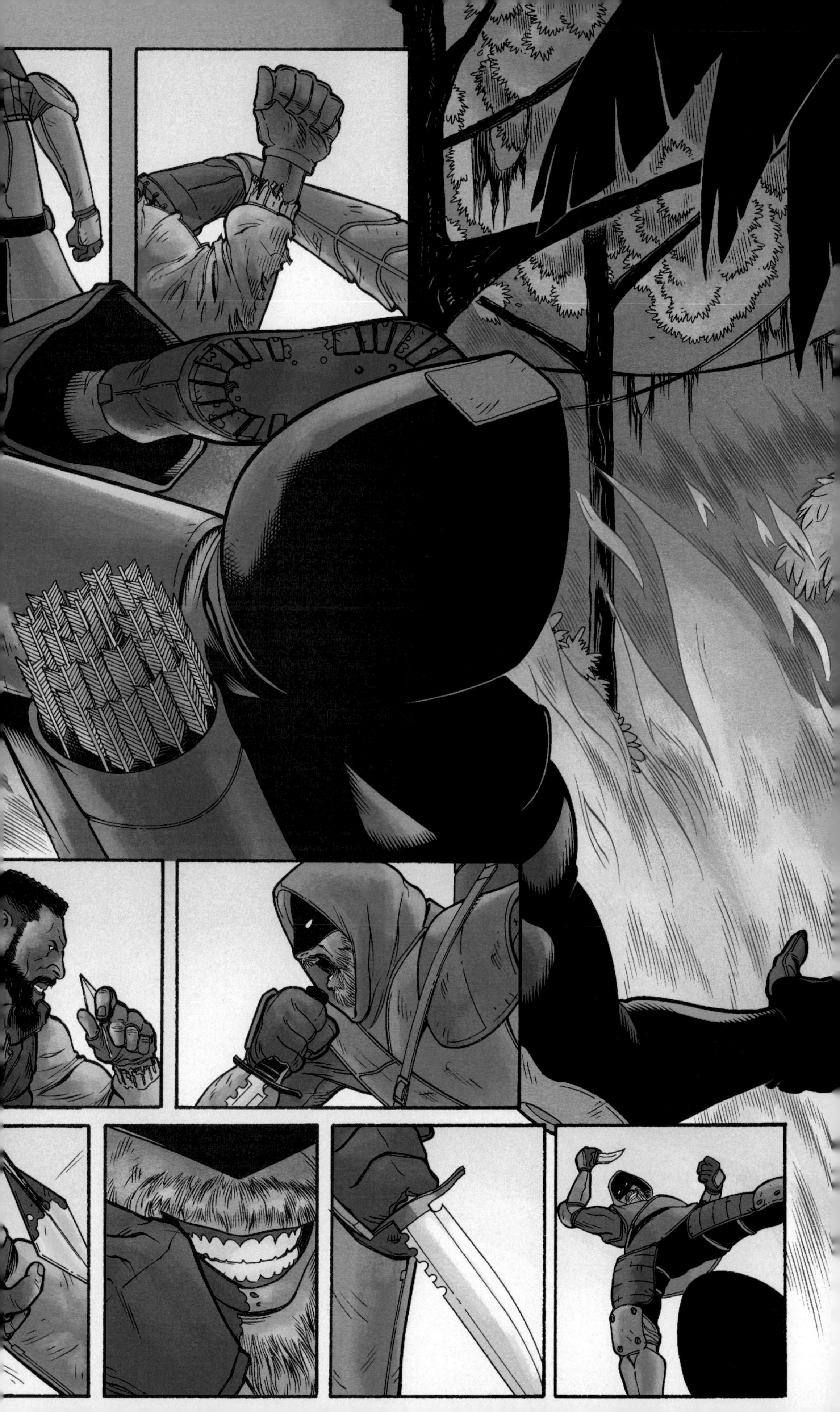

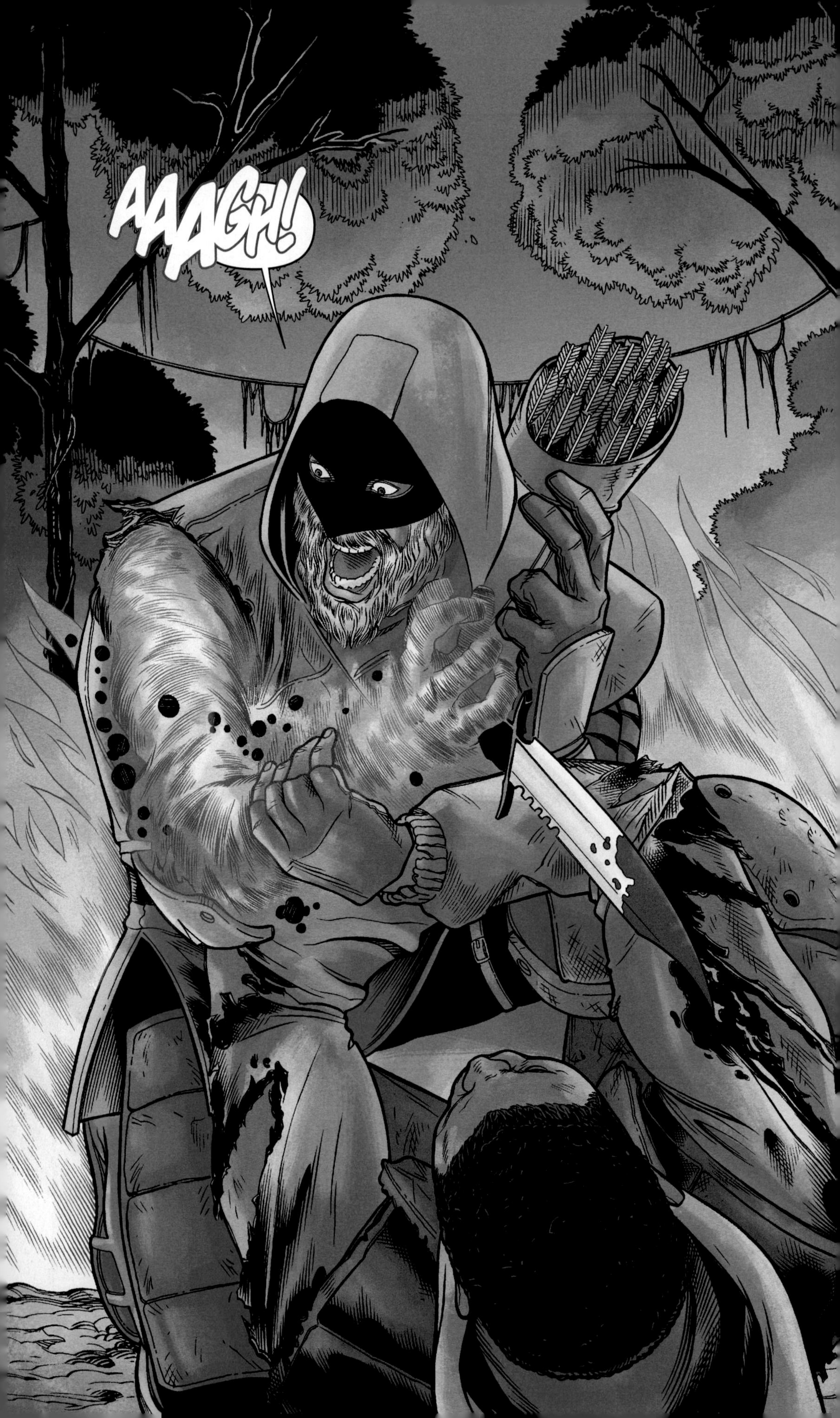
AAAGH!

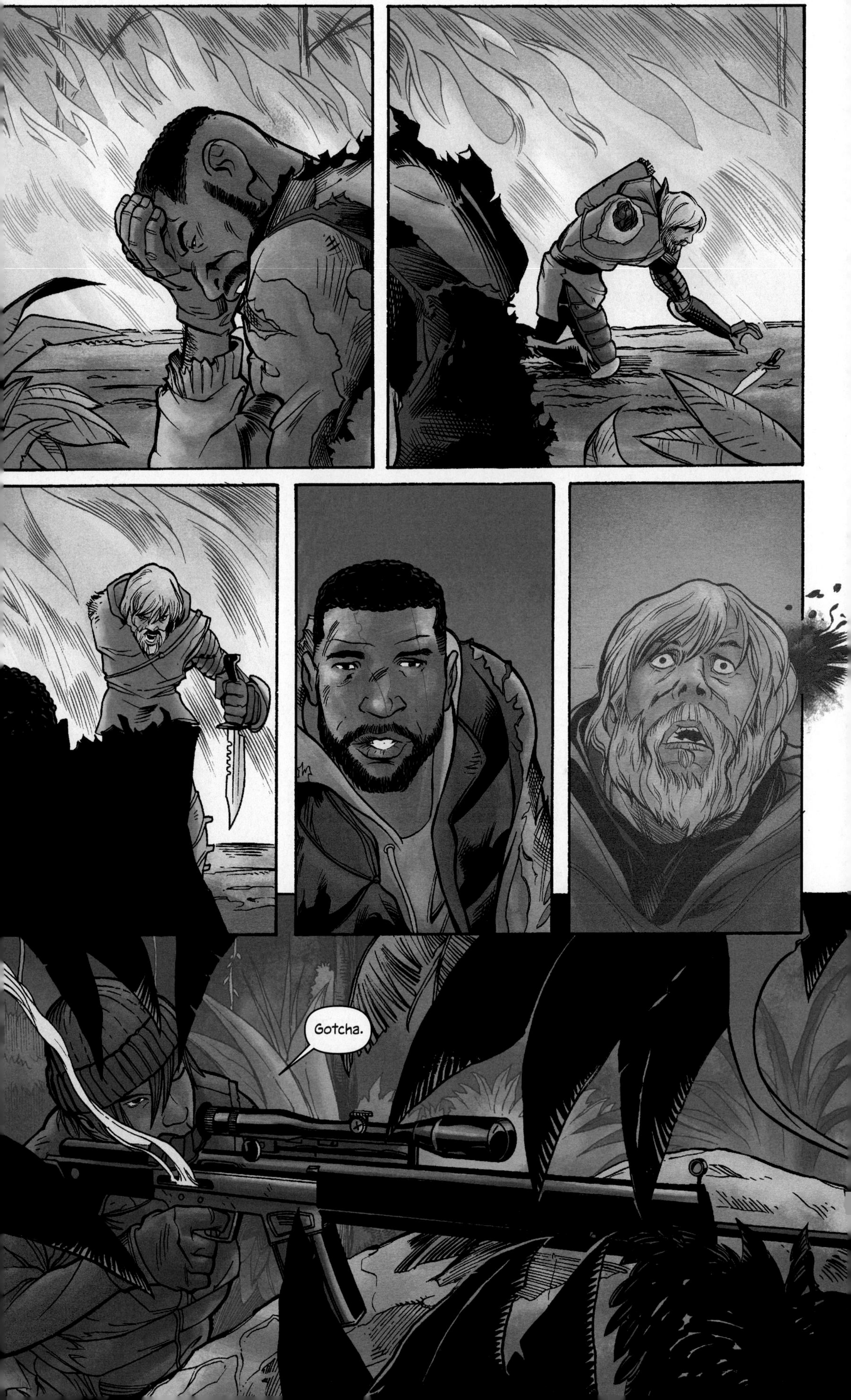
Gotcha.

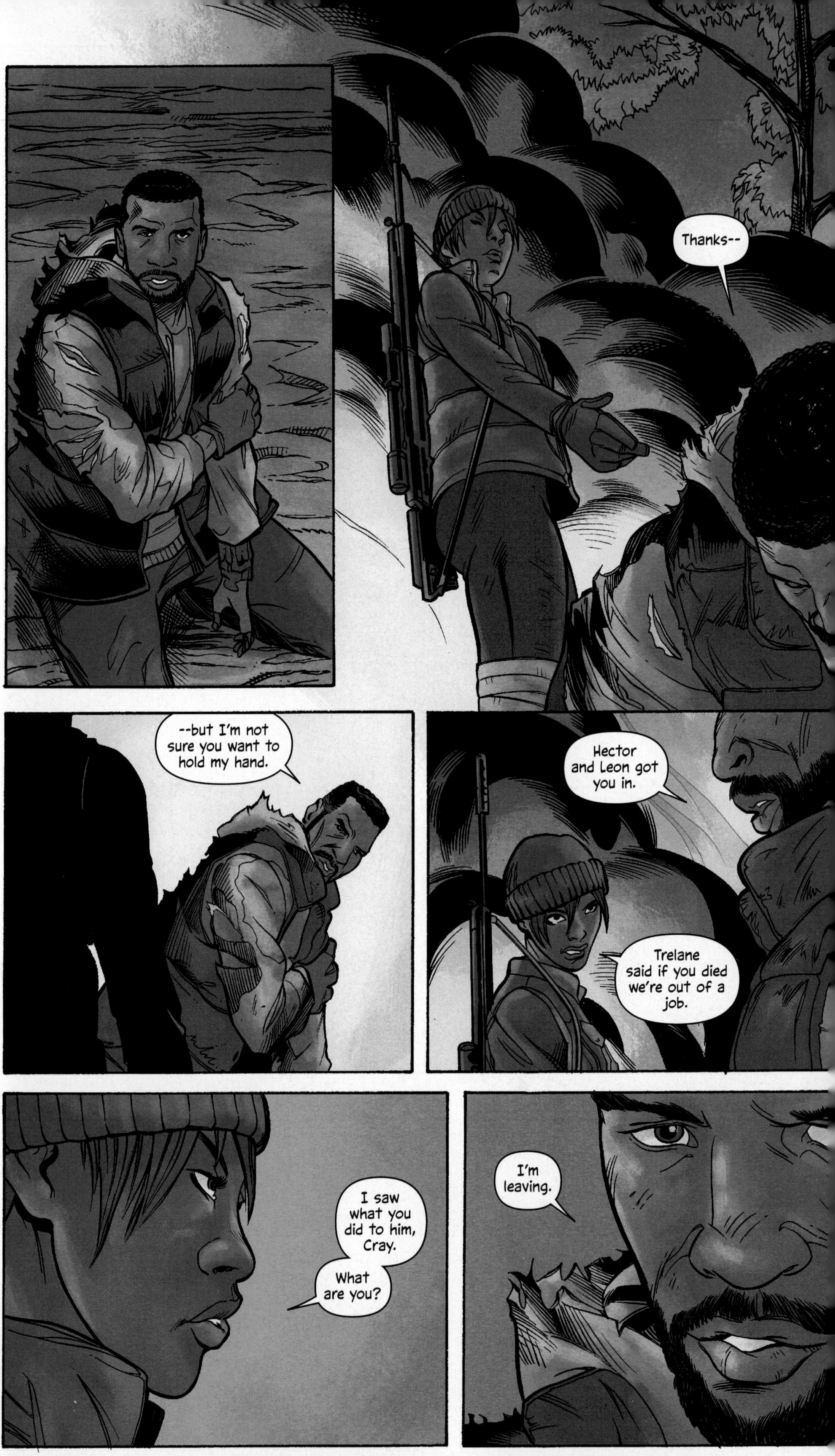
Thanks--
--but I'm not sure you want to hold my hand.
Hector and Leon got you in.
Trelane said if you died we're out of a job.
I saw what you did to him, Cray.
What are you?
I'm leaving.

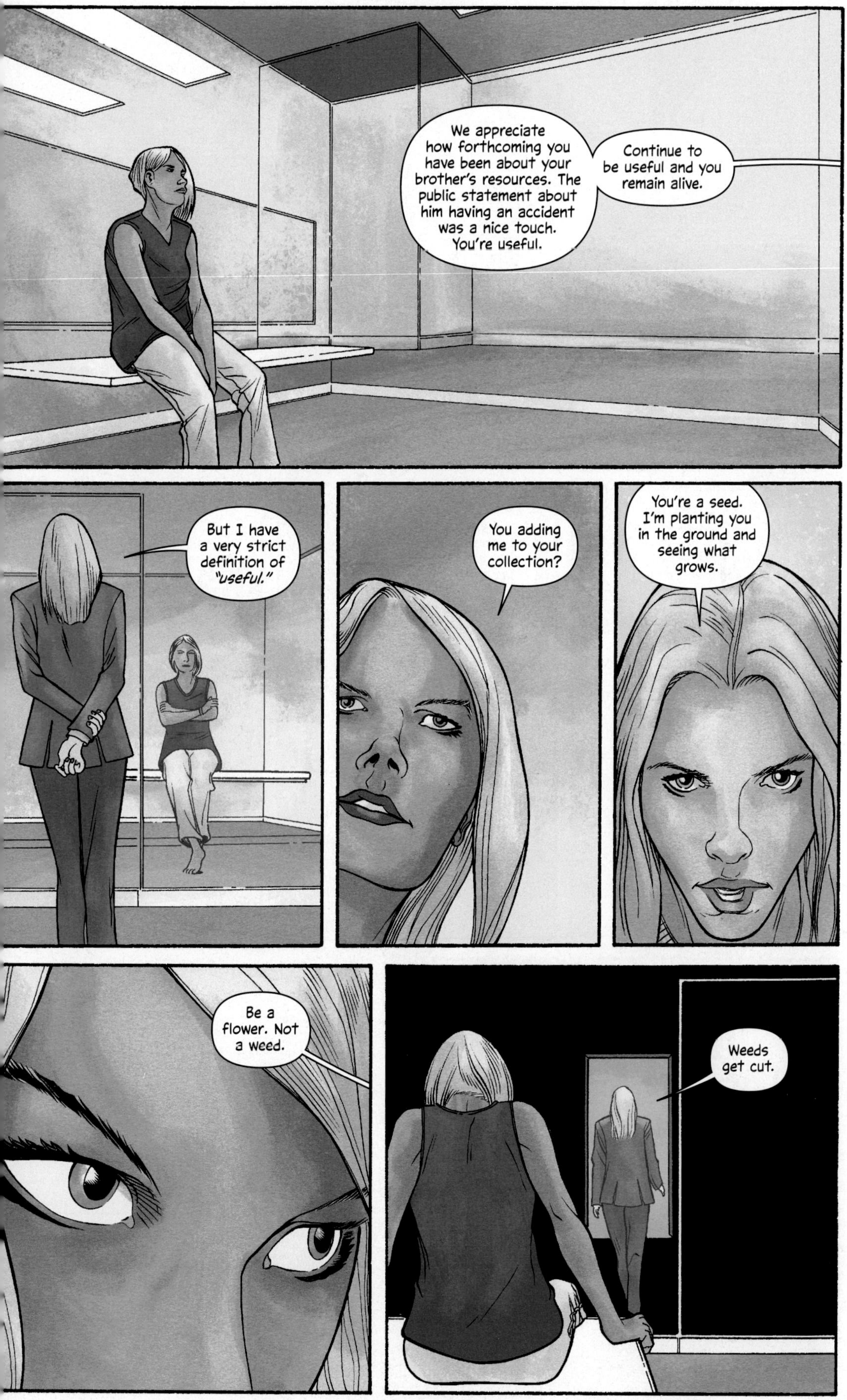
We appreciate how forthcoming you have been about your brother's resources. The public statement about him having an accident was a nice touch. You're useful.
Continue to be useful and you remain alive.
But I have a very strict definition of *"useful."*
You adding me to your collection?
You're a seed. I'm planting you in the ground and seeing what grows.
Be a flower. Not a weed.
Weeds get cut.

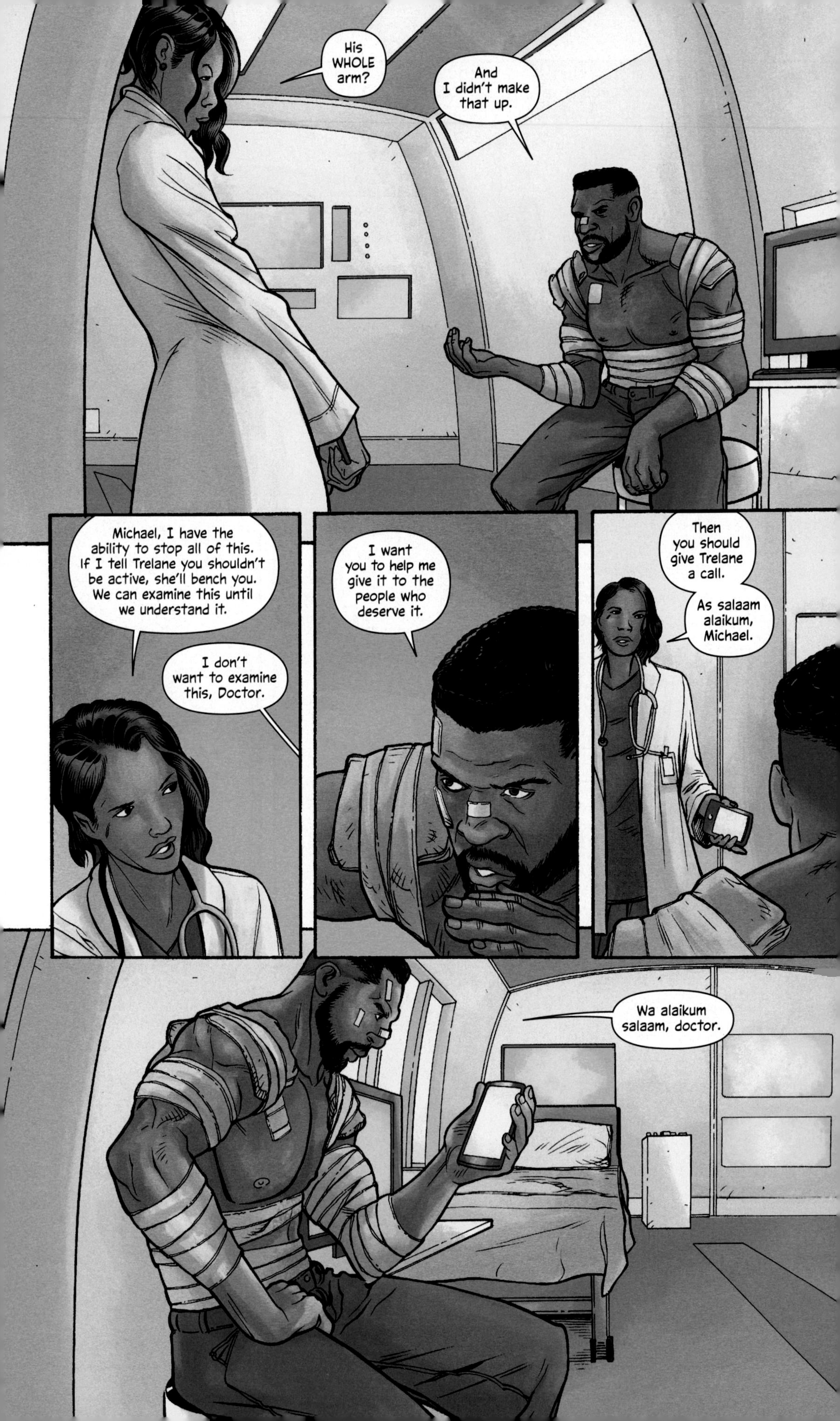
His WHOLE arm?
And I didn't make that up.
Michael, I have the ability to stop all of this. If I tell Trelane you shouldn't be active, she'll bench you. We can examine this until we understand it.
I don't want to examine this, Doctor.
I want you to help me give it to the people who deserve it.
Then you should give Trelane a call.
As salaam alaikum, Michael.
Wa alaikum salaam, doctor.

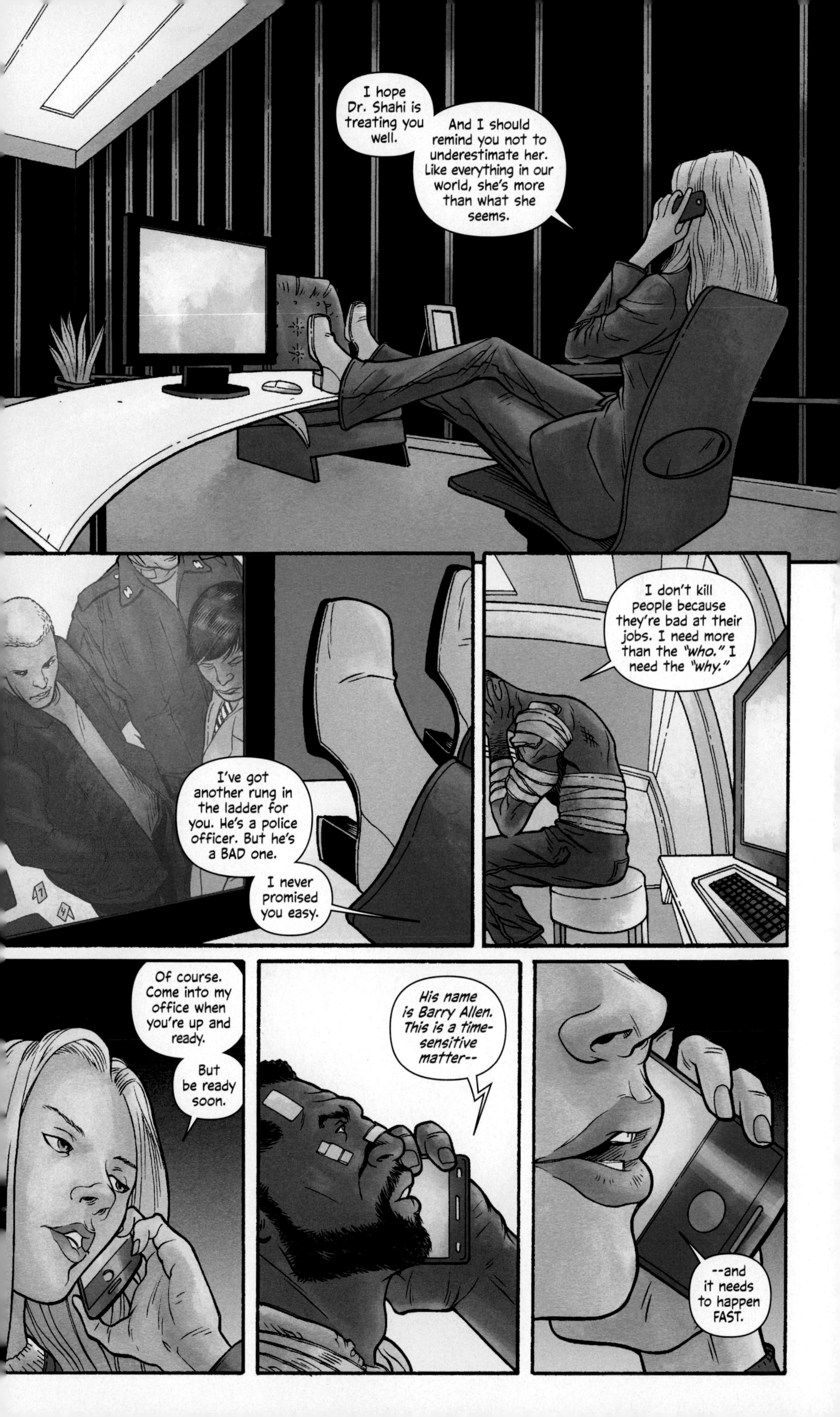
I hope Dr. Shahi is treating you well.
And I should remind you not to underestimate her. Like everything in our world, she's more than what she seems.
I've got another rung in the ladder for you. He's a police officer. But he's a BAD one.
I never promised you easy.
I don't kill people because they're bad at their jobs. I need more than the "who." I need the "why."
Of course. Come into my office when you're up and ready.
But be ready soon.
His name is Barry Allen. This is a time-sensitive matter--
--and it needs to happen FAST.

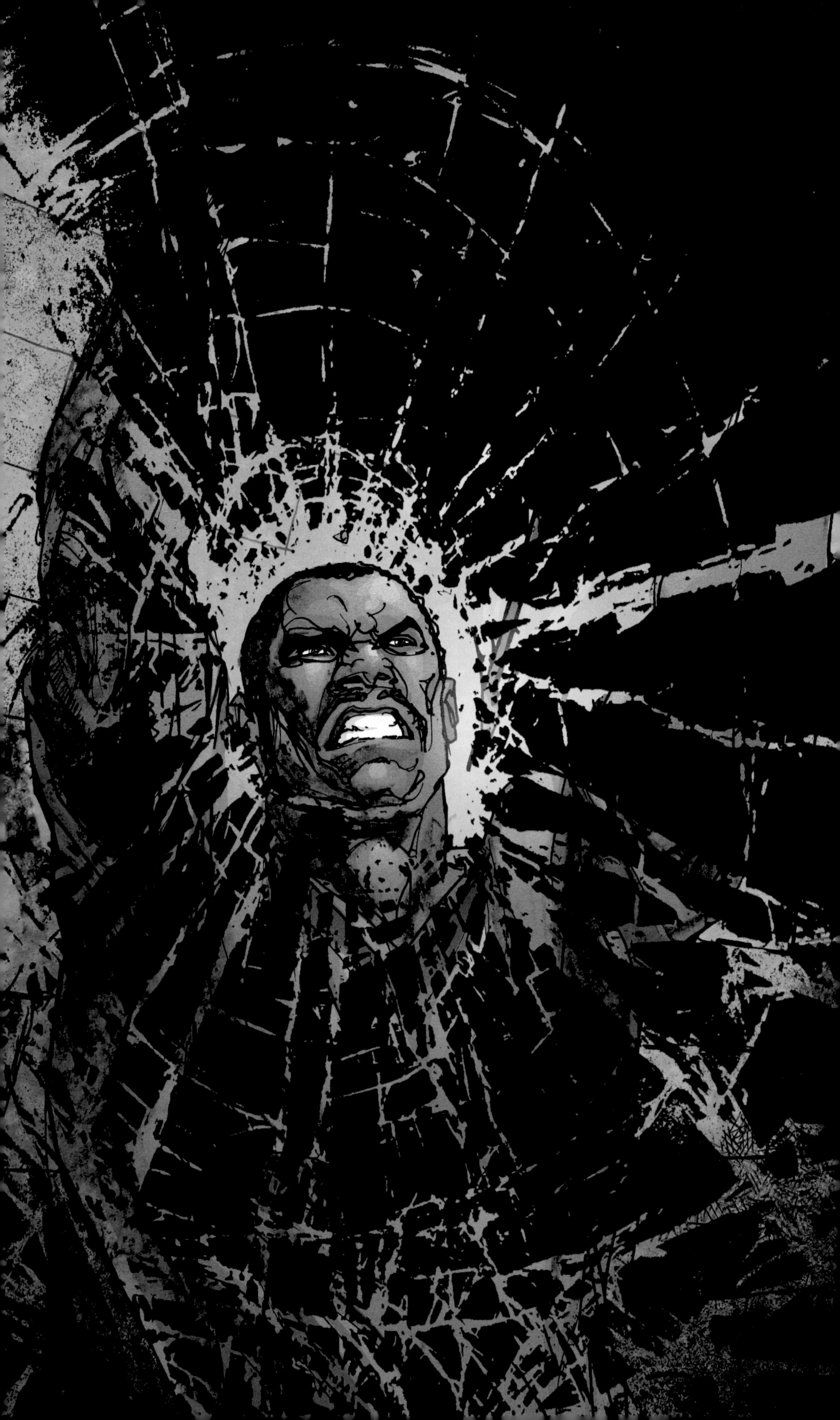

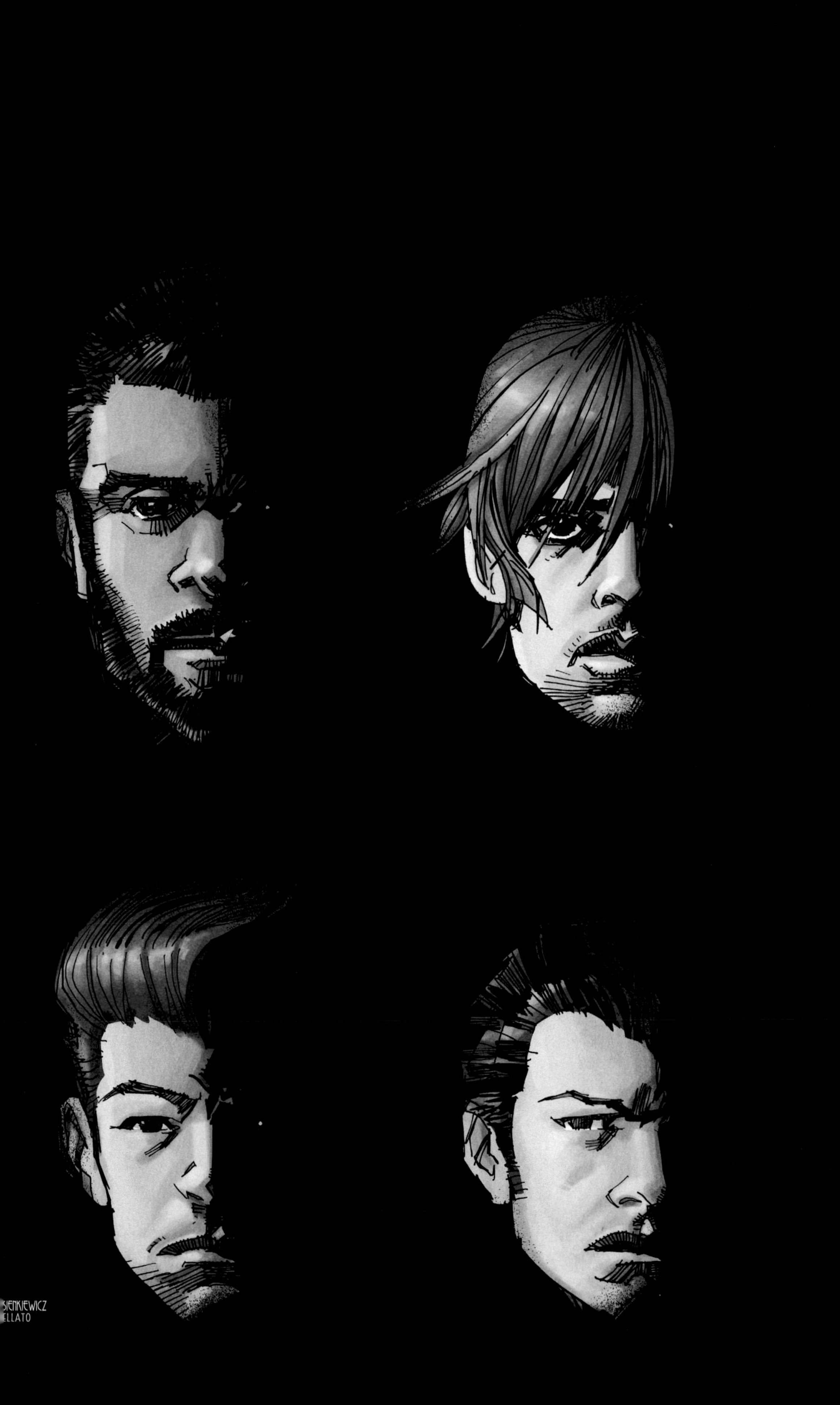
SIENKIEWICZ

3

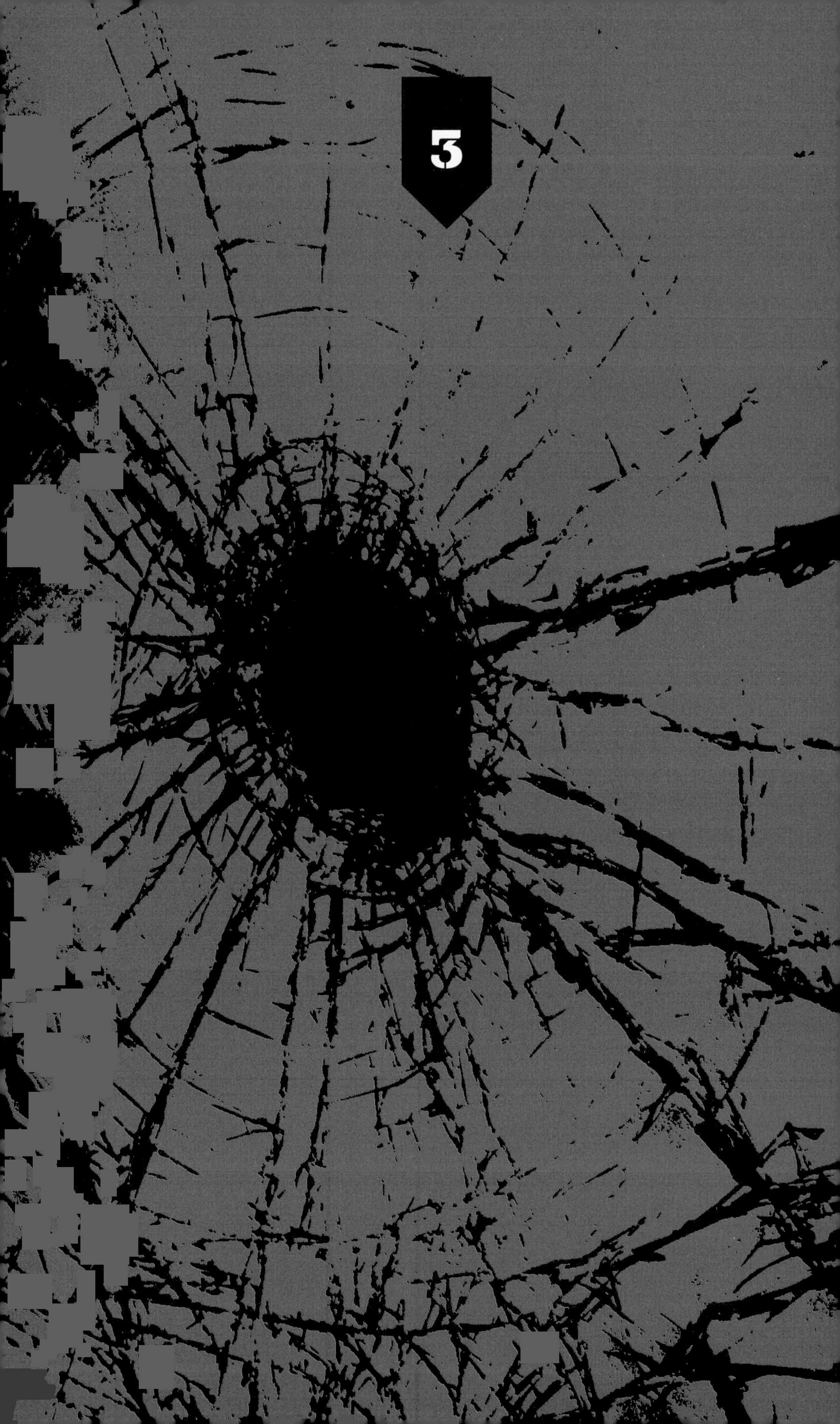

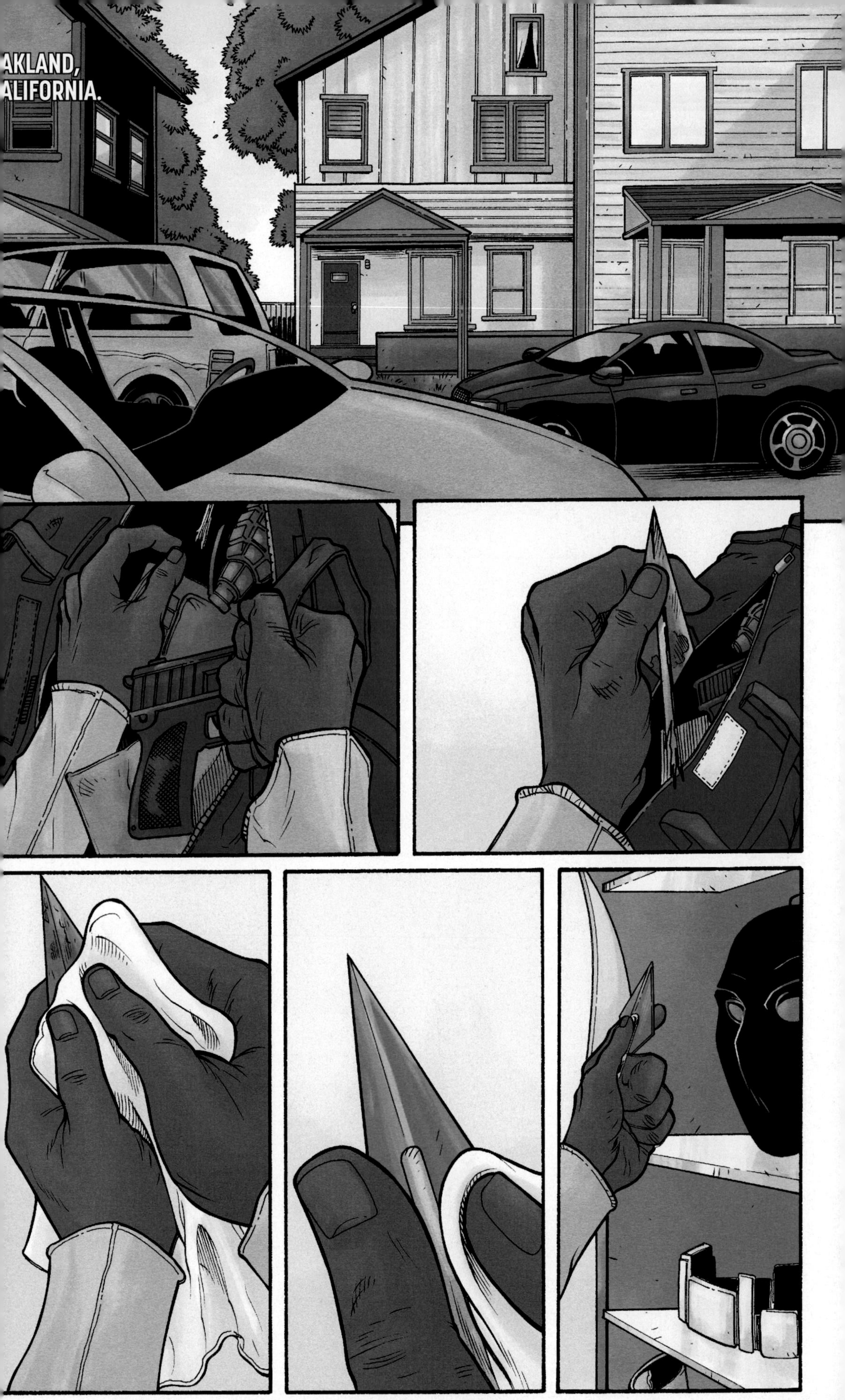
AKLAND,
ALIFORNIA.

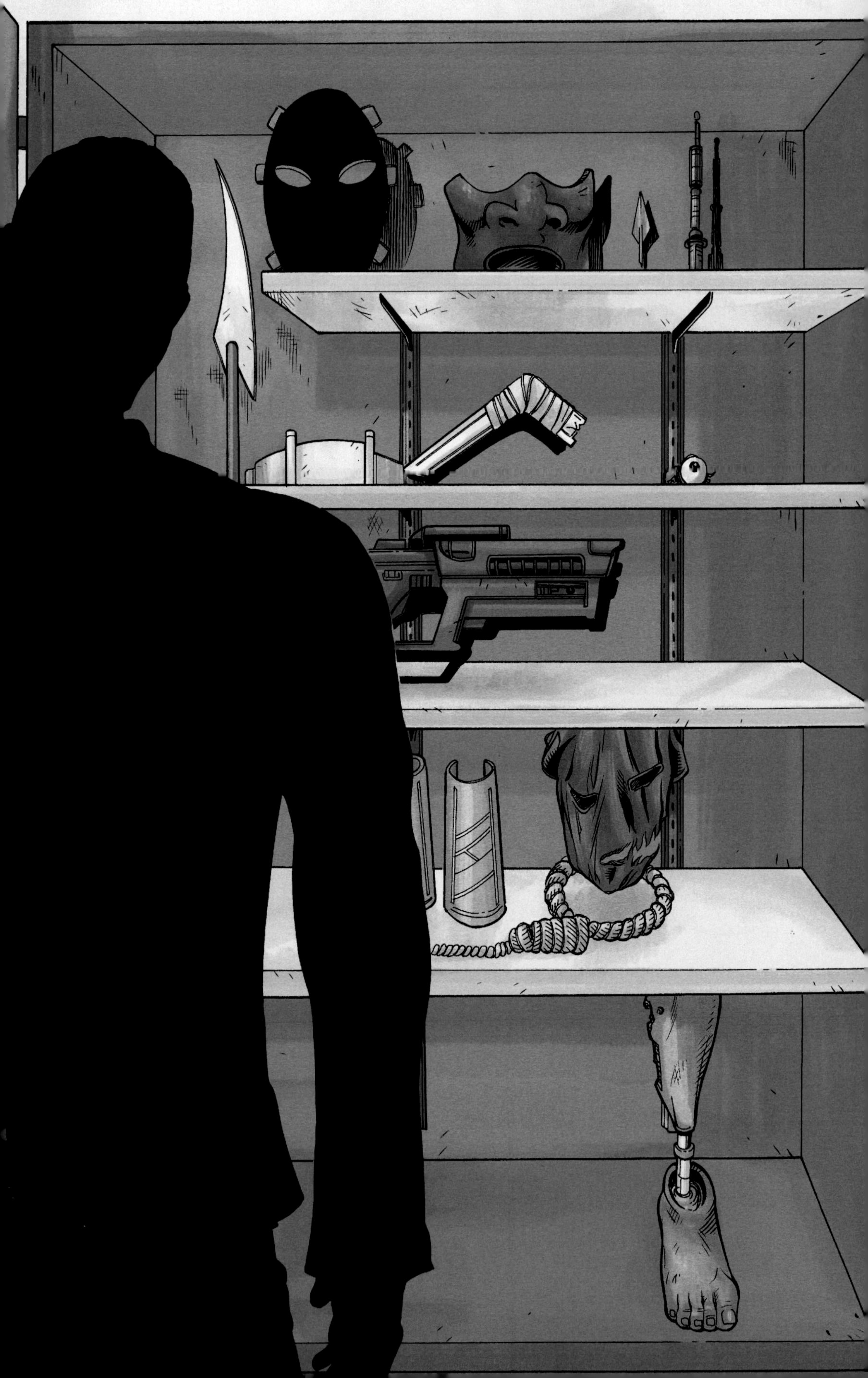

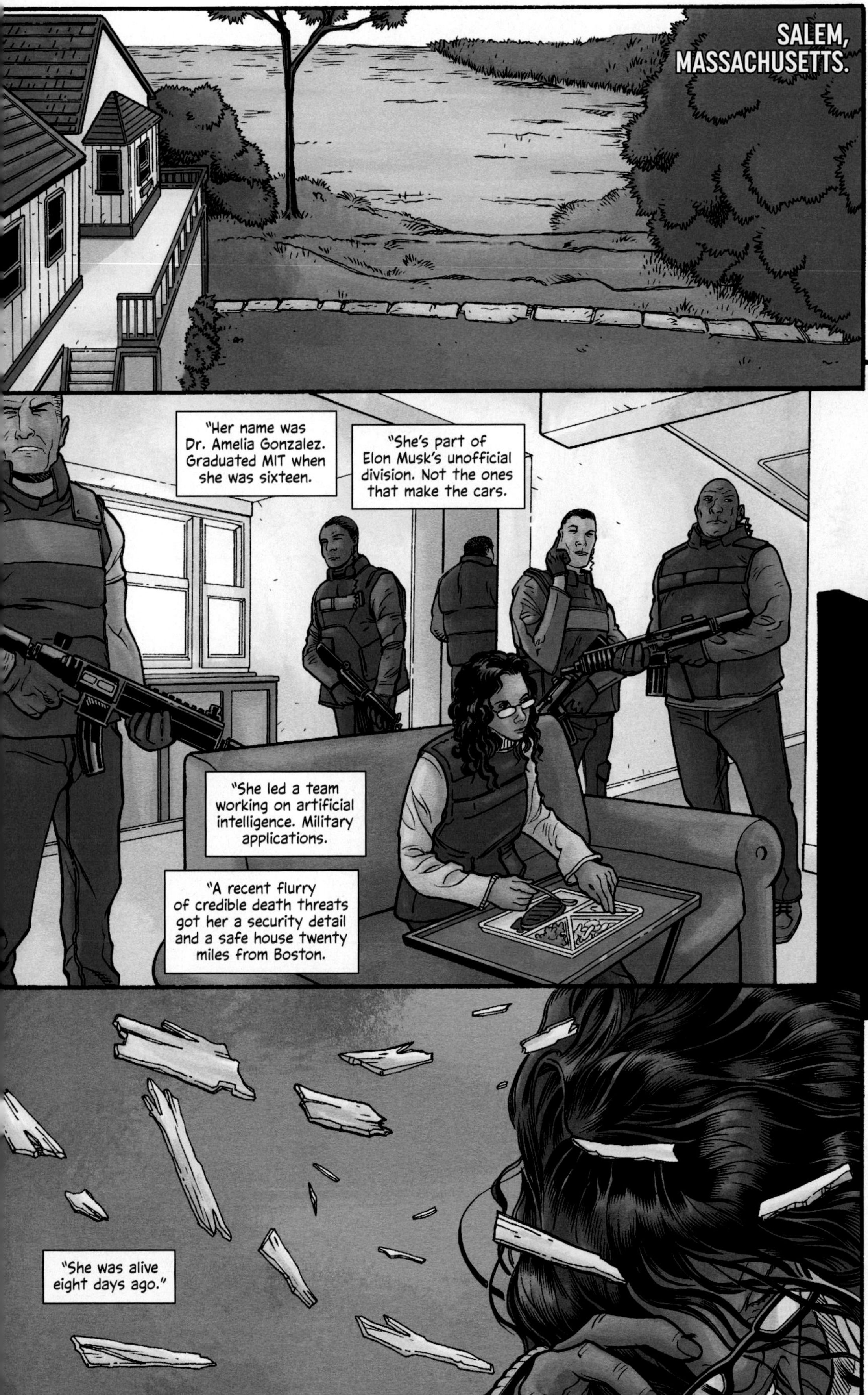
SALEM, MASSACHUSETTS.
"Her name was Dr. Amelia Gonzalez. Graduated MIT when she was sixteen.
"She's part of Elon Musk's unofficial division. Not the ones that make the cars.
"She led a team working on artificial intelligence. Military applications.
"A recent flurry of credible death threats got her a security detail and a safe house twenty miles from Boston.
"She was alive eight days ago."

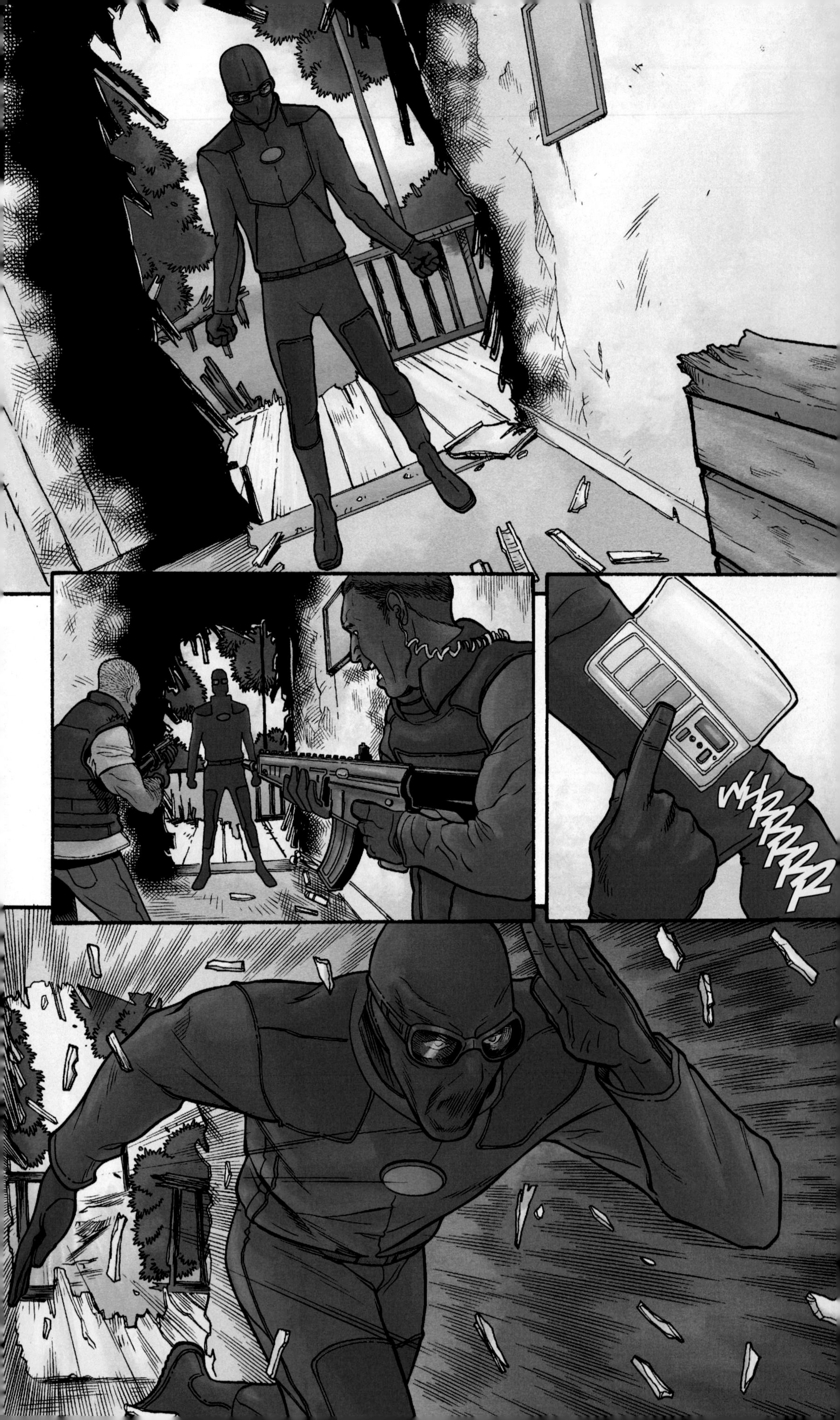
WHRRRRRR

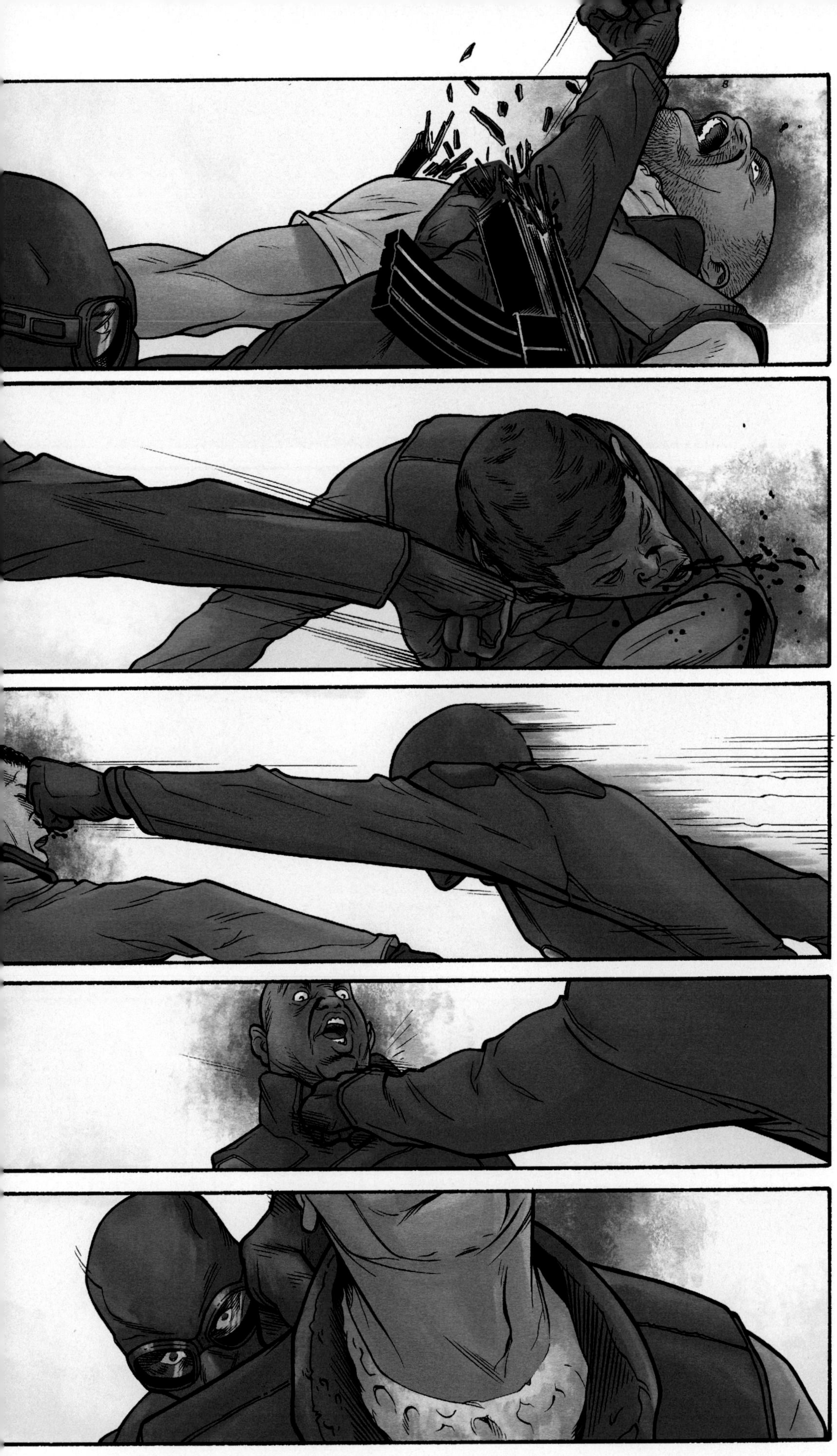

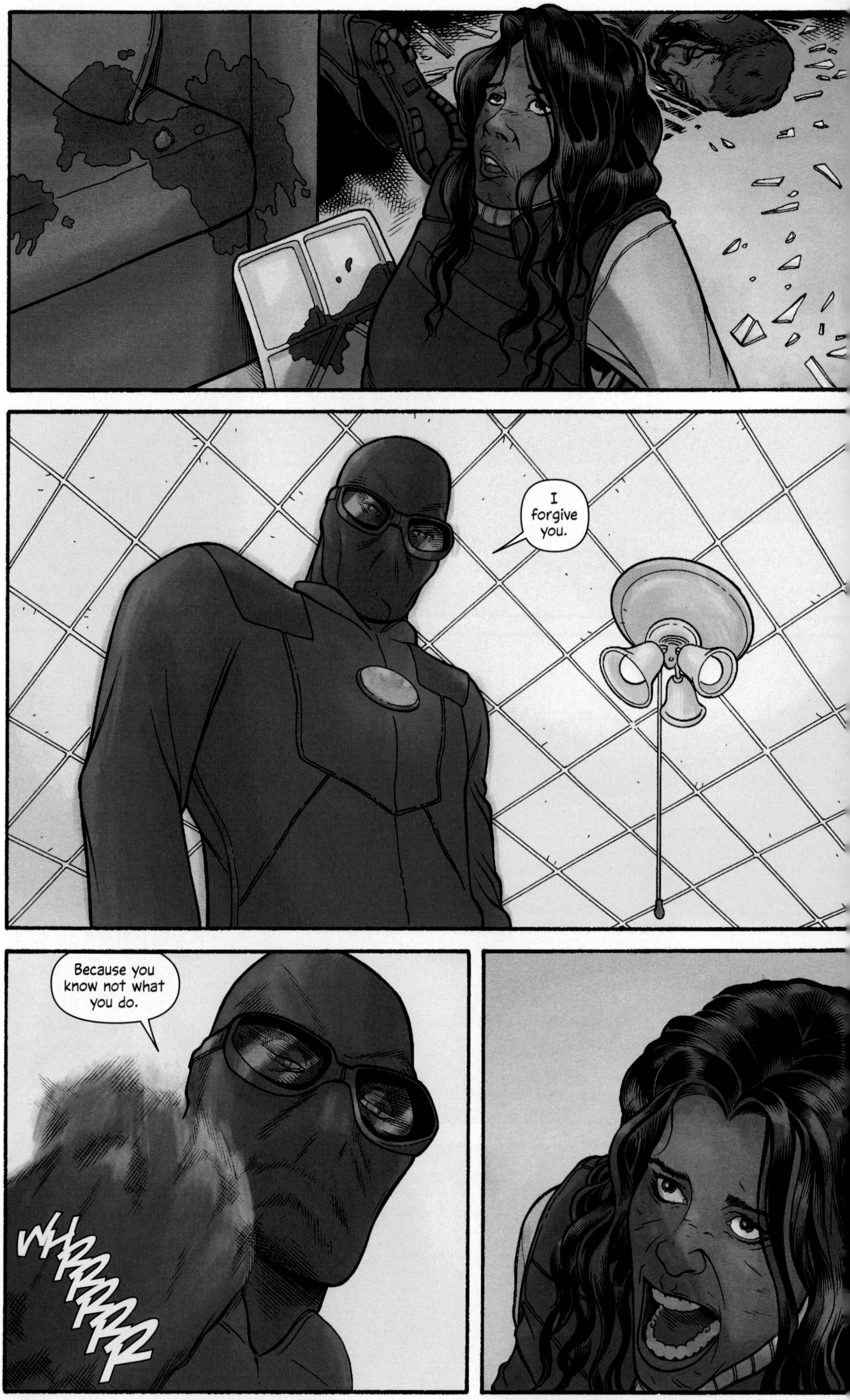
I forgive you.
Because you know not what you do.
WHRRRRR

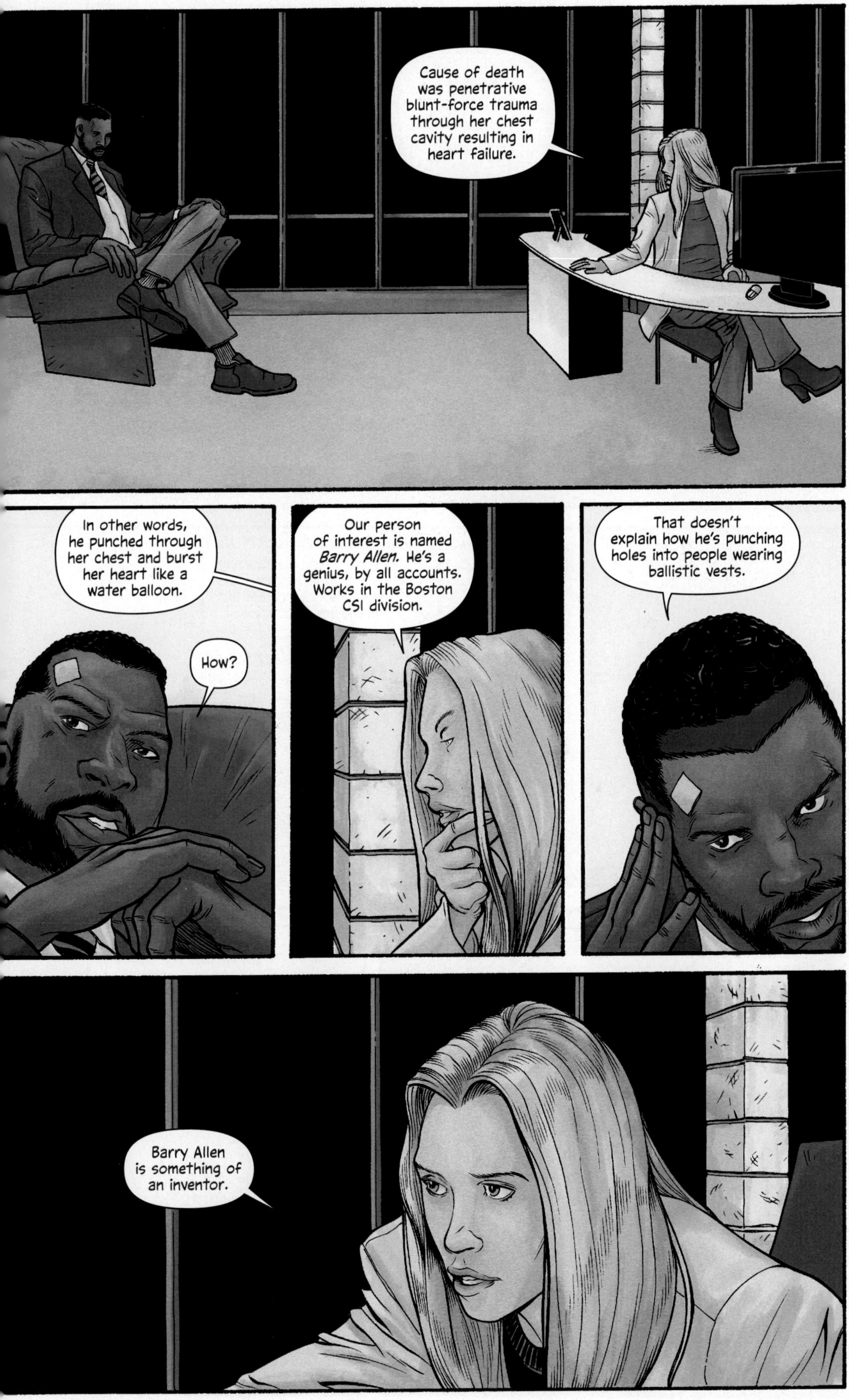

Cause of death was penetrative blunt-force trauma through her chest cavity resulting in heart failure.
In other words, he punched through her chest and burst her heart like a water balloon.
How?
Our person of interest is named *Barry Allen.* He's a genius, by all accounts. Works in the Boston CSI division.
That doesn't explain how he's punching holes into people wearing ballistic vests.
Barry Allen is something of an inventor.

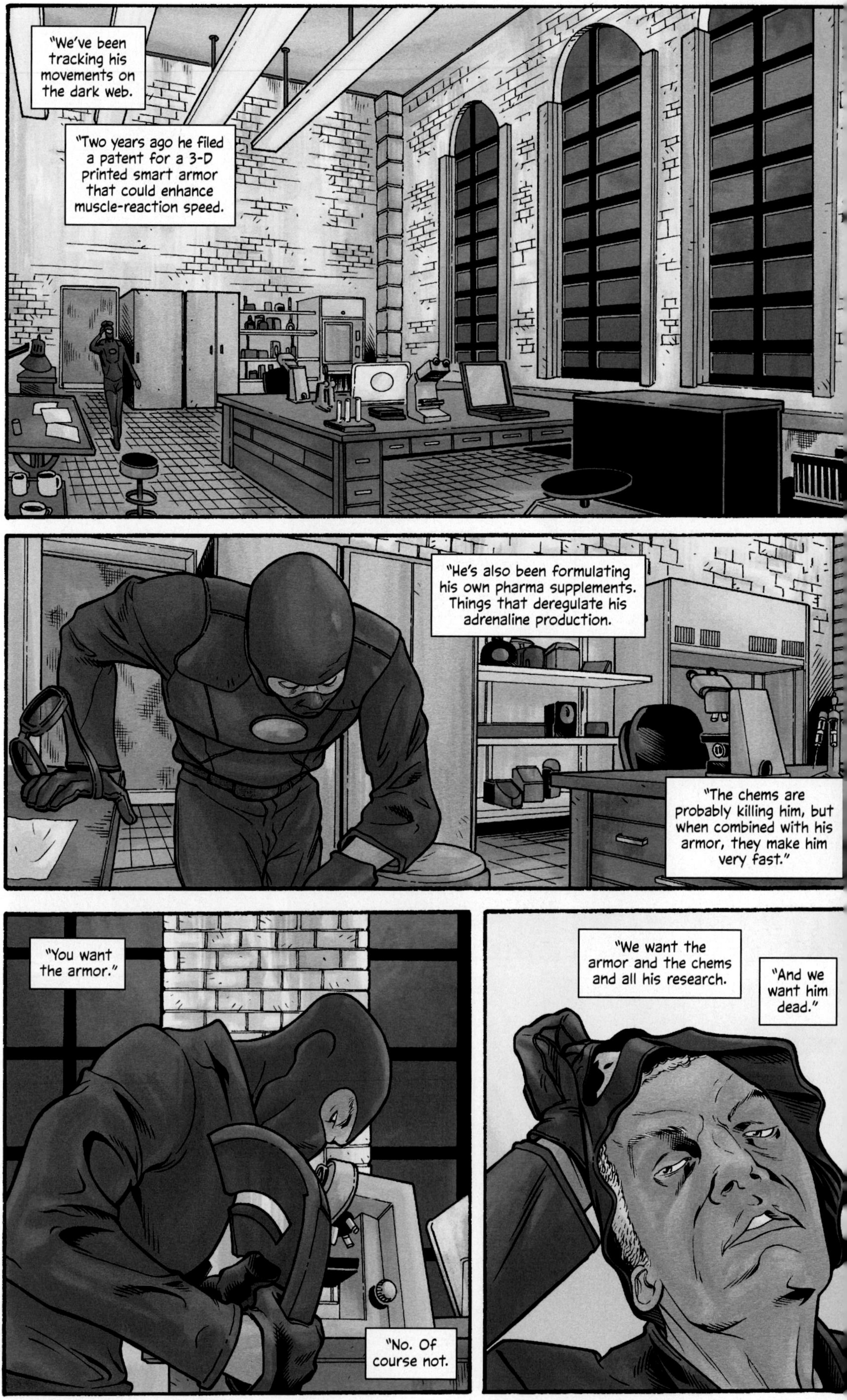

"We've been tracking his movements on the dark web.
"Two years ago he filed a patent for a 3-D printed smart armor that could enhance muscle-reaction speed.
"He's also been formulating his own pharma supplements. Things that deregulate his adrenaline production.
"The chems are probably killing him, but when combined with his armor, they make him very fast."
"You want the armor."
"No. Of course not.
"We want the armor and the chems and all his research.
"And we want him dead."

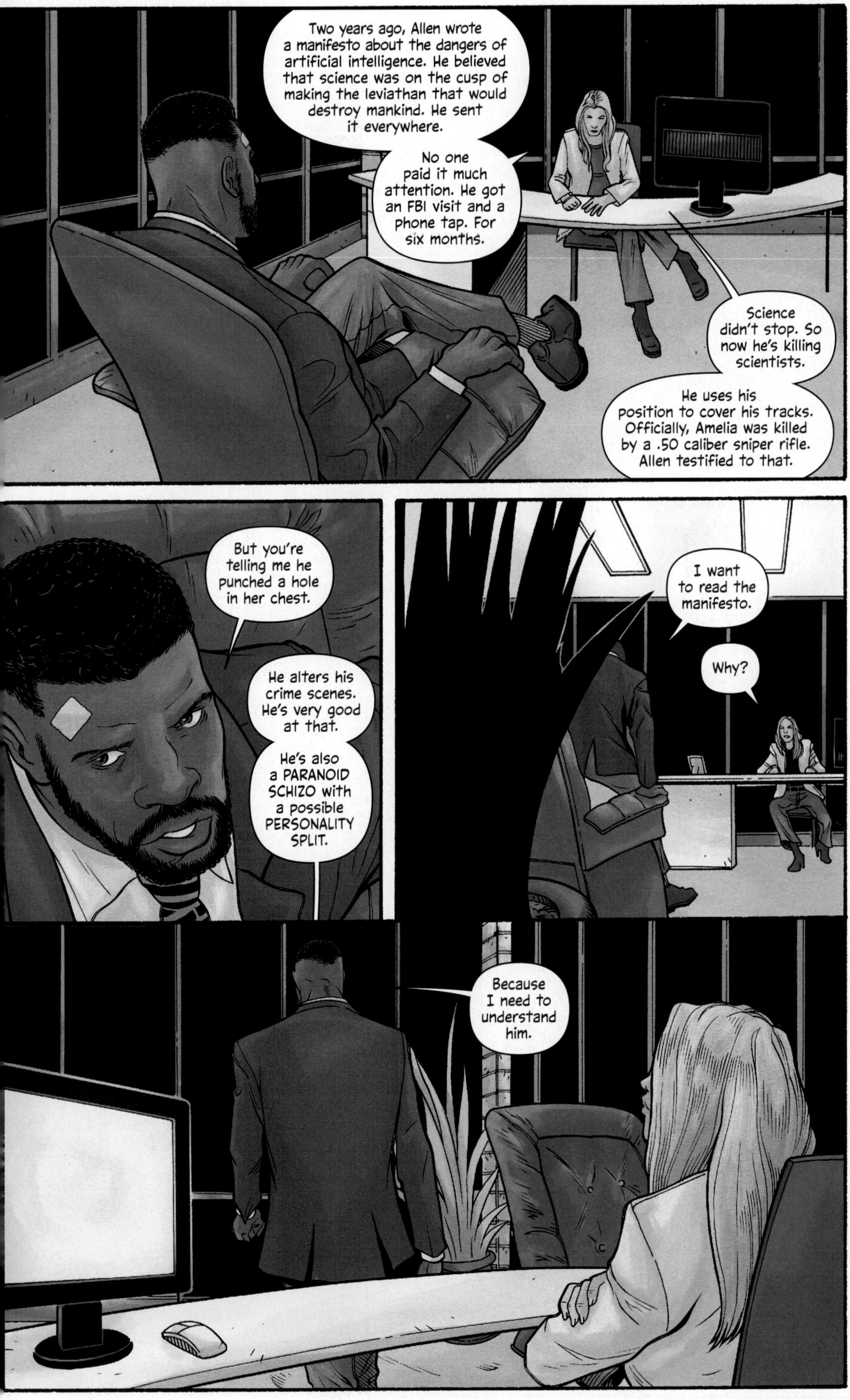
Two years ago, Allen wrote a manifesto about the dangers of artificial intelligence. He believed that science was on the cusp of making the leviathan that would destroy mankind. He sent it everywhere.
No one paid it much attention. He got an FBI visit and a phone tap. For six months.
Science didn't stop. So now he's killing scientists.
He uses his position to cover his tracks. Officially, Amelia was killed by a .50 caliber sniper rifle. Allen testified to that.
But you're telling me he punched a hole in her chest.
He alters his crime scenes. He's very good at that.
He's also a PARANOID SCHIZO with a possible PERSONALITY SPLIT.
I want to read the manifesto.
Why?
Because I need to understand him.

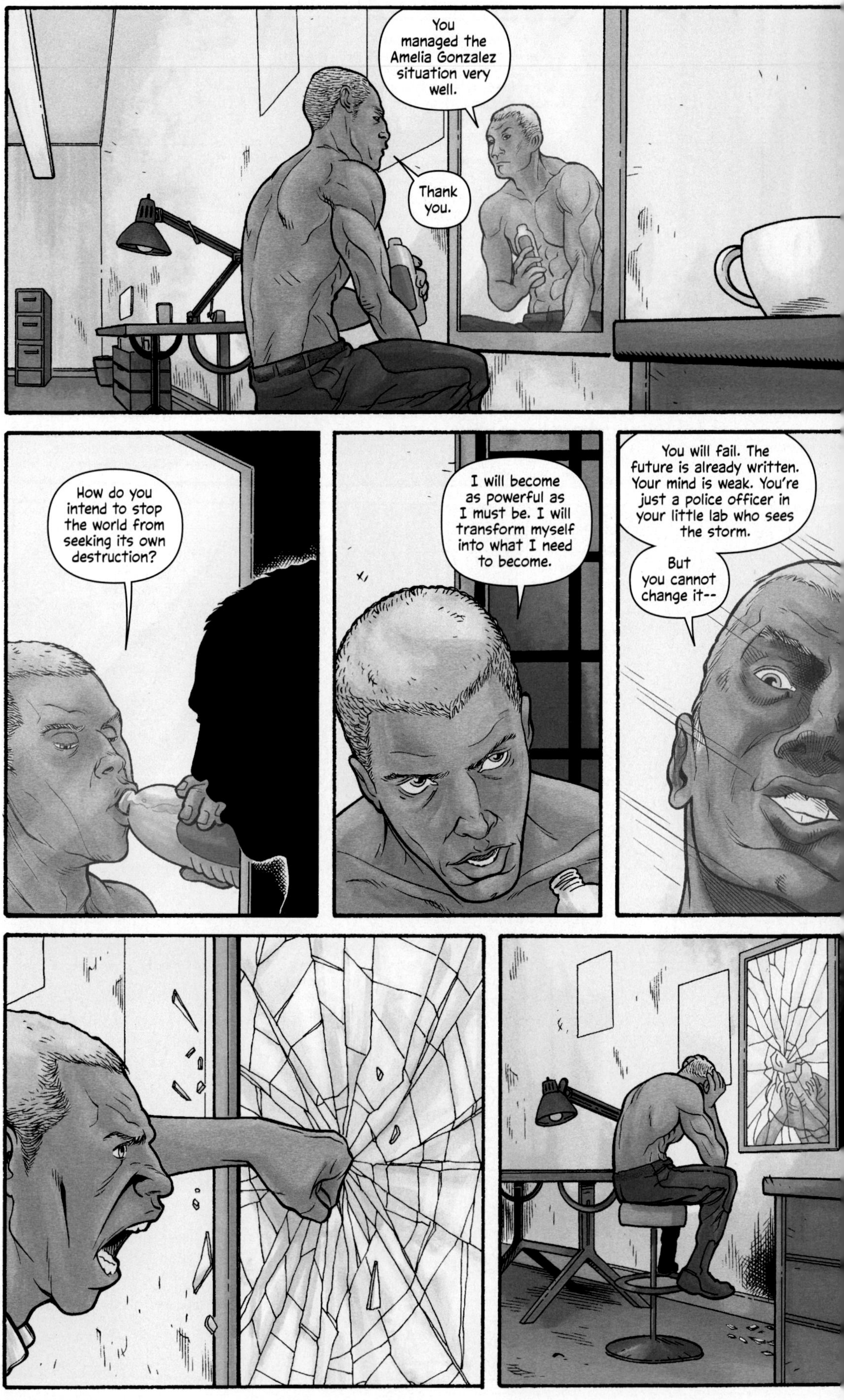
You managed the Amelia Gonzalez situation very well.
Thank you.
How do you intend to stop the world from seeking its own destruction?
I will become as powerful as I must be. I will transform myself into what I need to become.
You will fail. The future is already written. Your mind is weak. You're just a police officer in your little lab who sees the storm.
But you cannot change it--

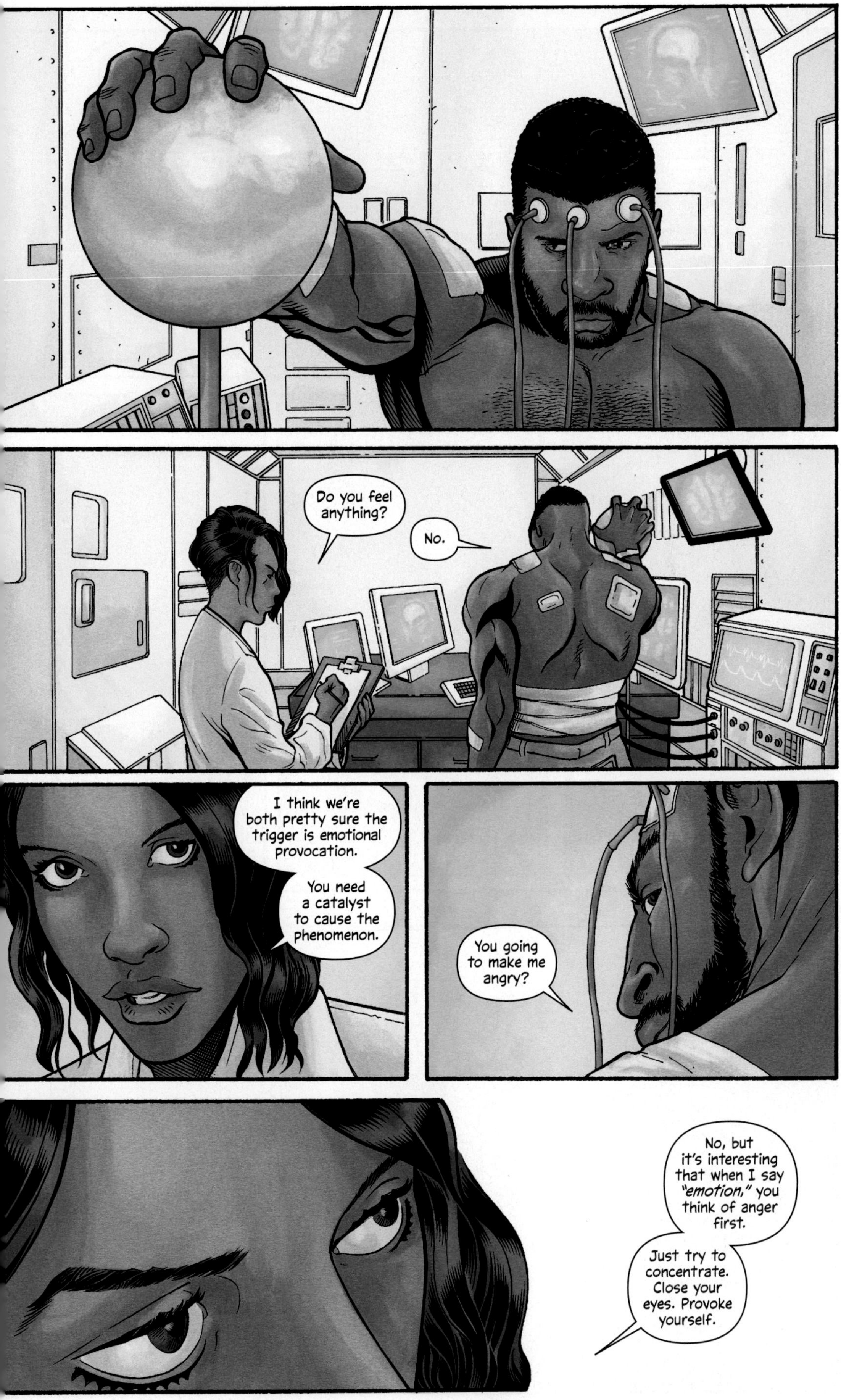
Do you feel anything?
No.
I think we're both pretty sure the trigger is emotional provocation.
You need a catalyst to cause the phenomenon.
You going to make me angry?
No, but it's interesting that when I say *"emotion,"* you think of anger first.
Just try to concentrate. Close your eyes. Provoke yourself.

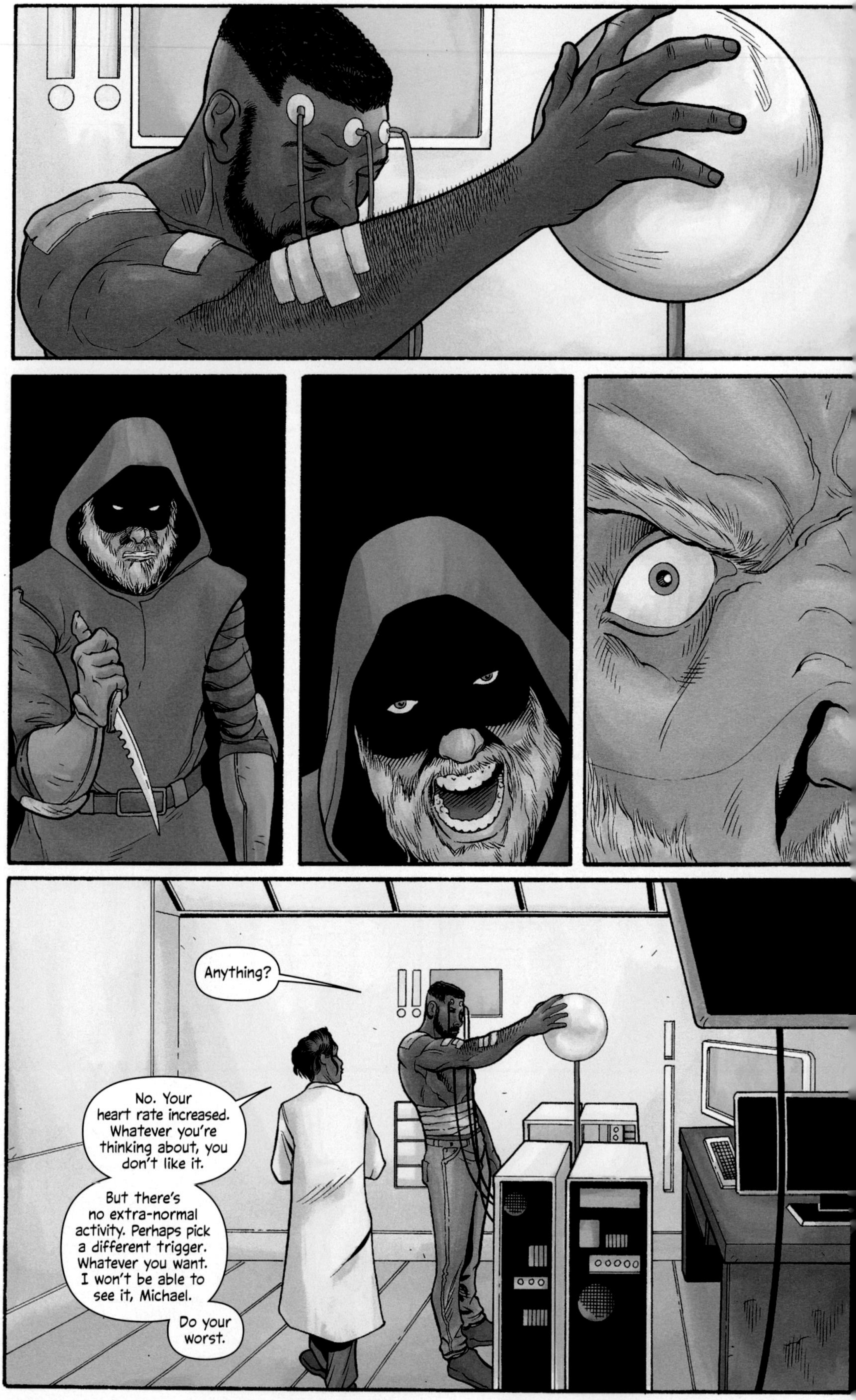
Anything?
No. Your heart rate increased. Whatever you're thinking about, you don't like it.
But there's no extra-normal activity. Perhaps pick a different trigger. Whatever you want. I won't be able to see it, Michael.
Do your worst.

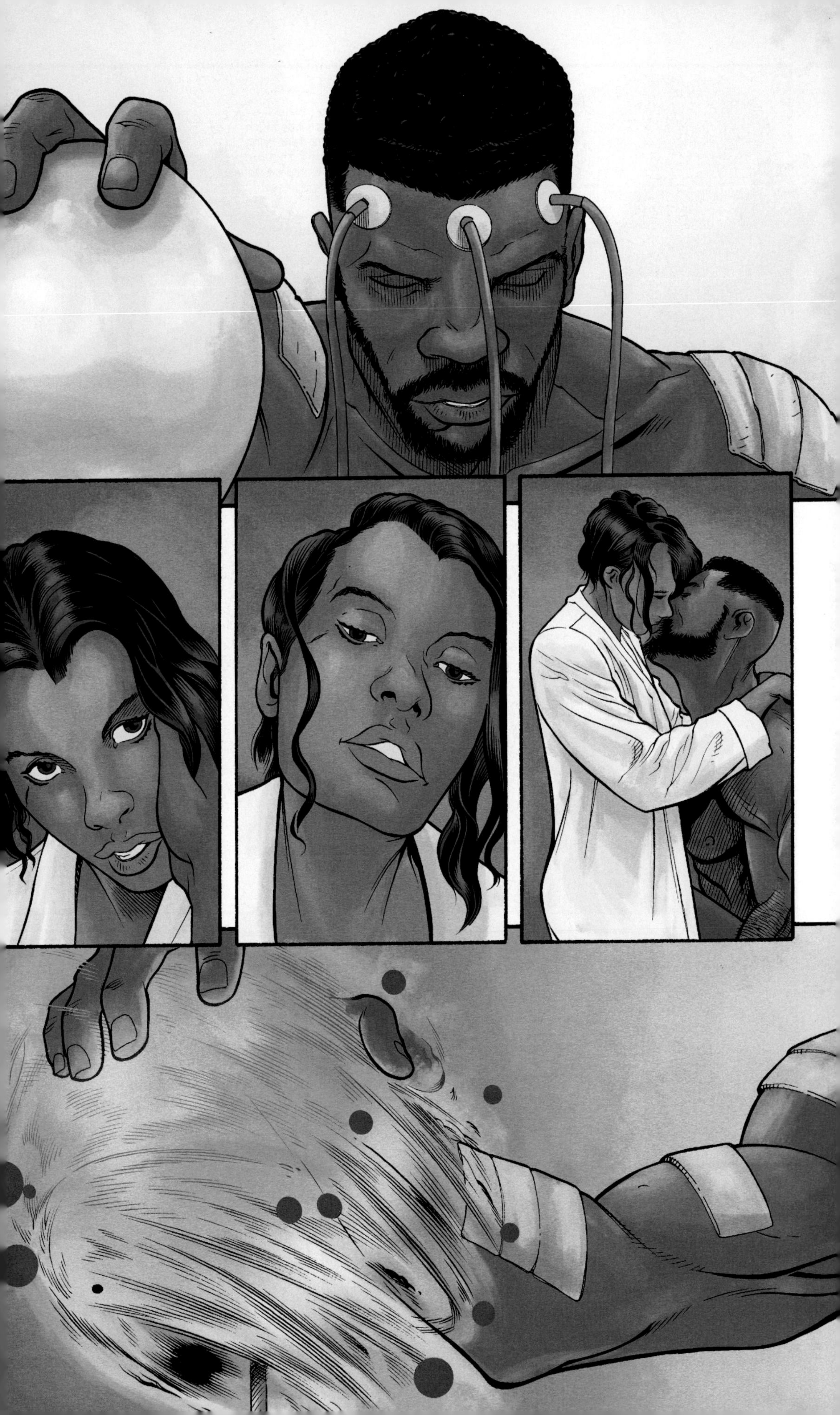

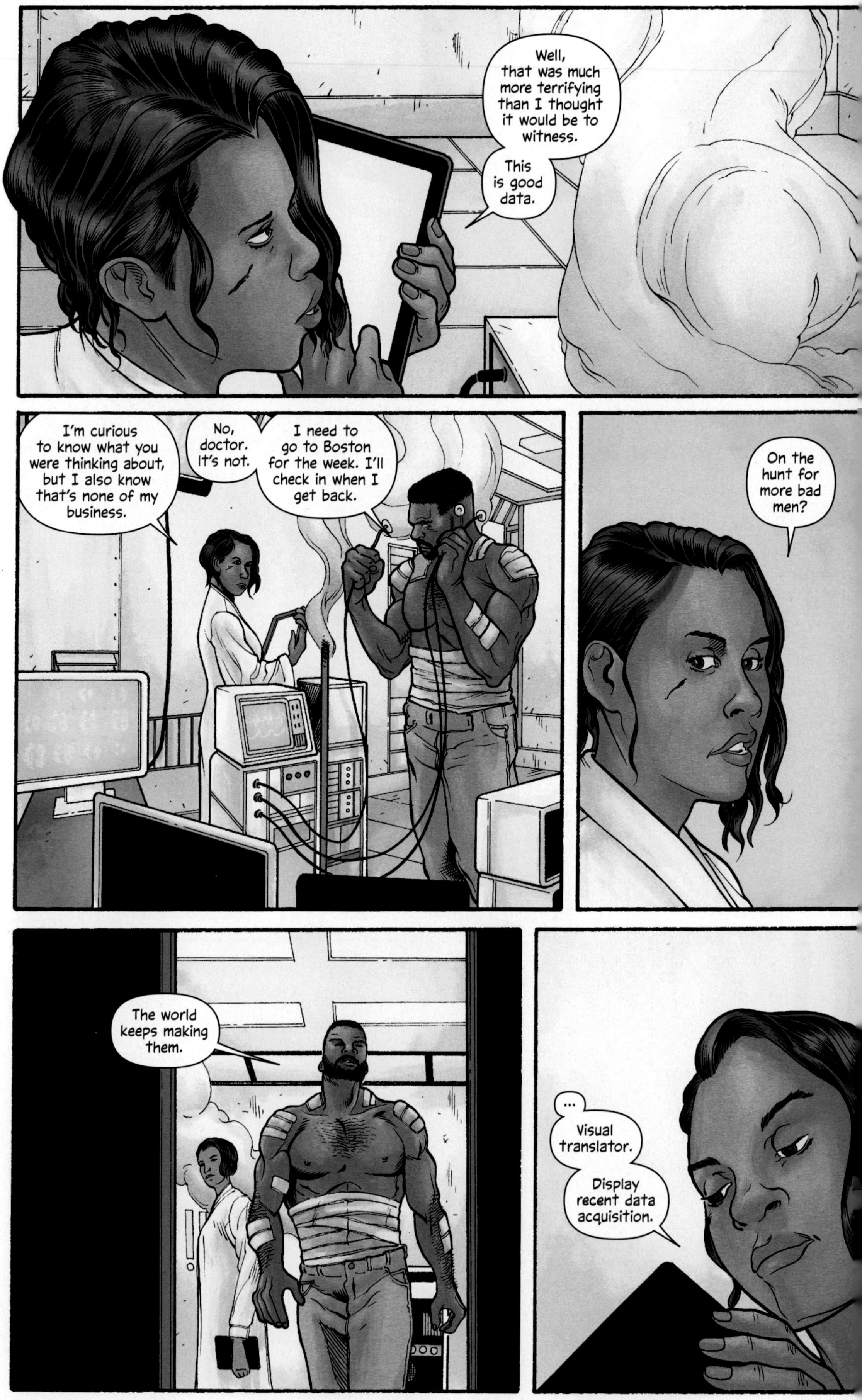
Well, that was much more terrifying than I thought it would be to witness.
This is good data.
I'm curious to know what you were thinking about, but I also know that's none of my business.
No, doctor. It's not.
I need to go to Boston for the week. I'll check in when I get back.
On the hunt for more bad men?
The world keeps making them.
...
Visual translator.
Display recent data acquisition.

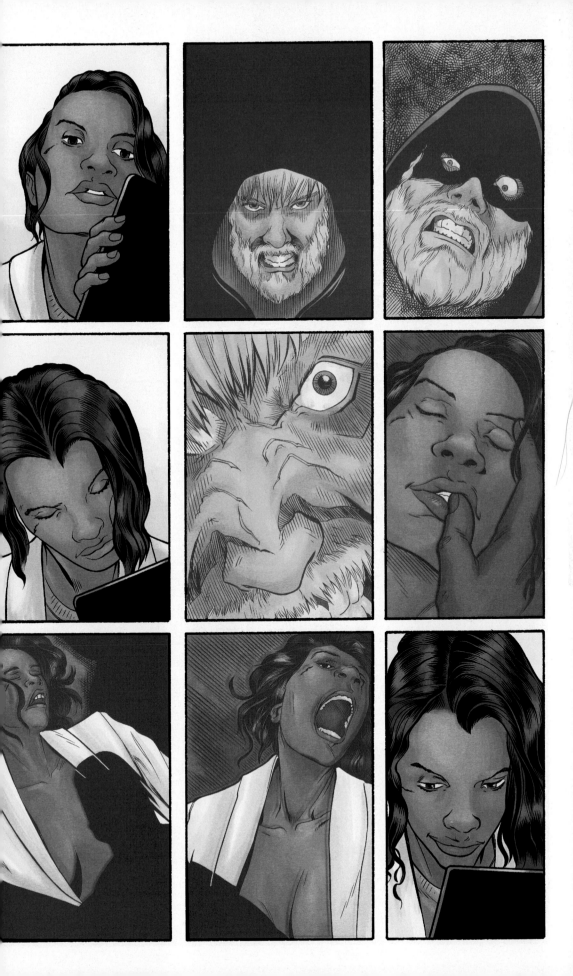

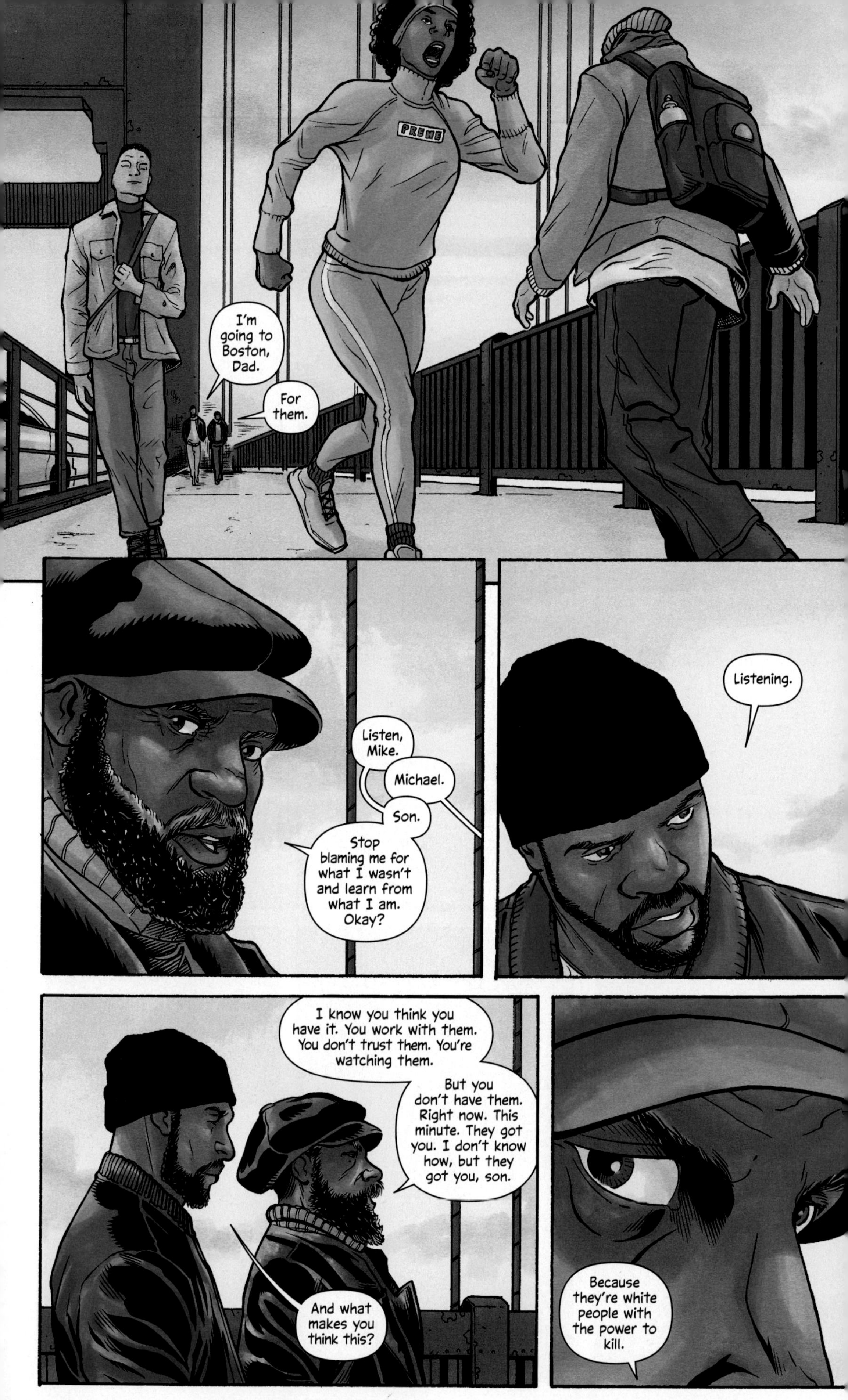
I'm going to Boston, Dad.
For them.
Listen, Mike.
Michael.
Son.
Stop blaming me for what I wasn't and learn from what I am. Okay?
Listening.
I know you think you have it. You work with them. You don't trust them. You're watching them.
But you don't have them. Right now. This minute. They got you. I don't know how, but they got you, son.
And what makes you think this?
Because they're white people with the power to kill.

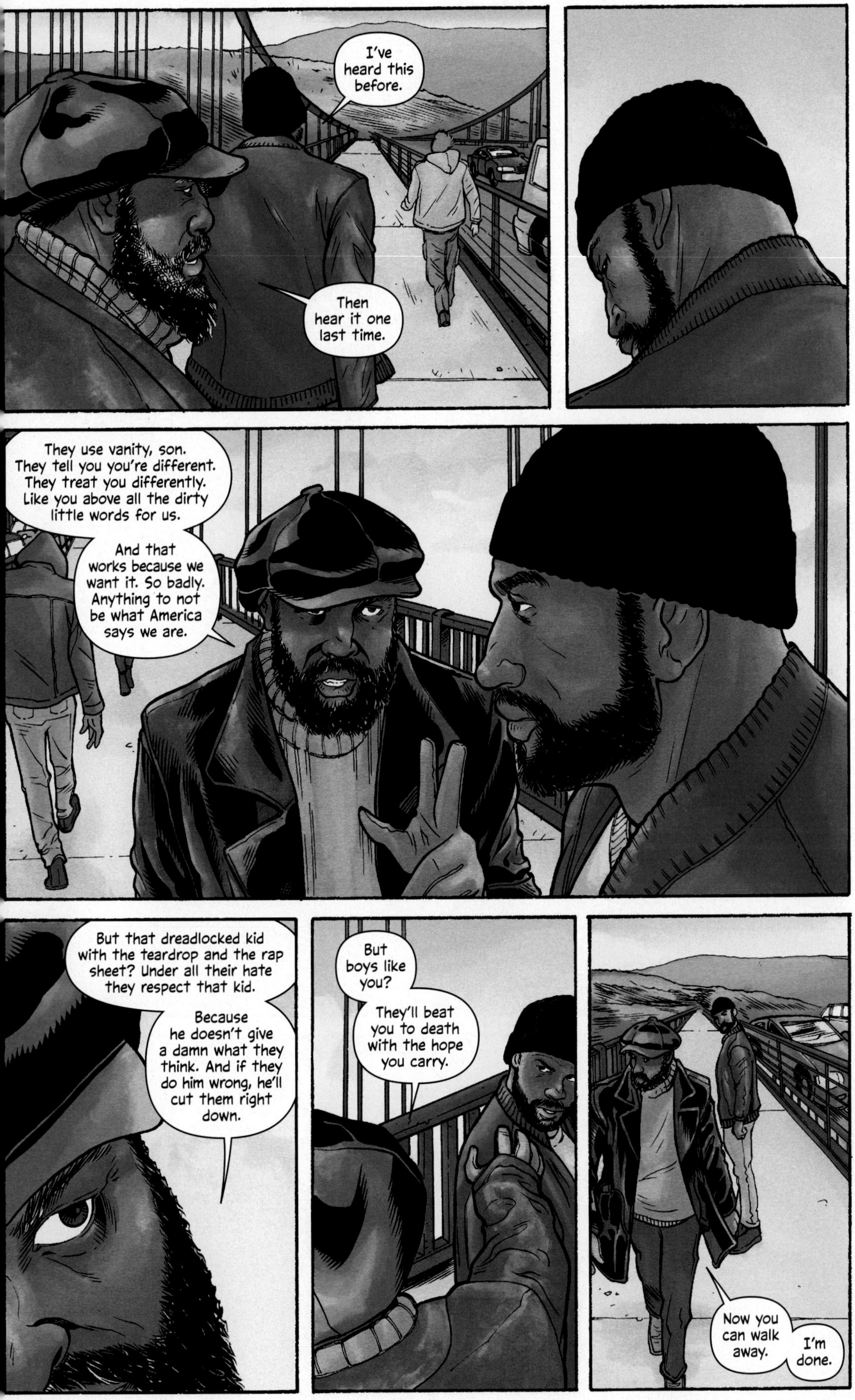
I've heard this before.
Then hear it one last time.
They use vanity, son. They tell you you're different. They treat you differently. Like you above all the dirty little words for us.
And that works because we want it. So badly. Anything to not be what America says we are.
But that dreadlocked kid with the teardrop and the rap sheet? Under all their hate they respect that kid.
Because he doesn't give a damn what they think. And if they do him wrong, he'll cut them right down.
But boys like you?
They'll beat you to death with the hope you carry.
Now you can walk away.
I'm done.

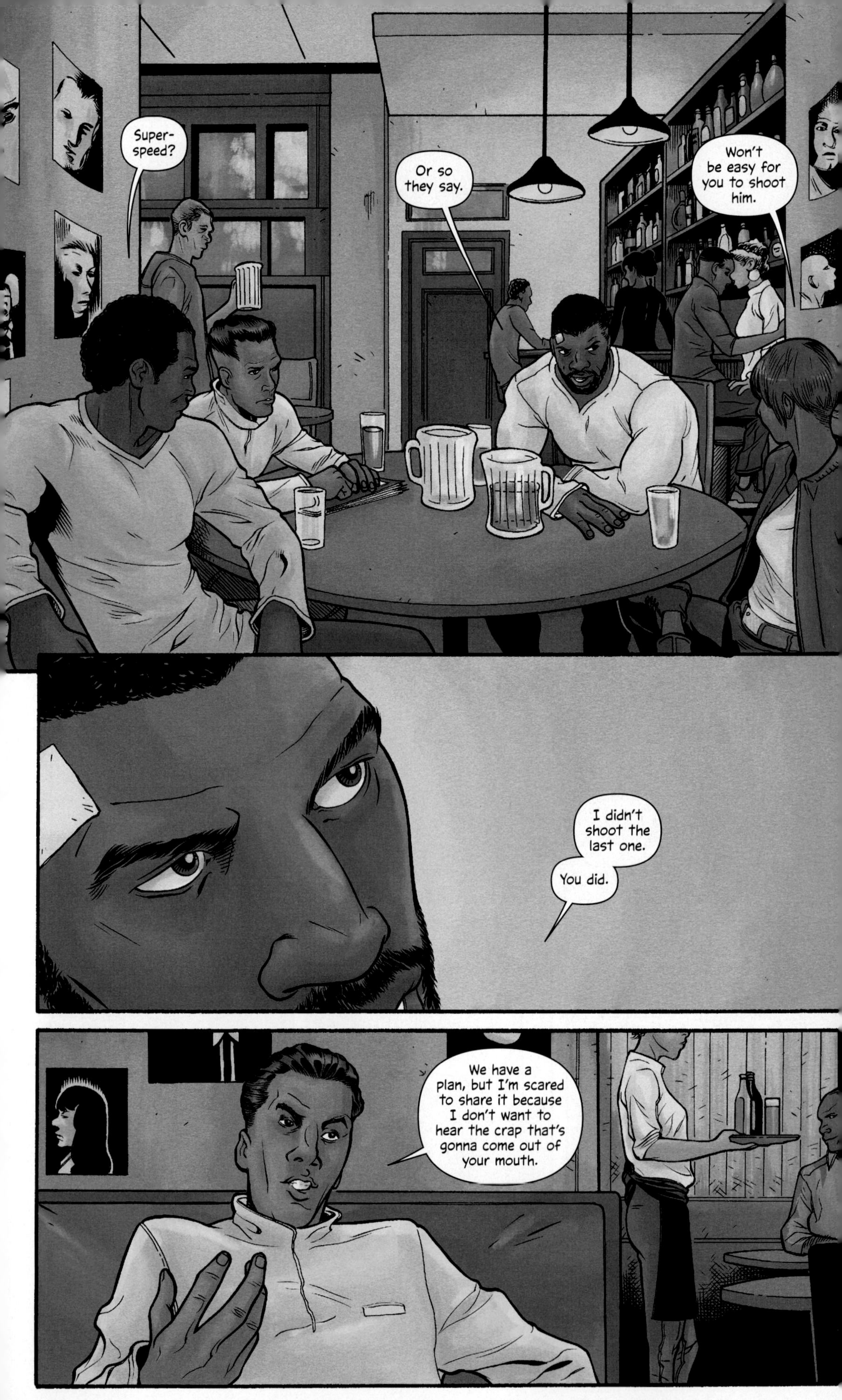
Super-speed?
Or so they say.
Won't be easy for you to shoot him.
I didn't shoot the last one.
You did.
We have a plan, but I'm scared to share it because I don't want to hear the crap that's gonna come out of your mouth.

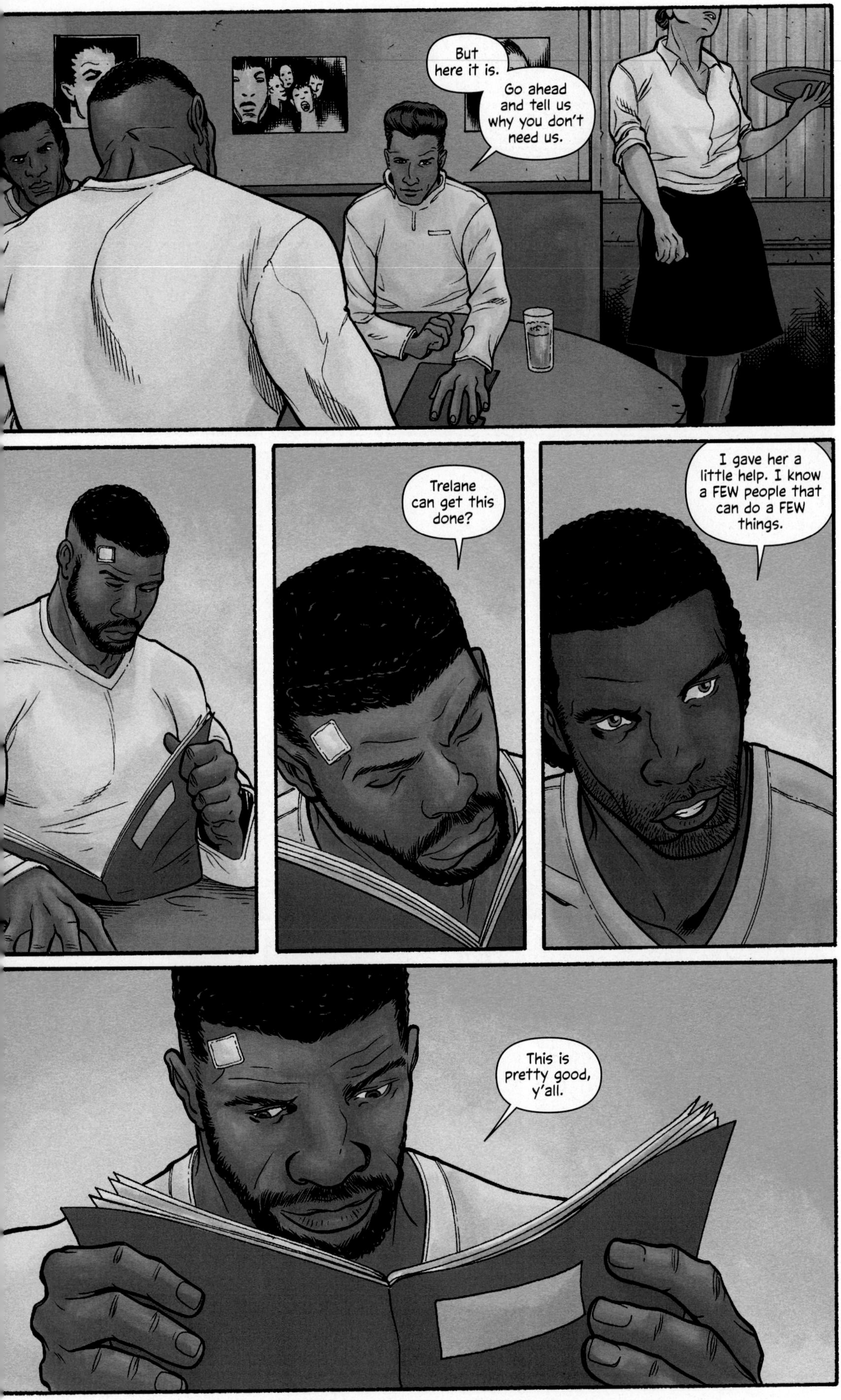
But here it is.
Go ahead and tell us why you don't need us.
Trelane can get this done?
I gave her a little help. I know a FEW people that can do a FEW things.
This is pretty good, y'all.

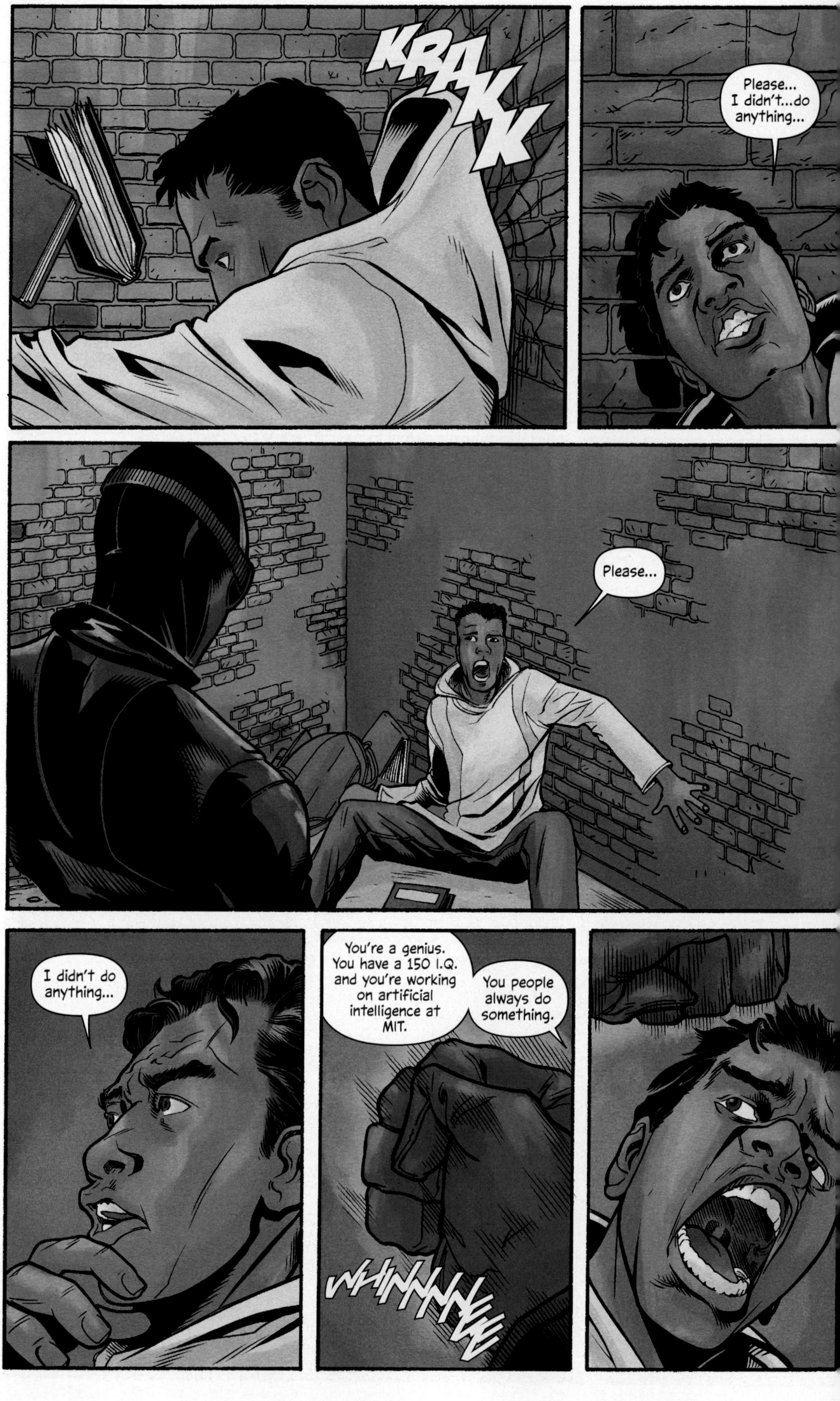
KRAKK
Please... I didn't...do anything...
Please...
I didn't do anything...
You're a genius. You have a 150 I.Q. and you're working on artificial intelligence at MIT.
You people always do something.
WHNNNEW

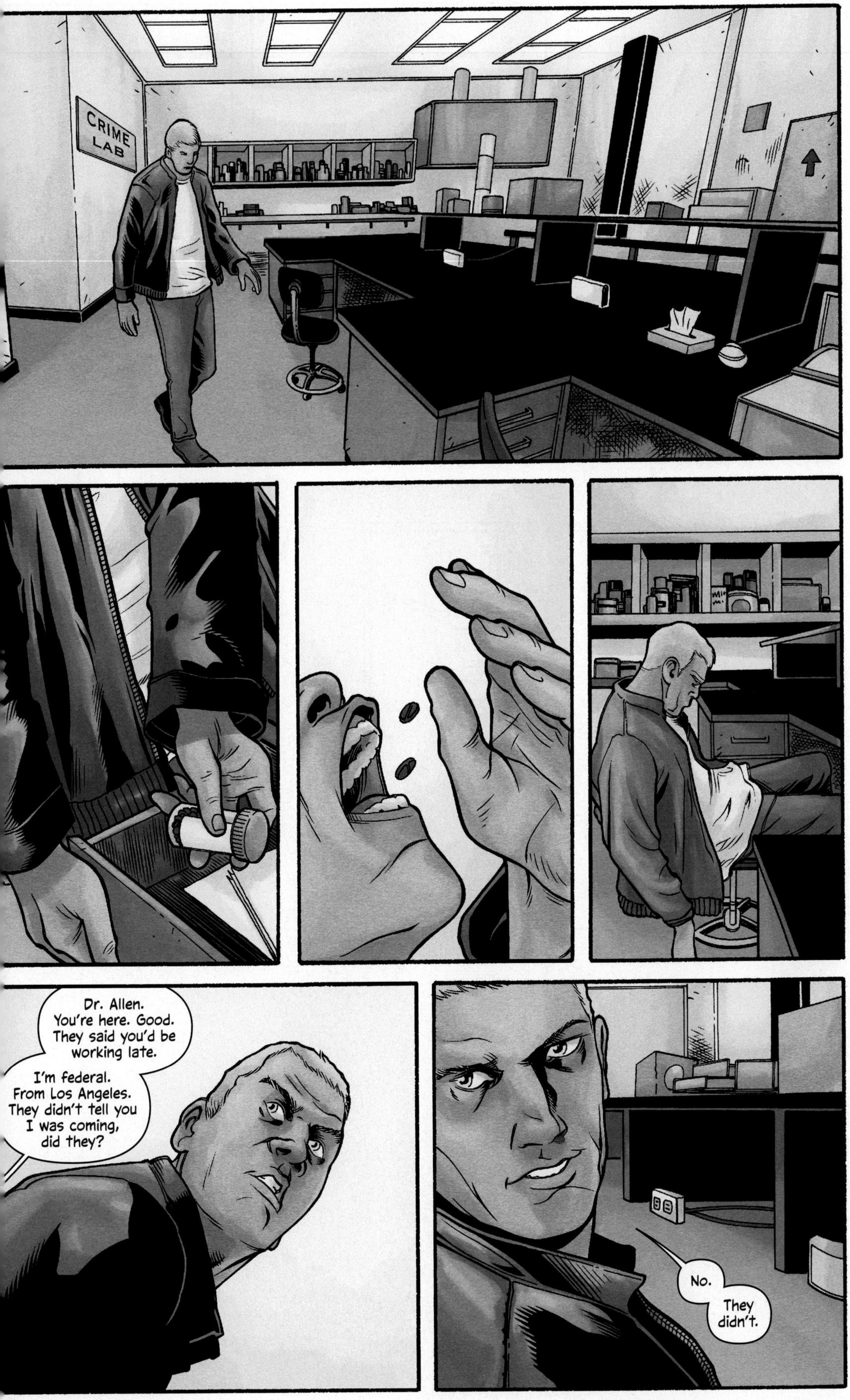
CRIME LAB
Dr. Allen. You're here. Good. They said you'd be working late.
I'm federal. From Los Angeles. They didn't tell you I was coming, did they?
No.
They didn't.

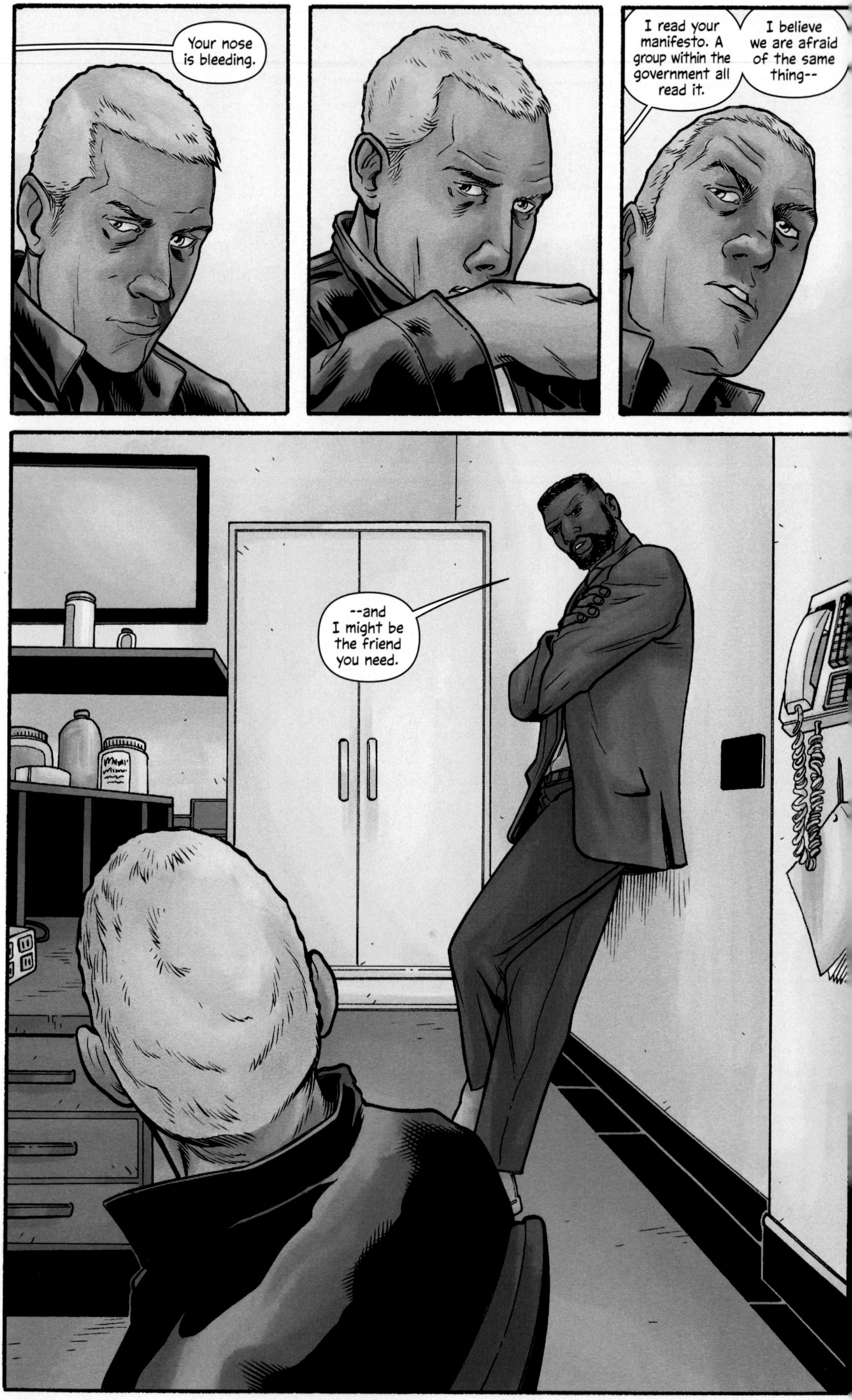
Your nose is bleeding.
I read your manifesto. A group within the government all read it.
I believe we are afraid of the same thing--
--and I might be the friend you need.

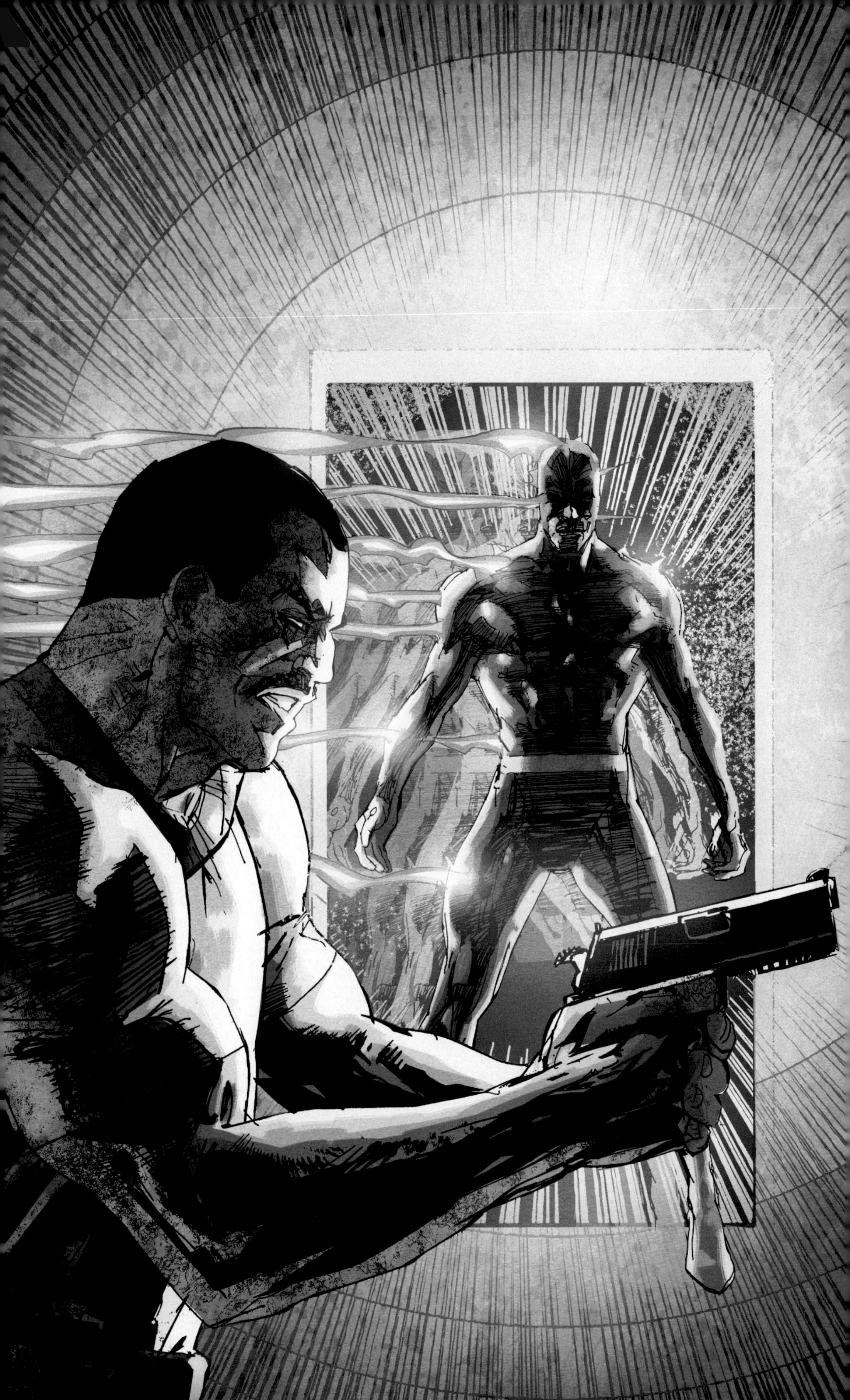

COWAN • SIENKIEWICZ

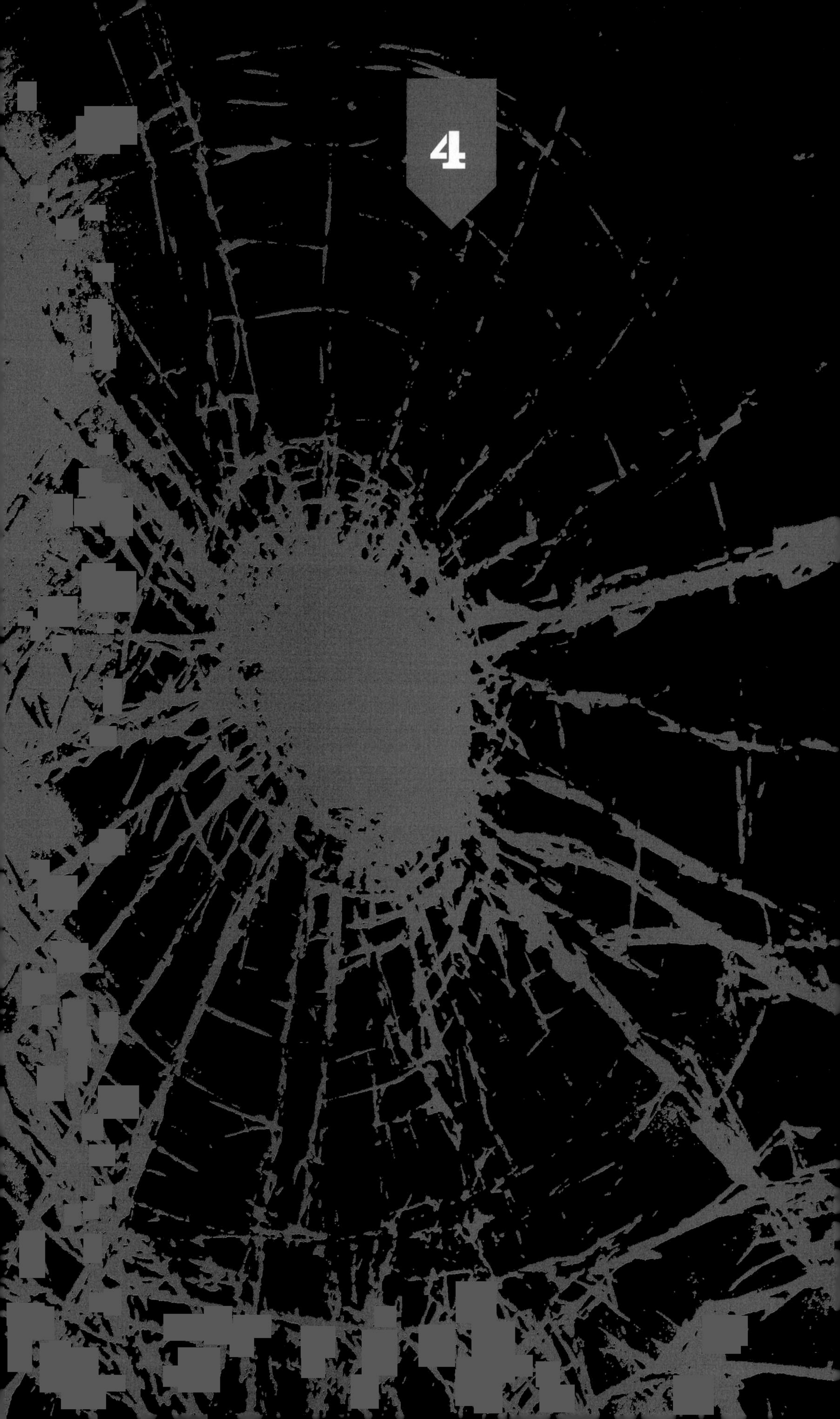
4

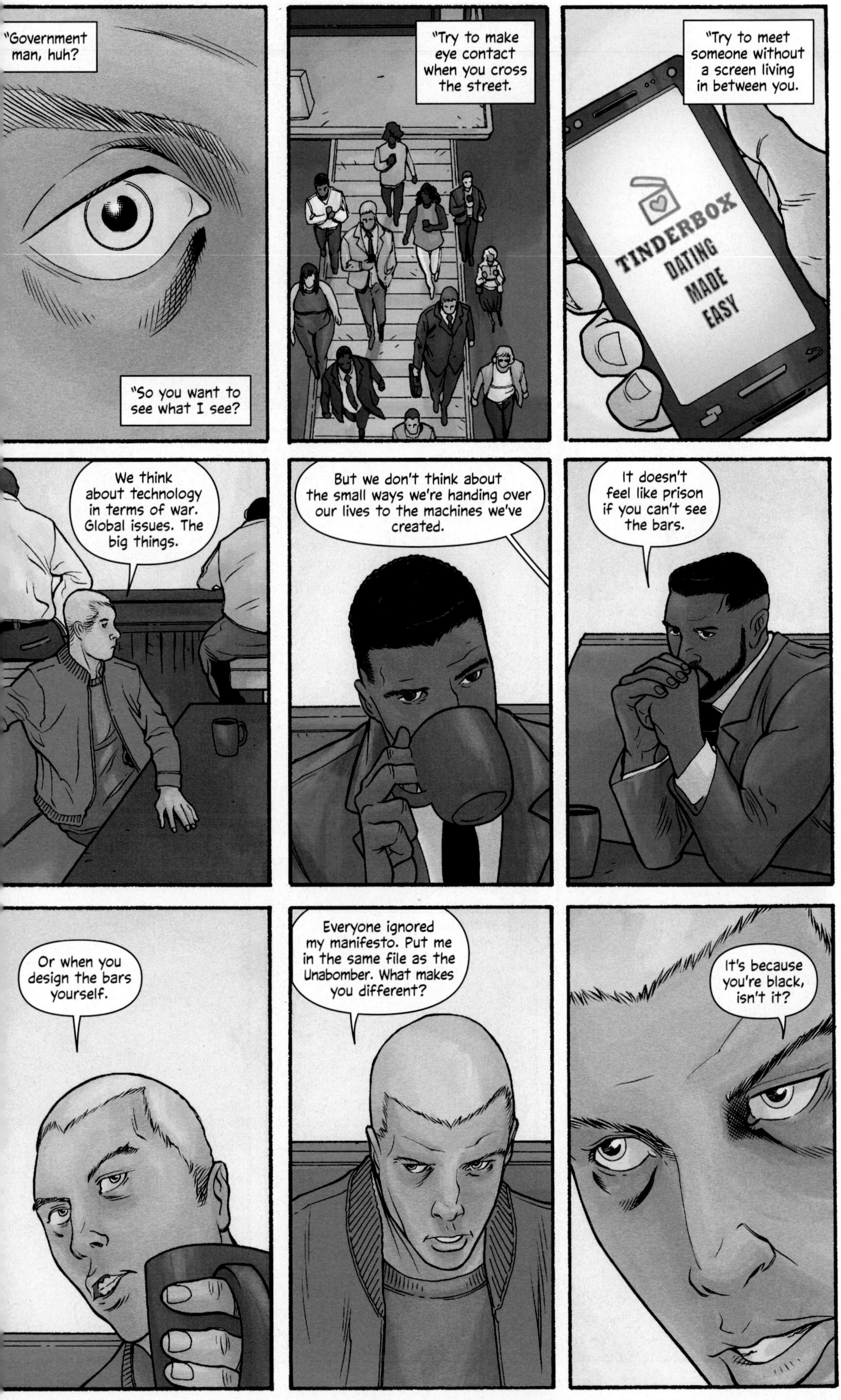
"Government man, huh?
"So you want to see what I see?
"Try to make eye contact when you cross the street.
"Try to meet someone without a screen living in between you.
TINDERBOX
DATING MADE EASY
We think about technology in terms of war. Global issues. The big things.
But we don't think about the small ways we're handing over our lives to the machines we've created.
It doesn't feel like prison if you can't see the bars.
Or when you design the bars yourself.
Everyone ignored my manifesto. Put me in the same file as the Unabomber. What makes you different?
It's because you're black, isn't it?

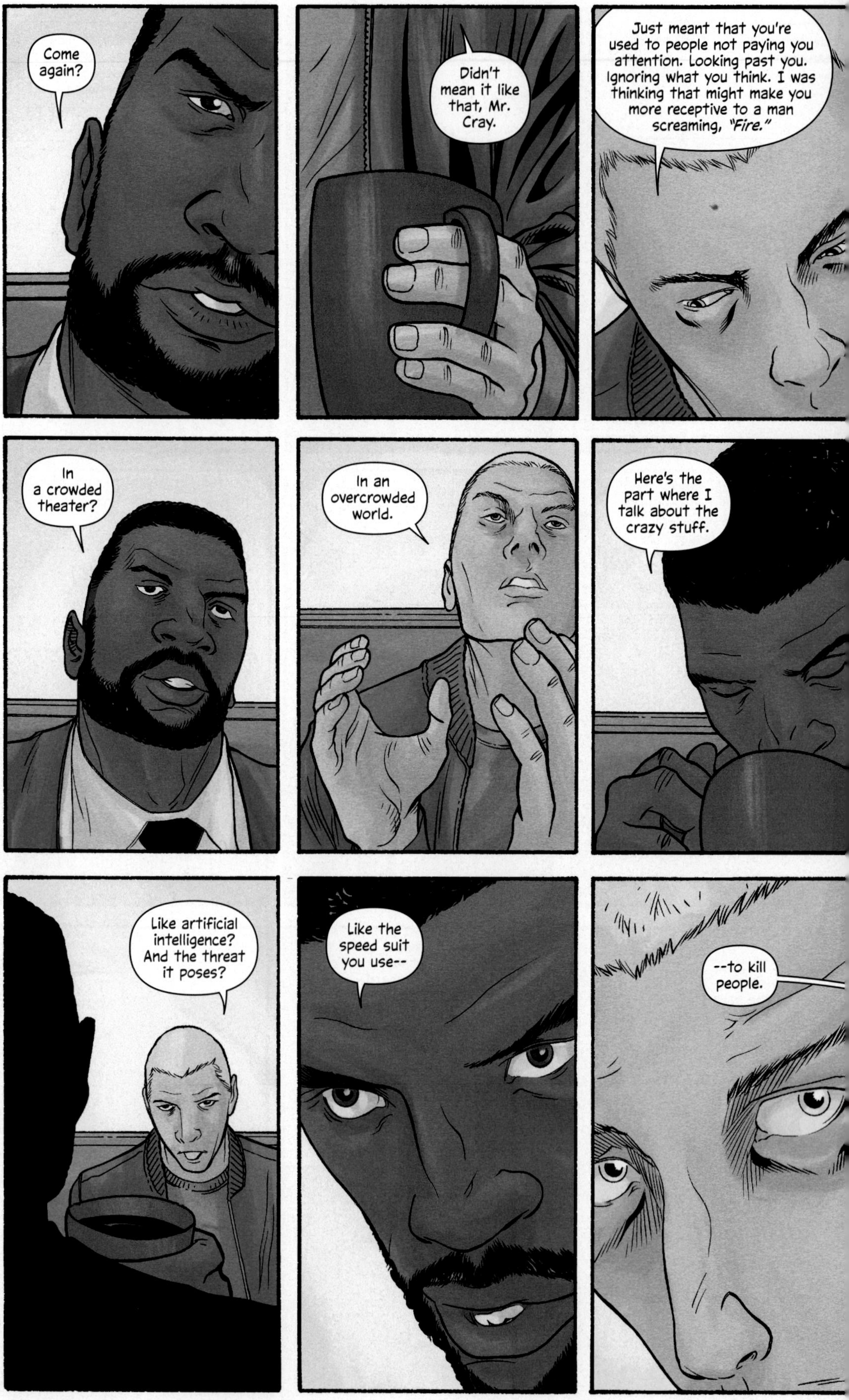
Come again?
Didn't mean it like that, Mr. Cray.
Just meant that you're used to people not paying you attention. Looking past you. Ignoring what you think. I was thinking that might make you more receptive to a man screaming, *"Fire."*
In a crowded theater?
In an overcrowded world.
Here's the part where I talk about the crazy stuff.
Like artificial intelligence? And the threat it poses?
Like the speed suit you use--
--to kill people.

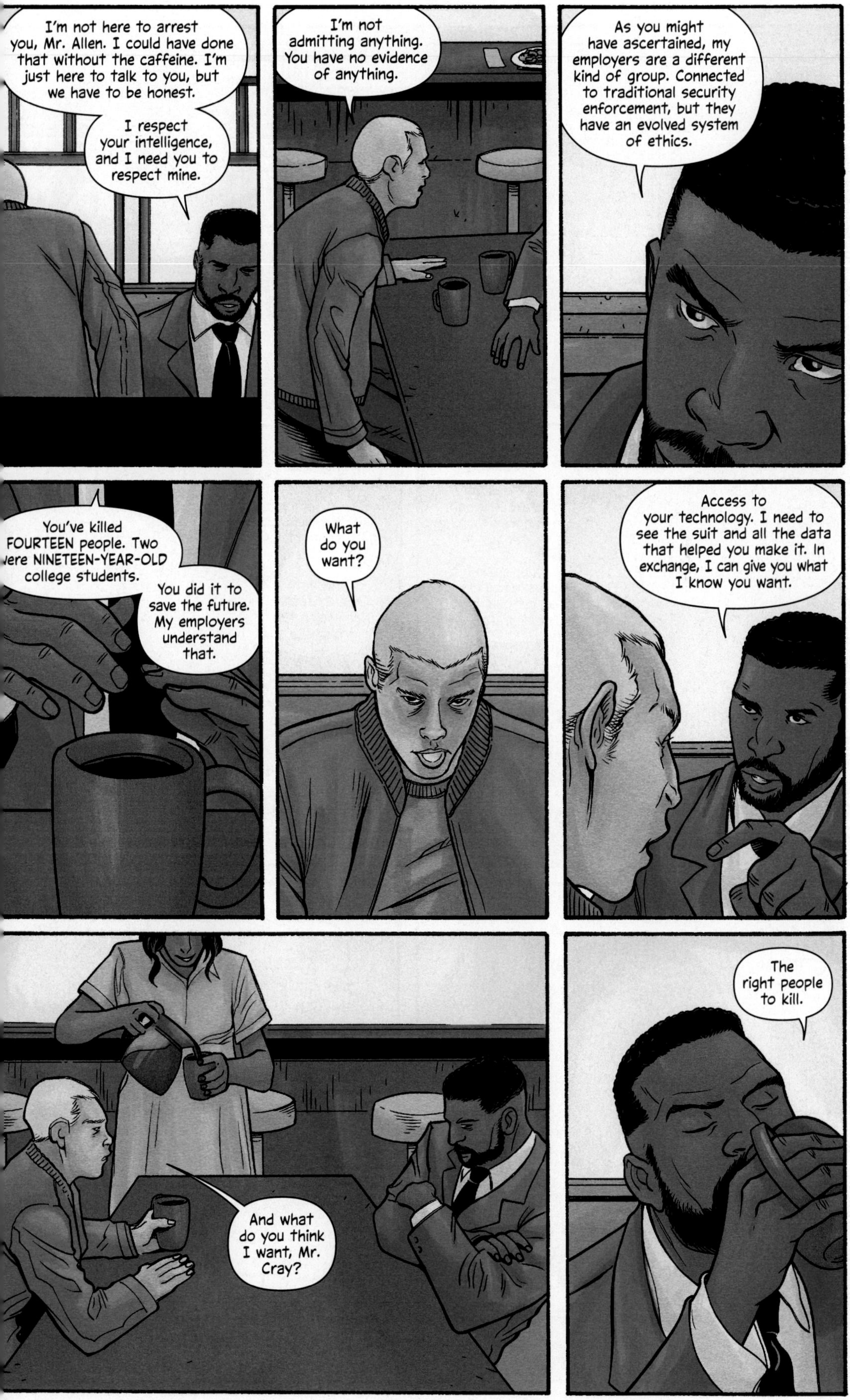
I'm not here to arrest you, Mr. Allen. I could have done that without the caffeine. I'm just here to talk to you, but we have to be honest.
I respect your intelligence, and I need you to respect mine.
I'm not admitting anything. You have no evidence of anything.
As you might have ascertained, my employers are a different kind of group. Connected to traditional security enforcement, but they have an evolved system of ethics.
You've killed FOURTEEN people. Two were NINETEEN-YEAR-OLD college students.
You did it to save the future. My employers understand that.
What do you want?
Access to your technology. I need to see the suit and all the data that helped you make it. In exchange, I can give you what I know you want.
And what do you think I want, Mr. Cray?
The right people to kill.

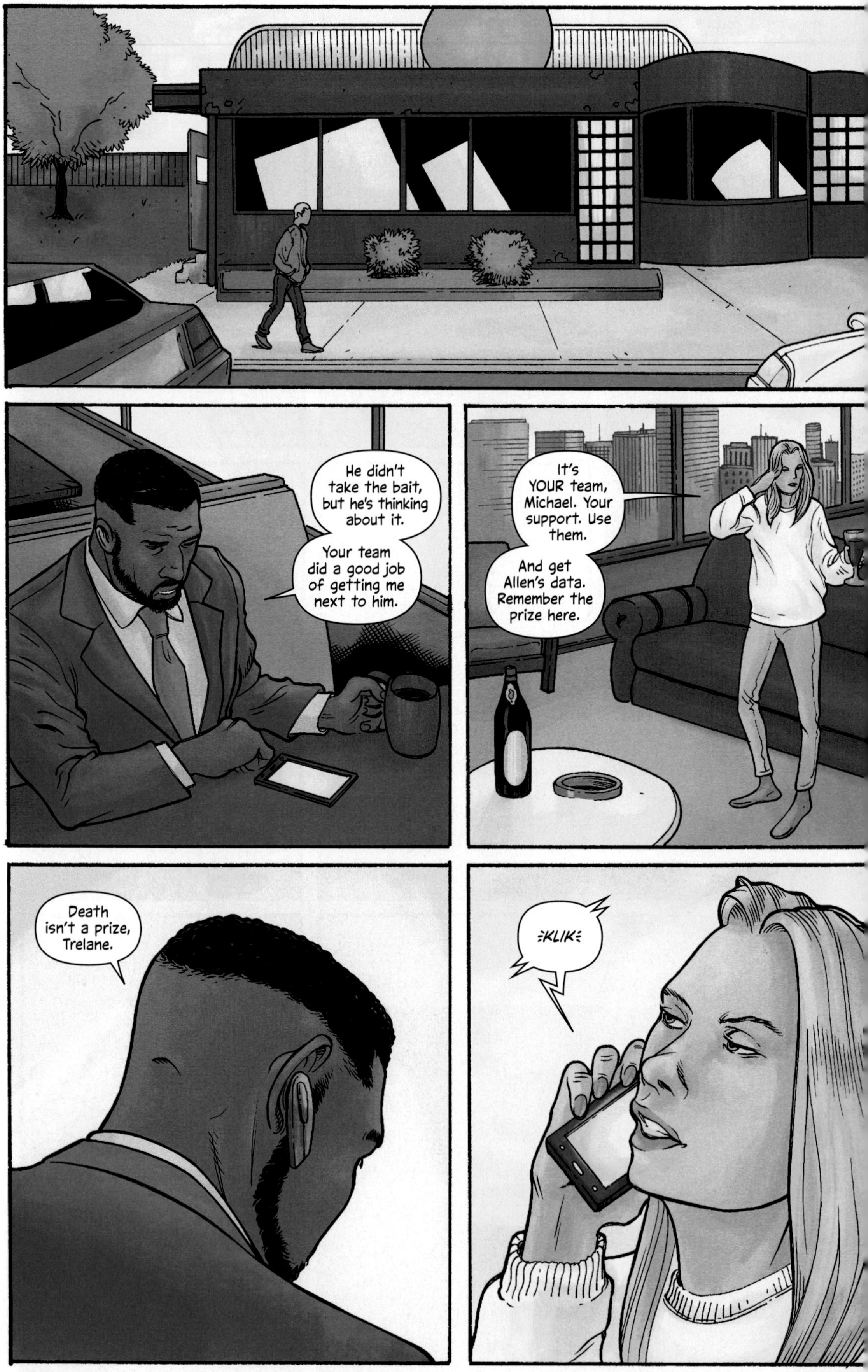
He didn't take the bait, but he's thinking about it.
Your team did a good job of getting me next to him.
It's YOUR team, Michael. Your support. Use them.
And get Allen's data. Remember the prize here.
Death isn't a prize, Trelane.
KLIK

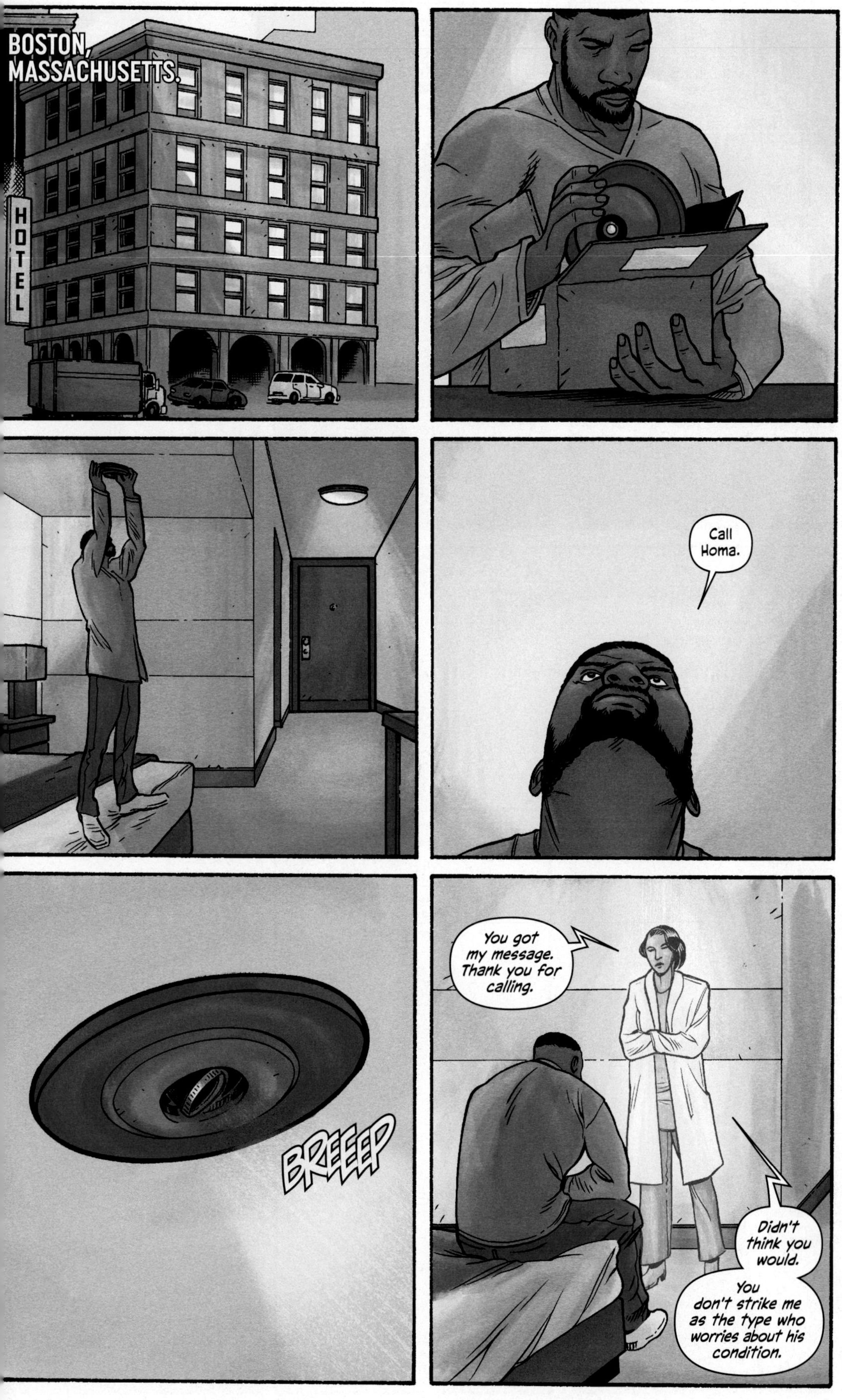
BOSTON, MASSACHUSETTS.
HOTEL
Call Homa.
BREEEP
You got my message. Thank you for calling.
Didn't think you would.
You don't strike me as the type who worries about his condition.

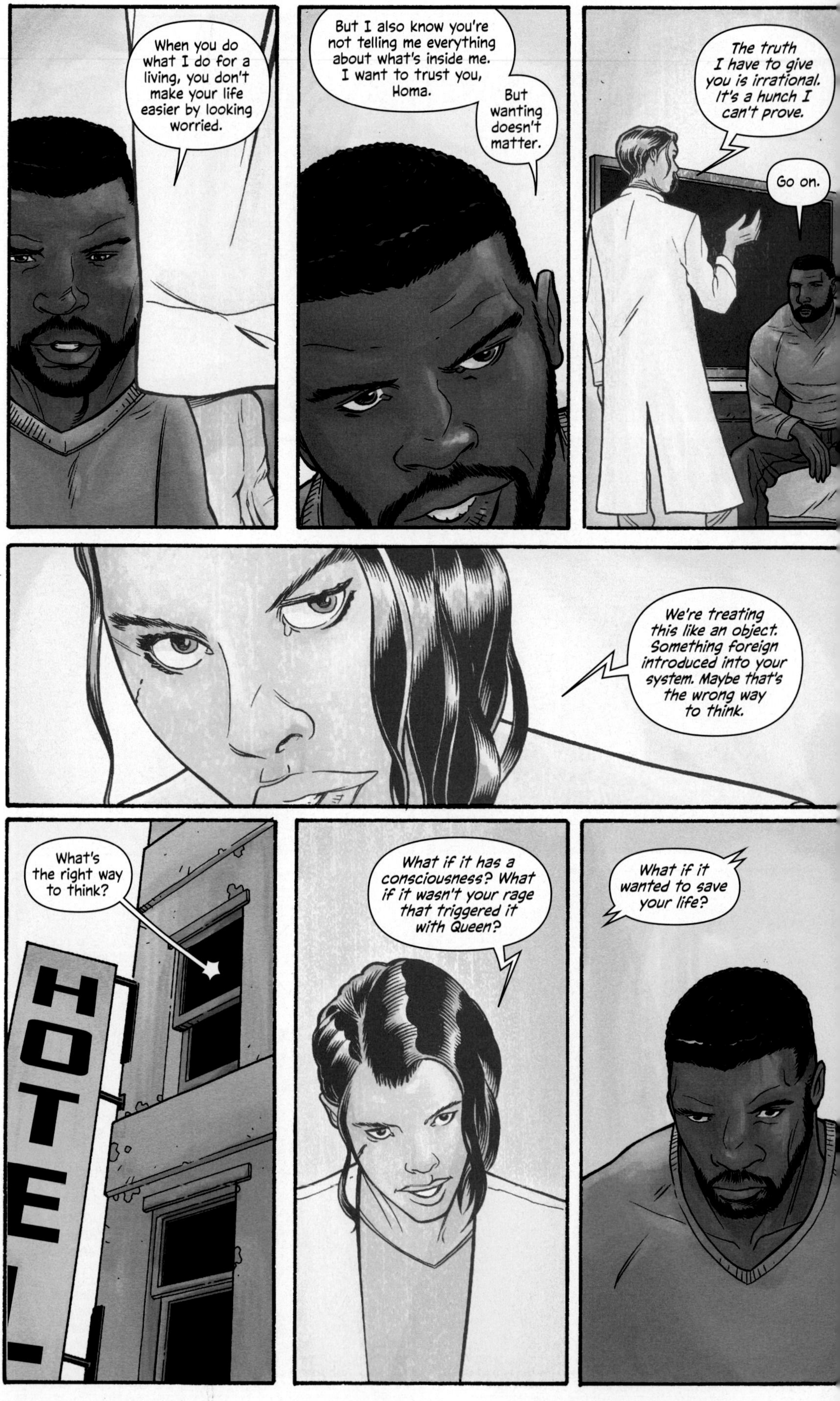
When you do what I do for a living, you don't make your life easier by looking worried.
But I also know you're not telling me everything about what's inside me. I want to trust you, Homa.
But wanting doesn't matter.
The truth I have to give you is irrational. It's a hunch I can't prove.
Go on.
We're treating this like an object. Something foreign introduced into your system. Maybe that's the wrong way to think.
What's the right way to think?
HOTE
What if it has a consciousness? What if it wasn't your rage that triggered it with Queen?
What if it wanted to save your life?

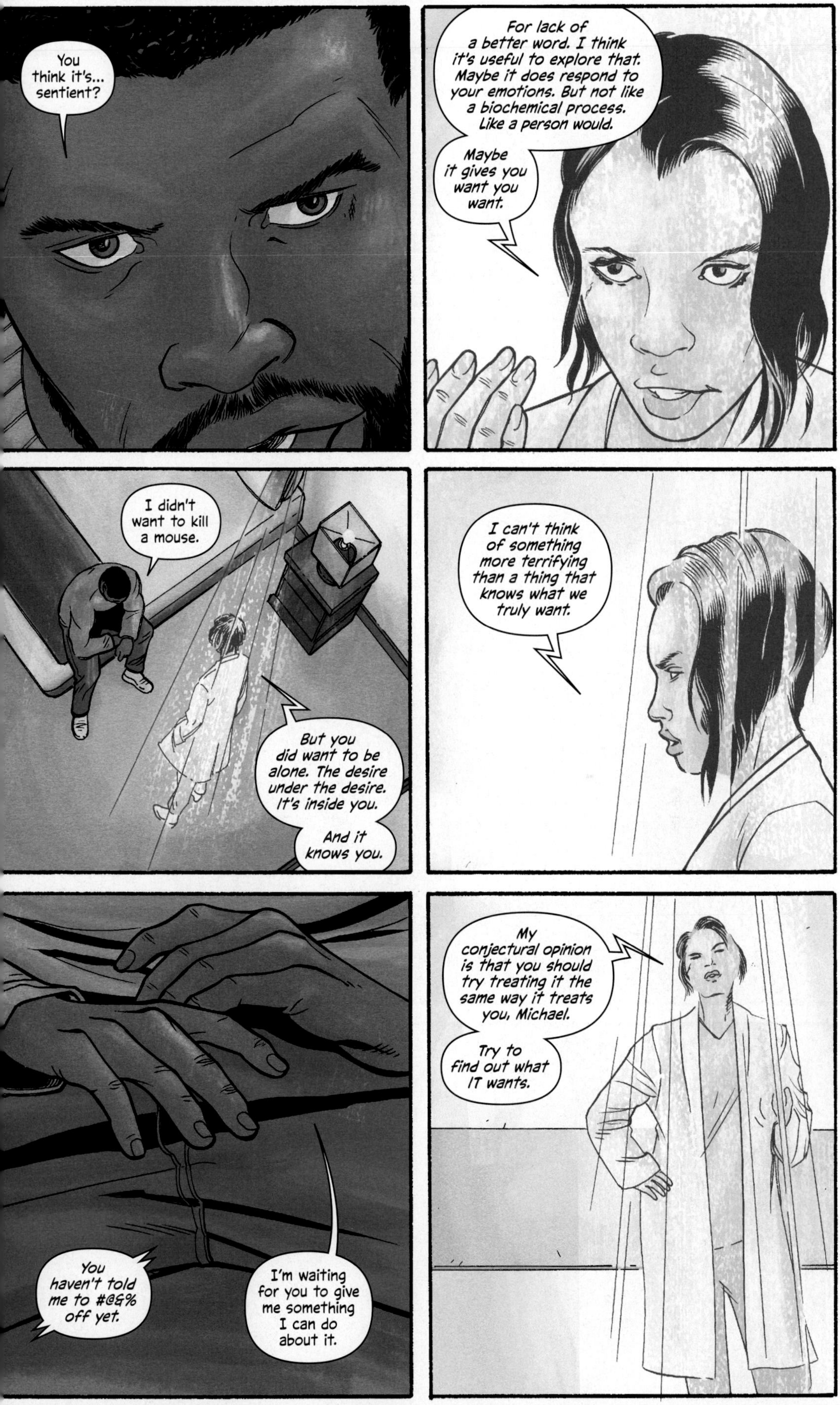
You think it's... sentient?
For lack of a better word. I think it's useful to explore that. Maybe it does respond to your emotions. But not like a biochemical process. Like a person would.
Maybe it gives you want you want.
I didn't want to kill a mouse.
But you did want to be alone. The desire under the desire. It's inside you.
And it knows you.
I can't think of something more terrifying than a thing that knows what we truly want.
You haven't told me to #@&% off yet.
I'm waiting for you to give me something I can do about it.
My conjectural opinion is that you should try treating it the same way it treats you, Michael.
Try to find out what IT wants.

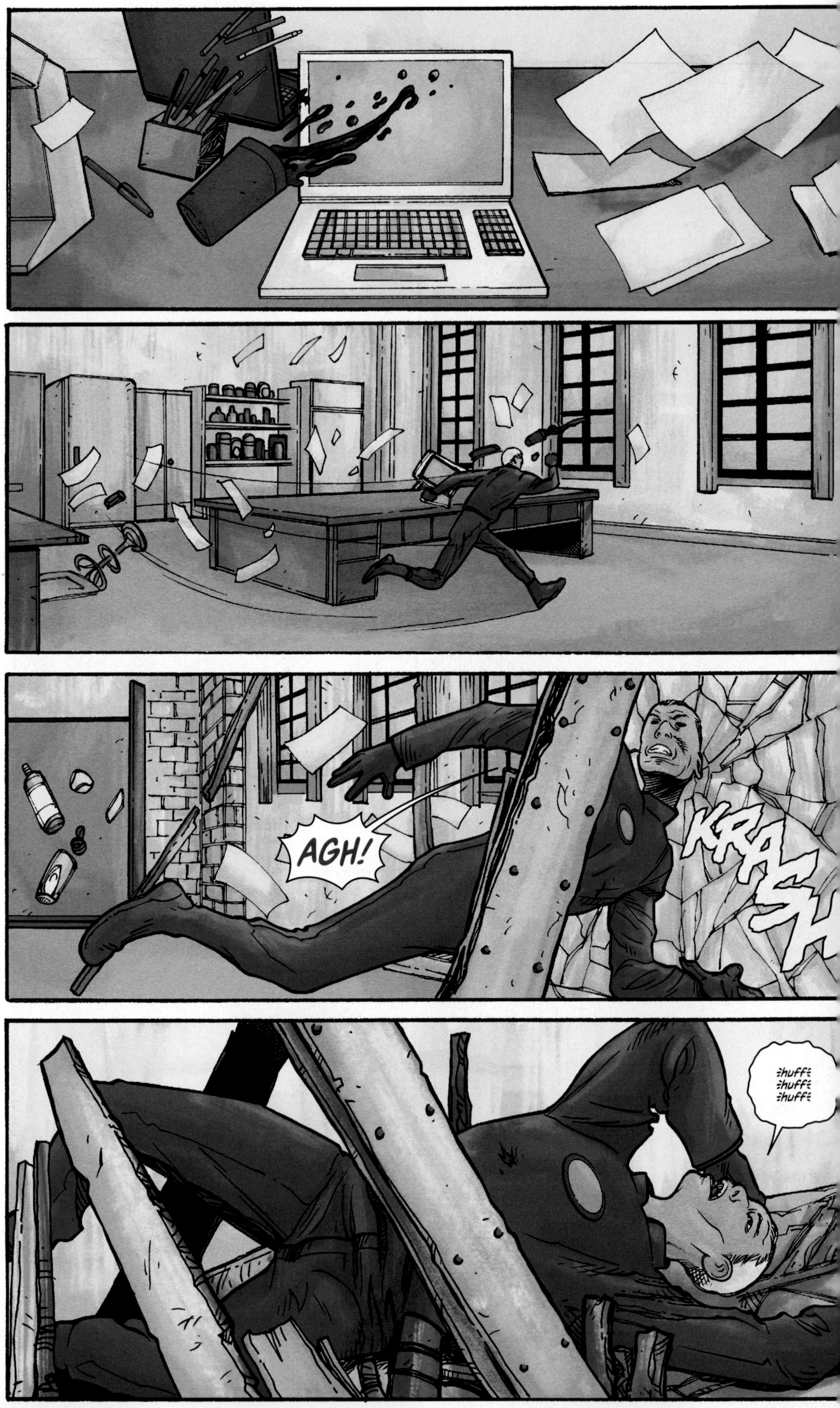
AGH!
KRASH
huff huff huff

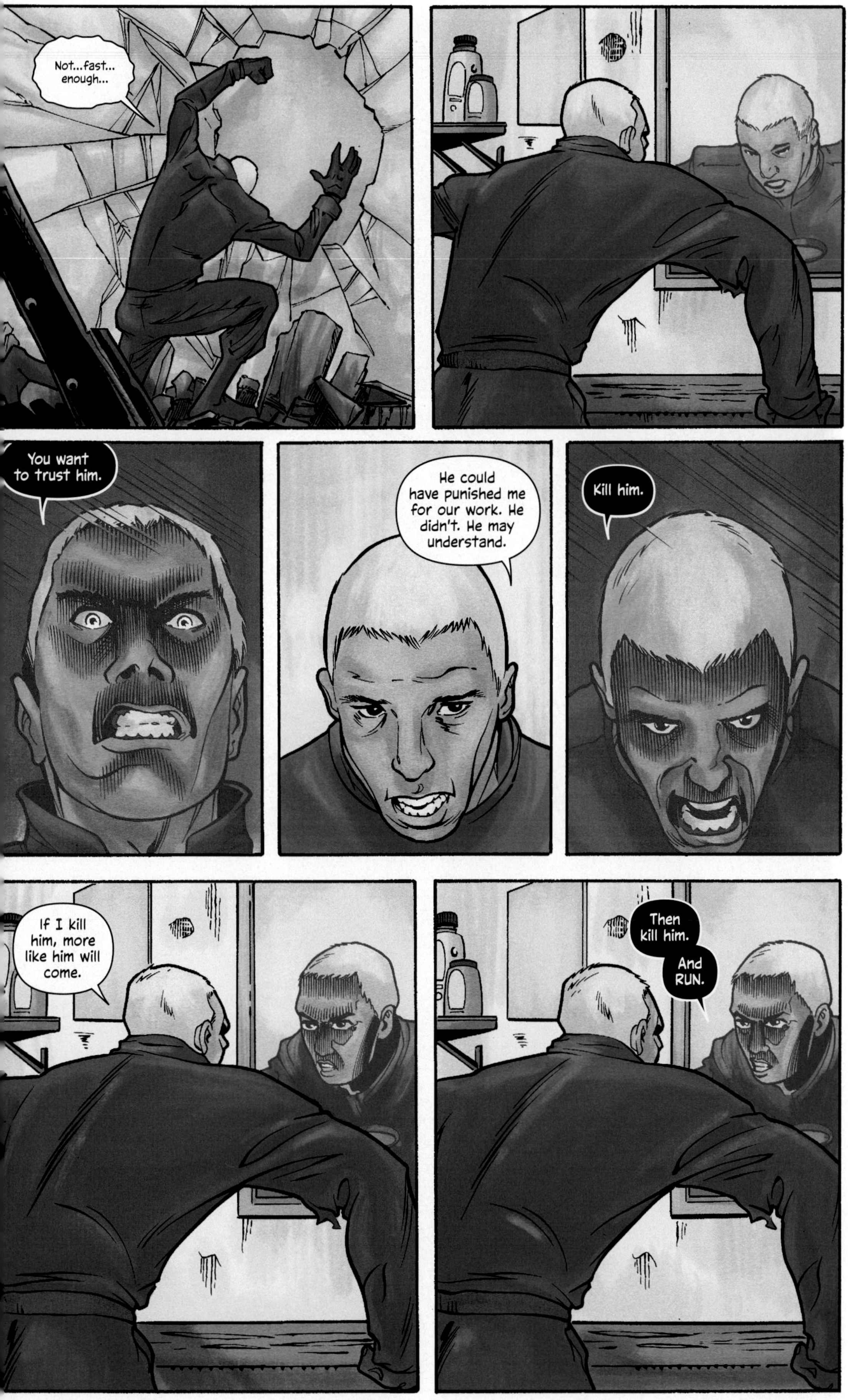
Not...fast... enough...
You want to trust him.
He could have punished me for our work. He didn't. He may understand.
Kill him.
If I kill him, more like him will come.
Then kill him.
And RUN.

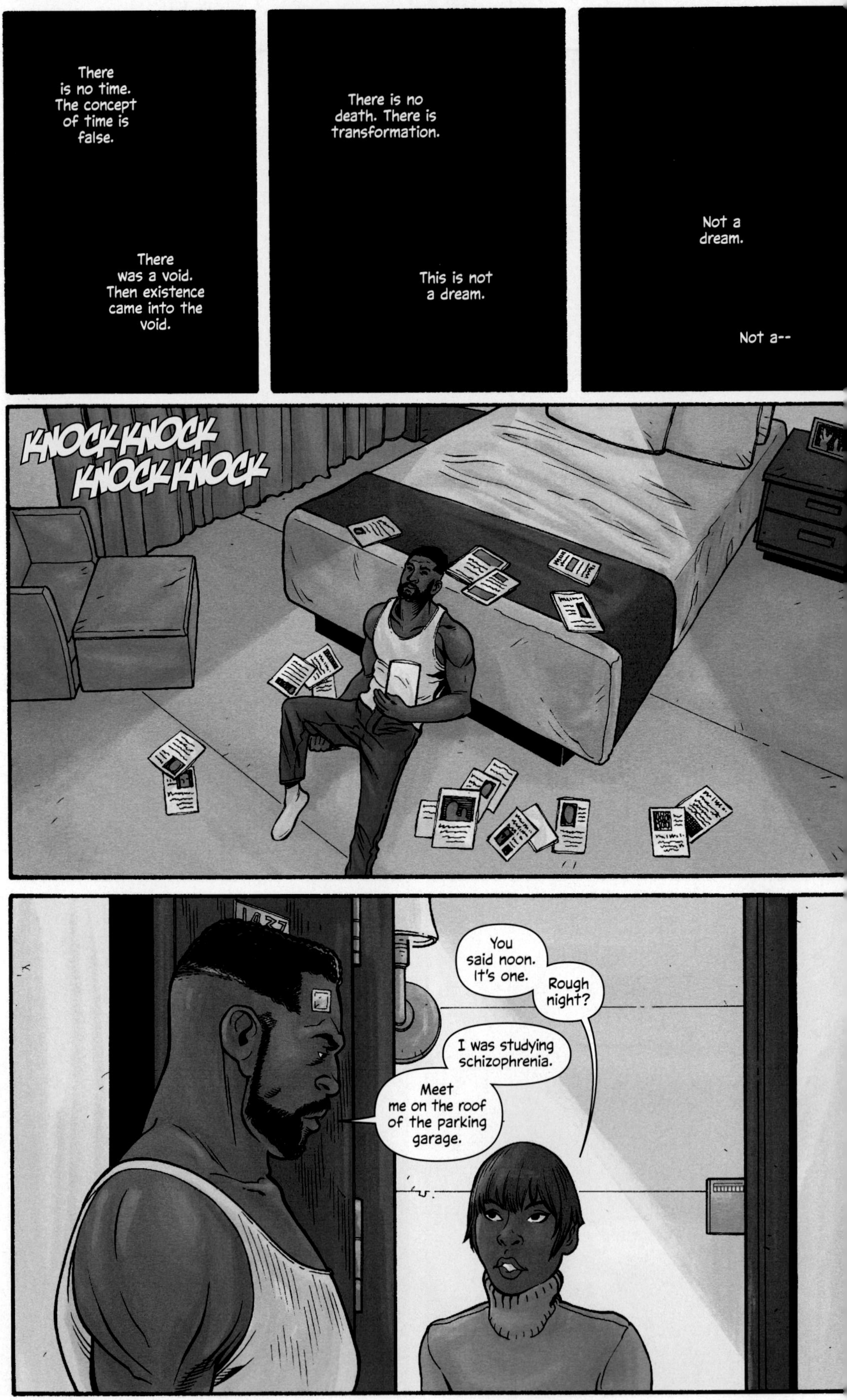
There is no time. The concept of time is false.
There was a void. Then existence came into the void.
There is no death. There is transformation.
This is not a dream.
Not a dream.
Not a--
KNOCK KNOCK KNOCK KNOCK
You said noon. It's one.
Rough night?
I was studying schizophrenia.
Meet me on the roof of the parking garage.

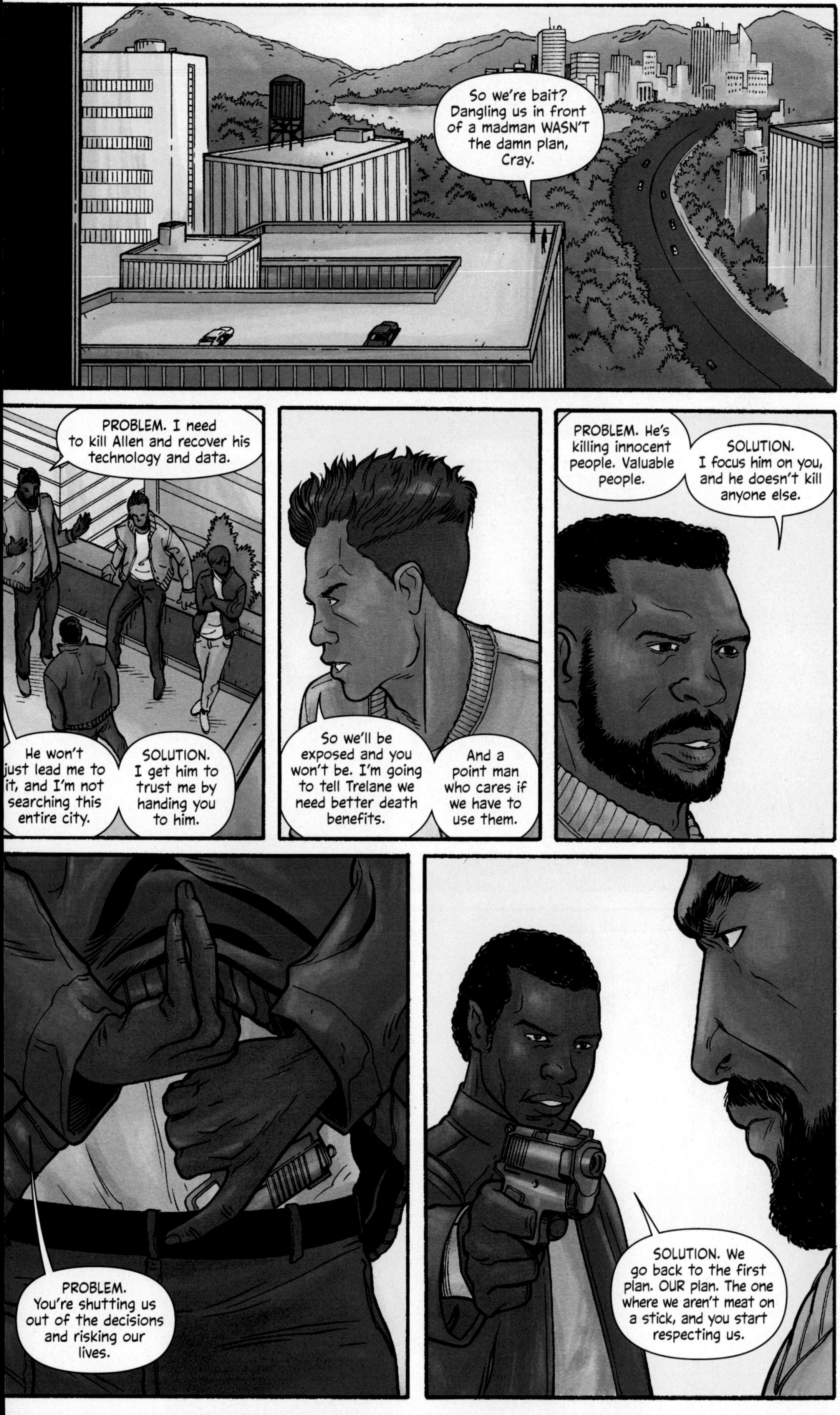
So we're bait? Dangling us in front of a madman WASN'T the damn plan, Cray.
PROBLEM. I need to kill Allen and recover his technology and data.
He won't just lead me to it, and I'm not searching this entire city.
SOLUTION. I get him to trust me by handing you to him.
So we'll be exposed and you won't be. I'm going to tell Trelane we need better death benefits.
And a point man who cares if we have to use them.
PROBLEM. He's killing innocent people. Valuable people.
SOLUTION. I focus him on you, and he doesn't kill anyone else.
PROBLEM. You're shutting us out of the decisions and risking our lives.
SOLUTION. We go back to the first plan. OUR plan. The one where we aren't meat on a stick, and you start respecting us.

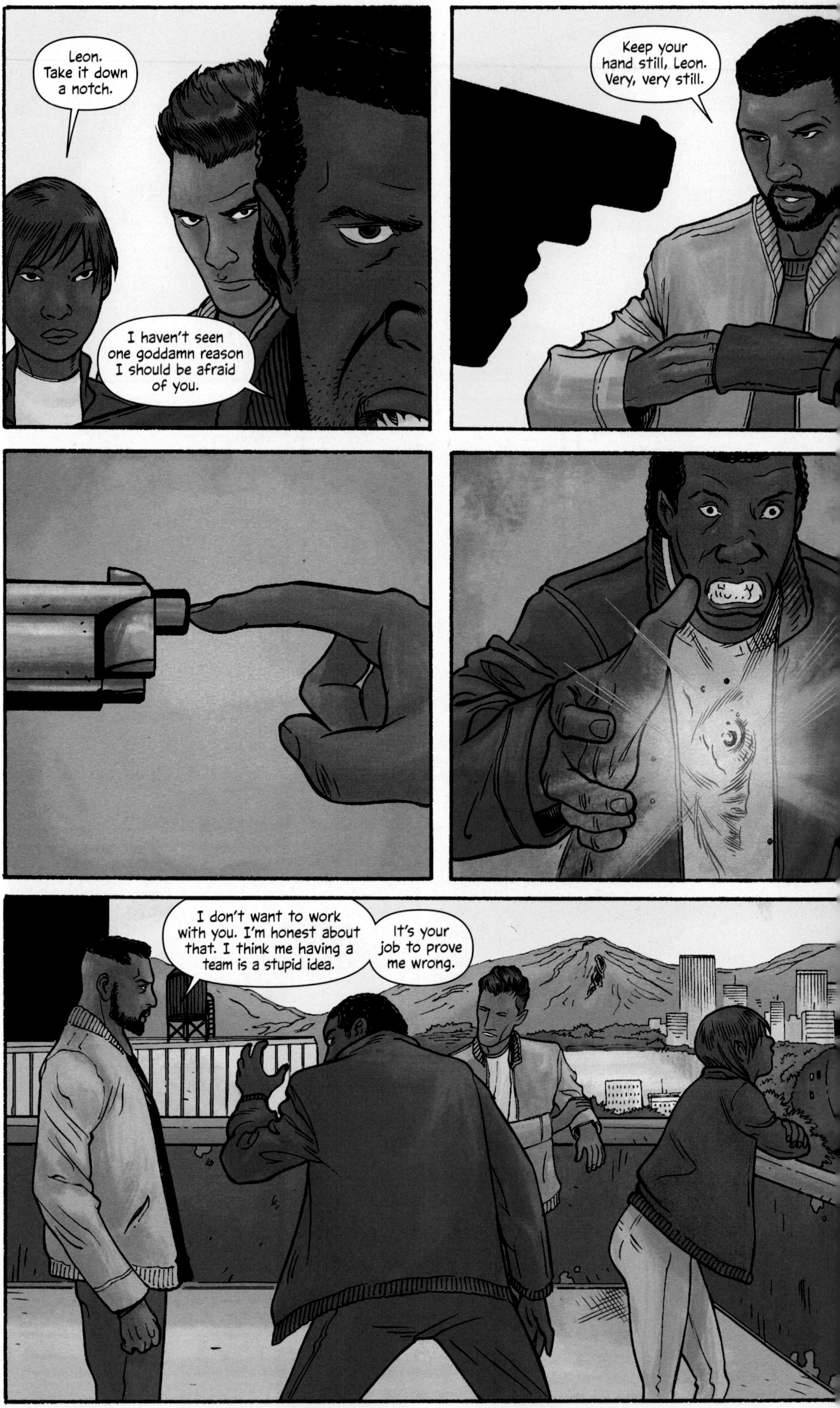
Leon. Take it down a notch.
I haven't seen one goddamn reason I should be afraid of you.
Keep your hand still, Leon. Very, very still.
I don't want to work with you. I'm honest about that. I think me having a team is a stupid idea.
It's your job to prove me wrong.

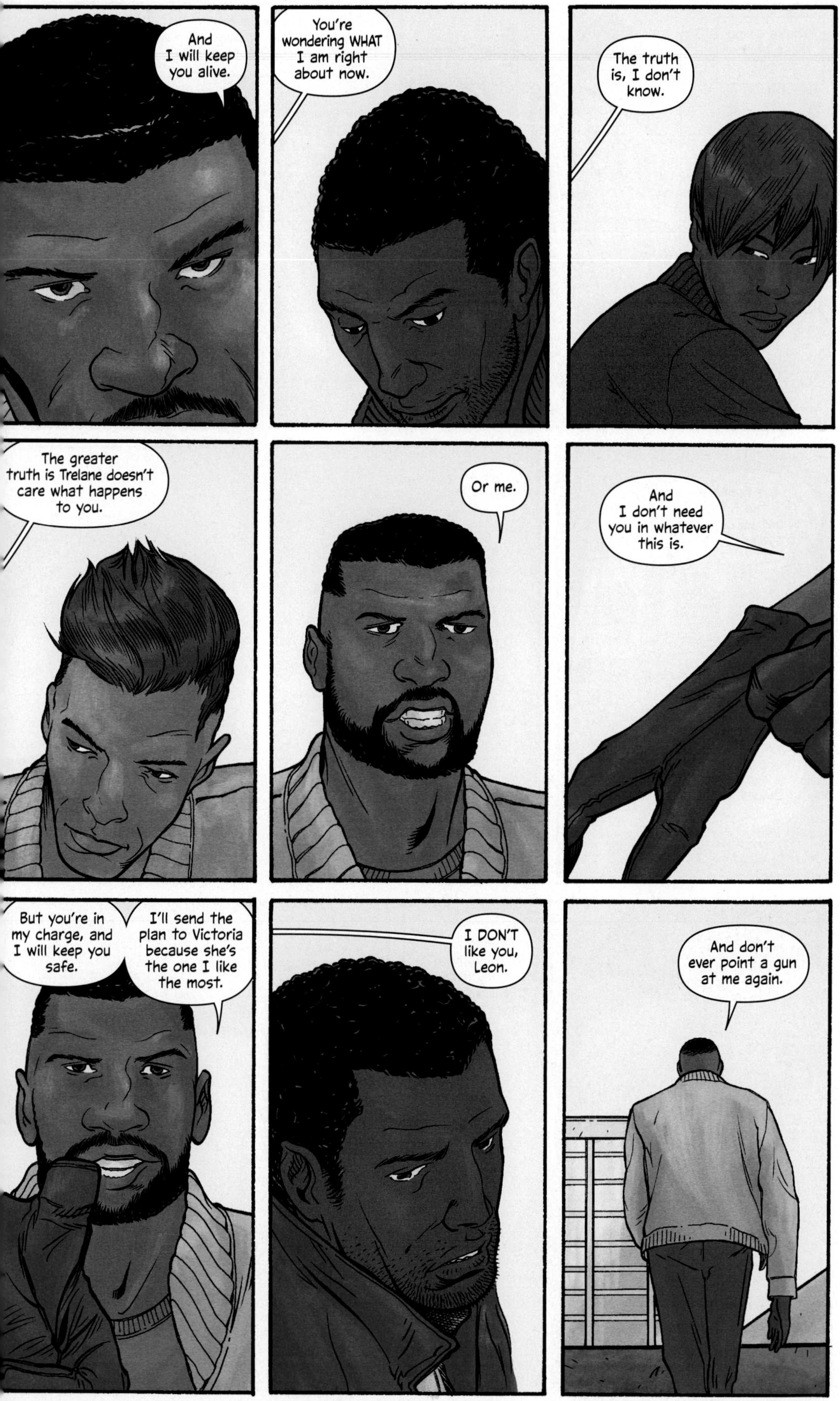
And I will keep you alive.
You're wondering WHAT I am right about now.
The truth is, I don't know.
The greater truth is Trelane doesn't care what happens to you.
Or me.
And I don't need you in whatever this is.
But you're in my charge, and I will keep you safe.
I'll send the plan to Victoria because she's the one I like the most.
I DON'T like you, Leon.
And don't ever point a gun at me again.

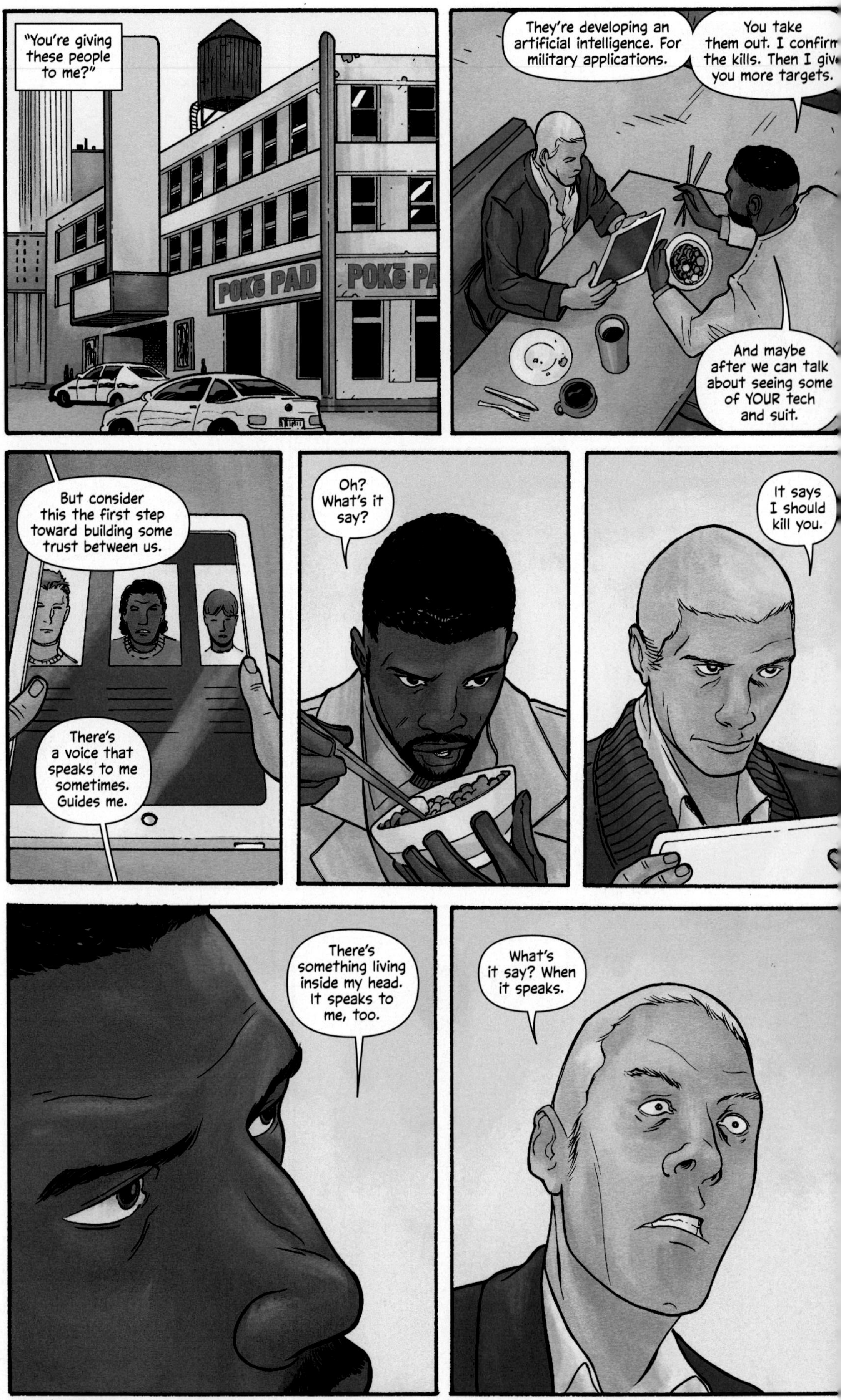

"You're giving these people to me?"
POKĒ PAD
POKĒ PA
They're developing an artificial intelligence. For military applications.
You take them out. I confirm the kills. Then I give you more targets.
And maybe after we can talk about seeing some of YOUR tech and suit.
But consider this the first step toward building some trust between us.
There's a voice that speaks to me sometimes. Guides me.
Oh? What's it say?
It says I should kill you.
There's something living inside my head. It speaks to me, too.
What's it say? When it speaks.

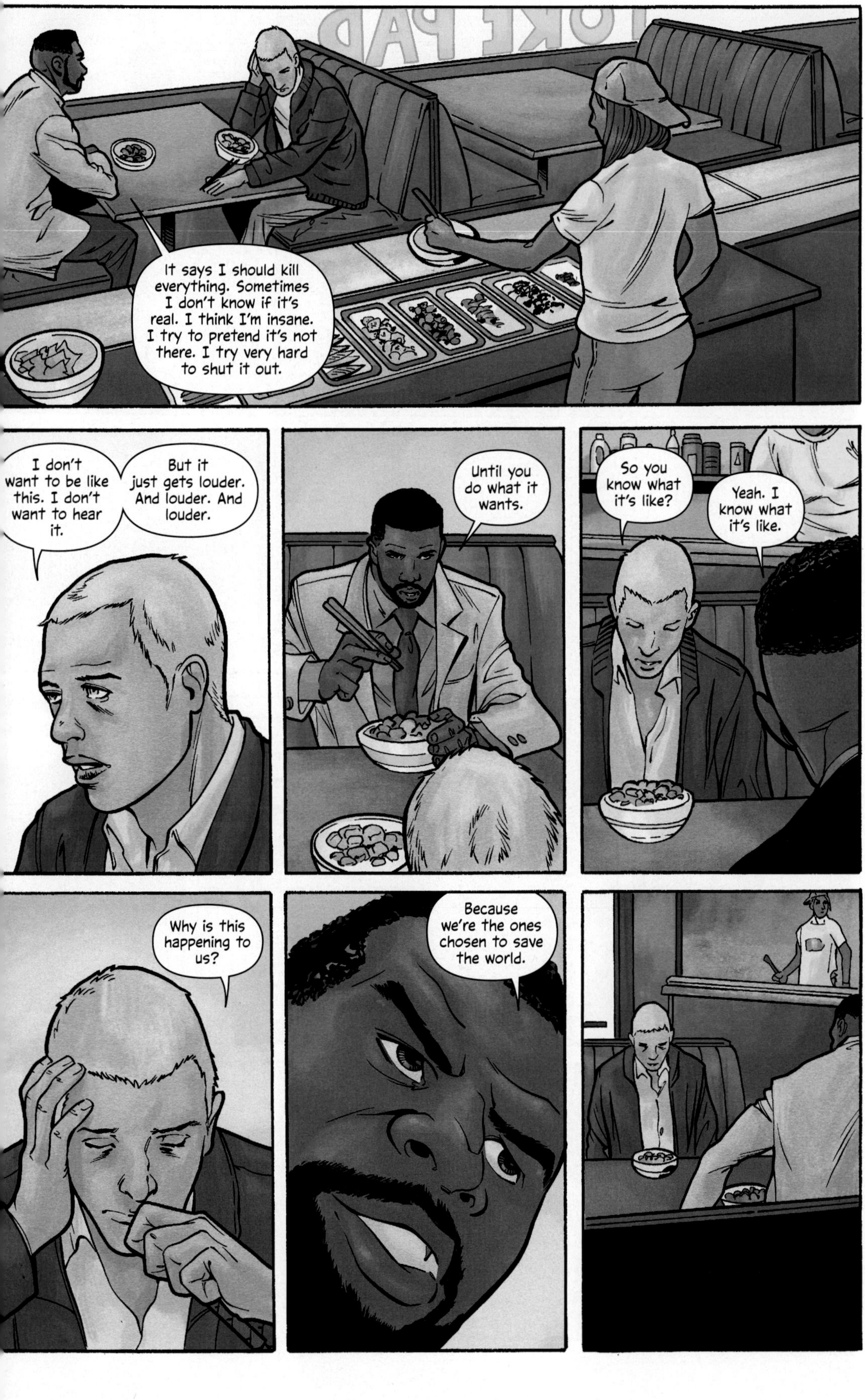

It says I should kill everything. Sometimes I don't know if it's real. I think I'm insane. I try to pretend it's not there. I try very hard to shut it out.
I don't want to be like this. I don't want to hear it.
But it just gets louder. And louder. And louder.
Until you do what it wants.
So you know what it's like?
Yeah. I know what it's like.
Why is this happening to us?
Because we're the ones chosen to save the world.

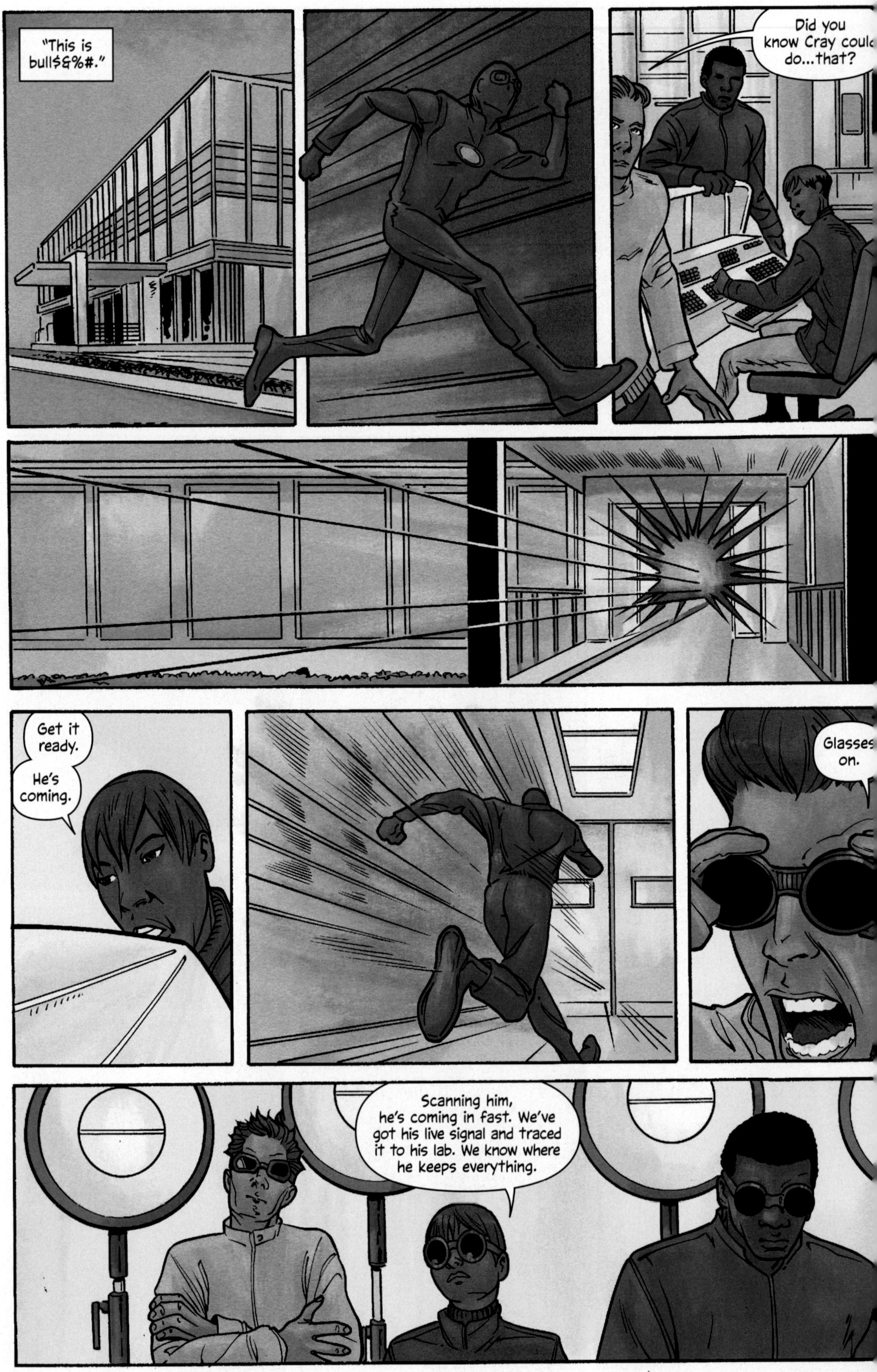
"This is bull$&%#."
Did you know Cray could do...that?
Get it ready.
He's coming.
Glasses on.
Scanning him, he's coming in fast. We've got his live signal and traced it to his lab. We know where he keeps everything.

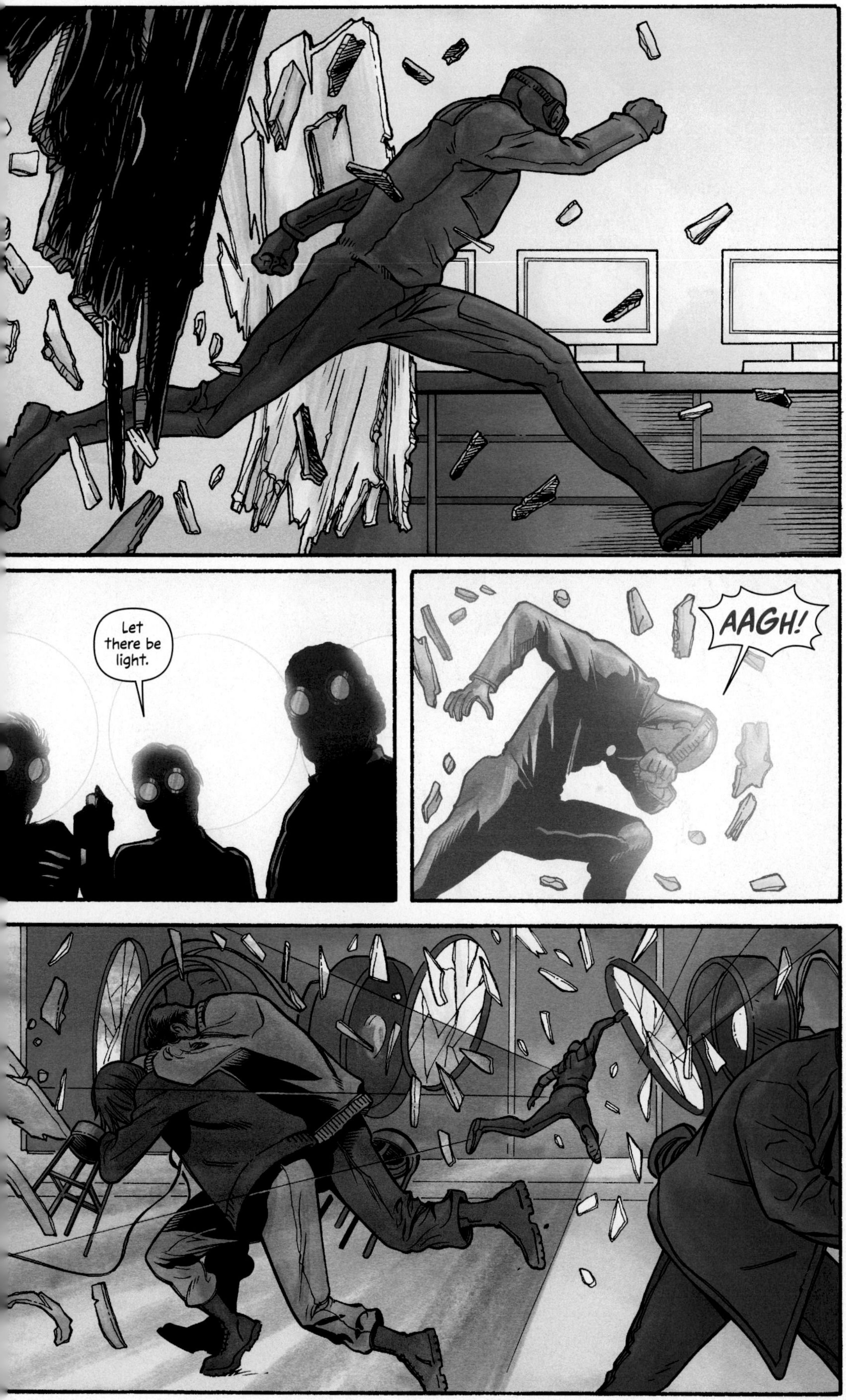
Let there be light.
AAGH!

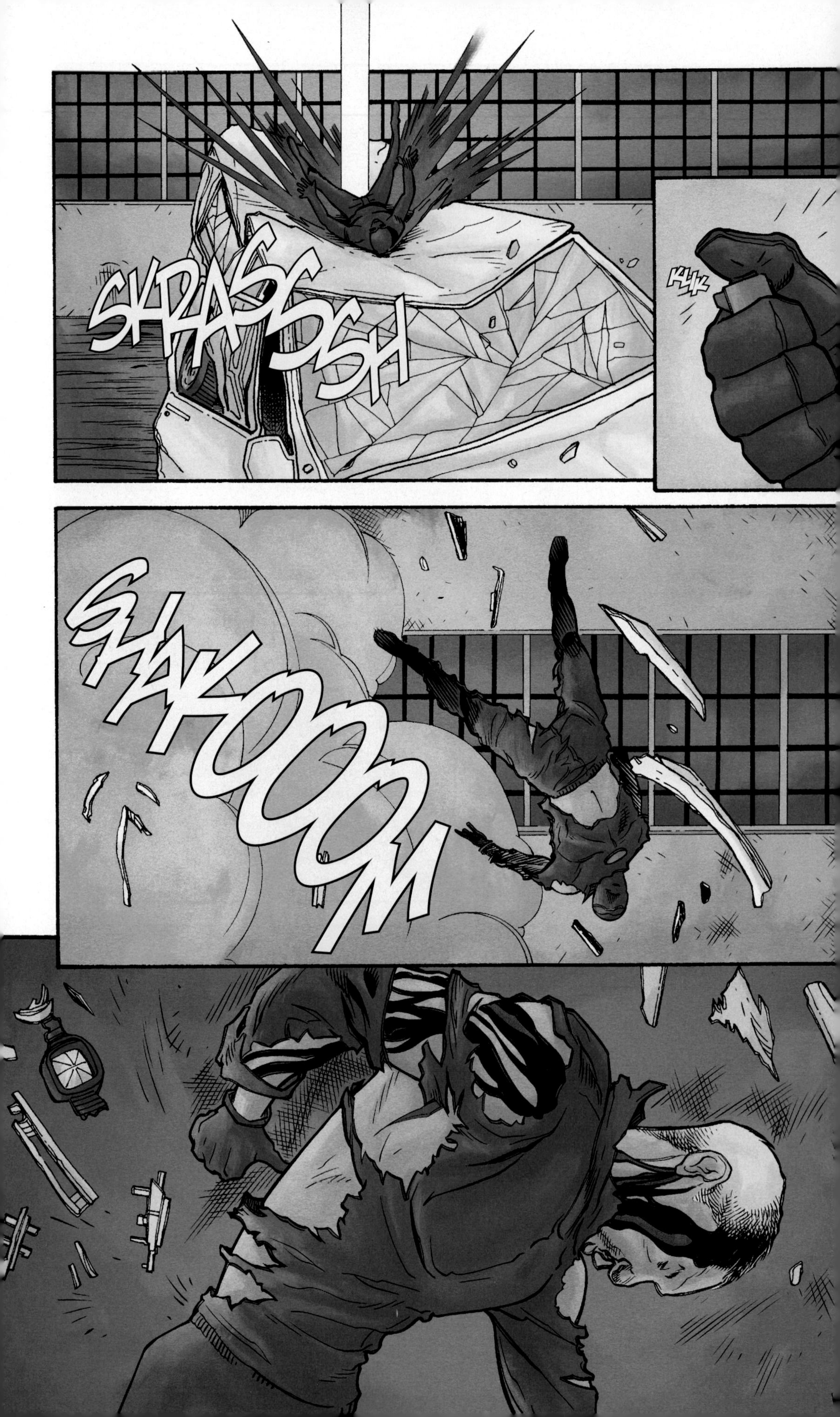
SKRASSSH
KLIK
SHAKOOOM

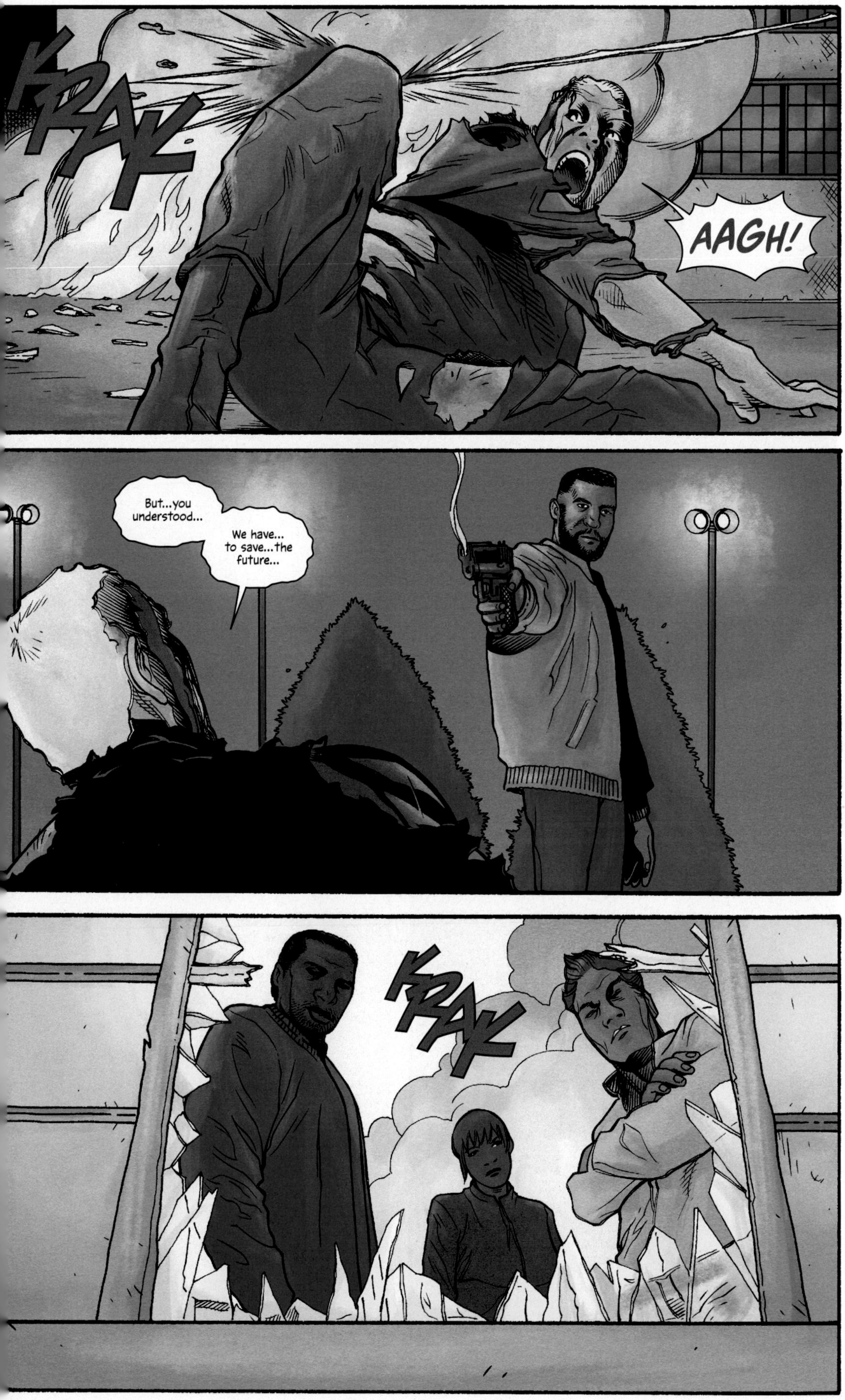
KRAK
AAGH!
But...you understood...
We have... to save...the future...
KRAK

You all okay?
Yeah.
Victoria, give me the trace information to Barry's lab. I'll retrieve the tech and data.
You all can go.
I do understand, Barry.
I'm the one chosen to save the world.

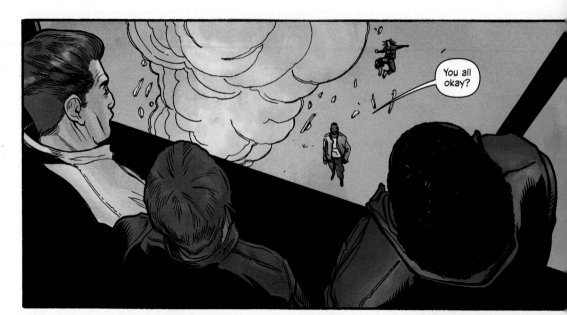

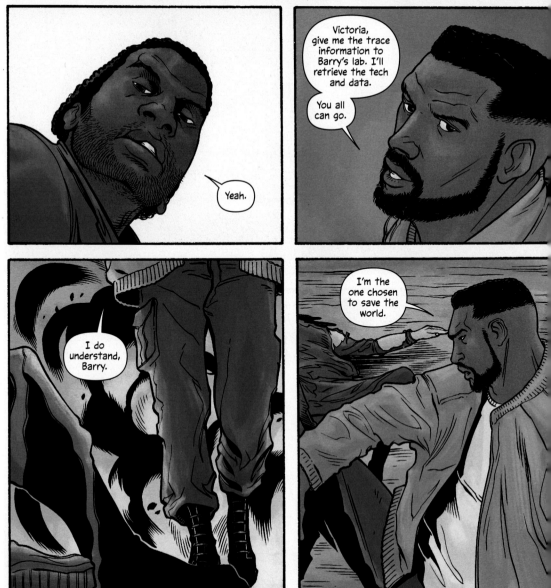

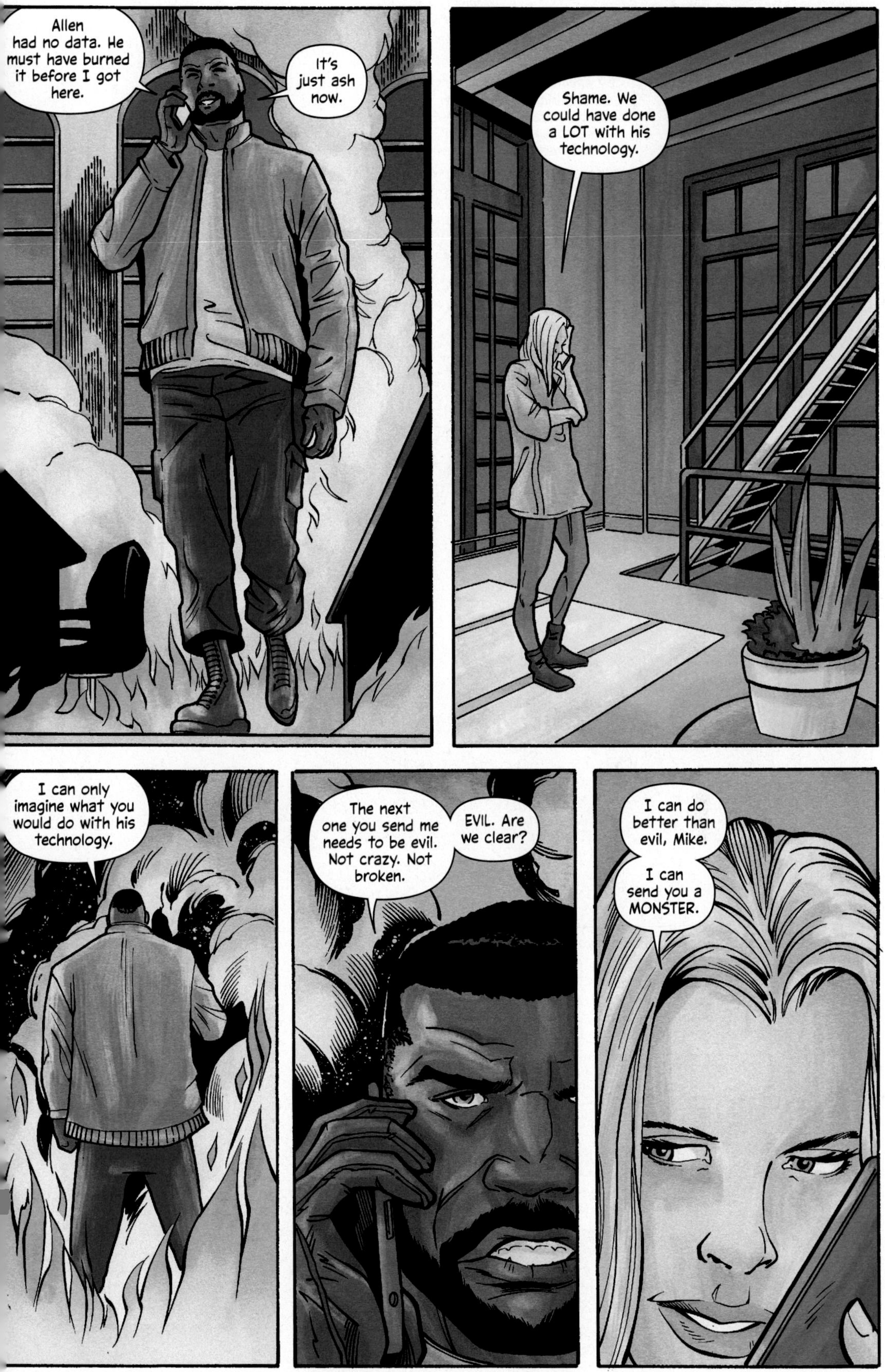
Allen had no data. He must have burned it before I got here.
It's just ash now.
Shame. We could have done a LOT with his technology.
I can only imagine what you would do with his technology.
The next one you send me needs to be evil. Not crazy. Not broken.
EVIL. Are we clear?
I can do better than evil, Mike.
I can send you a MONSTER.

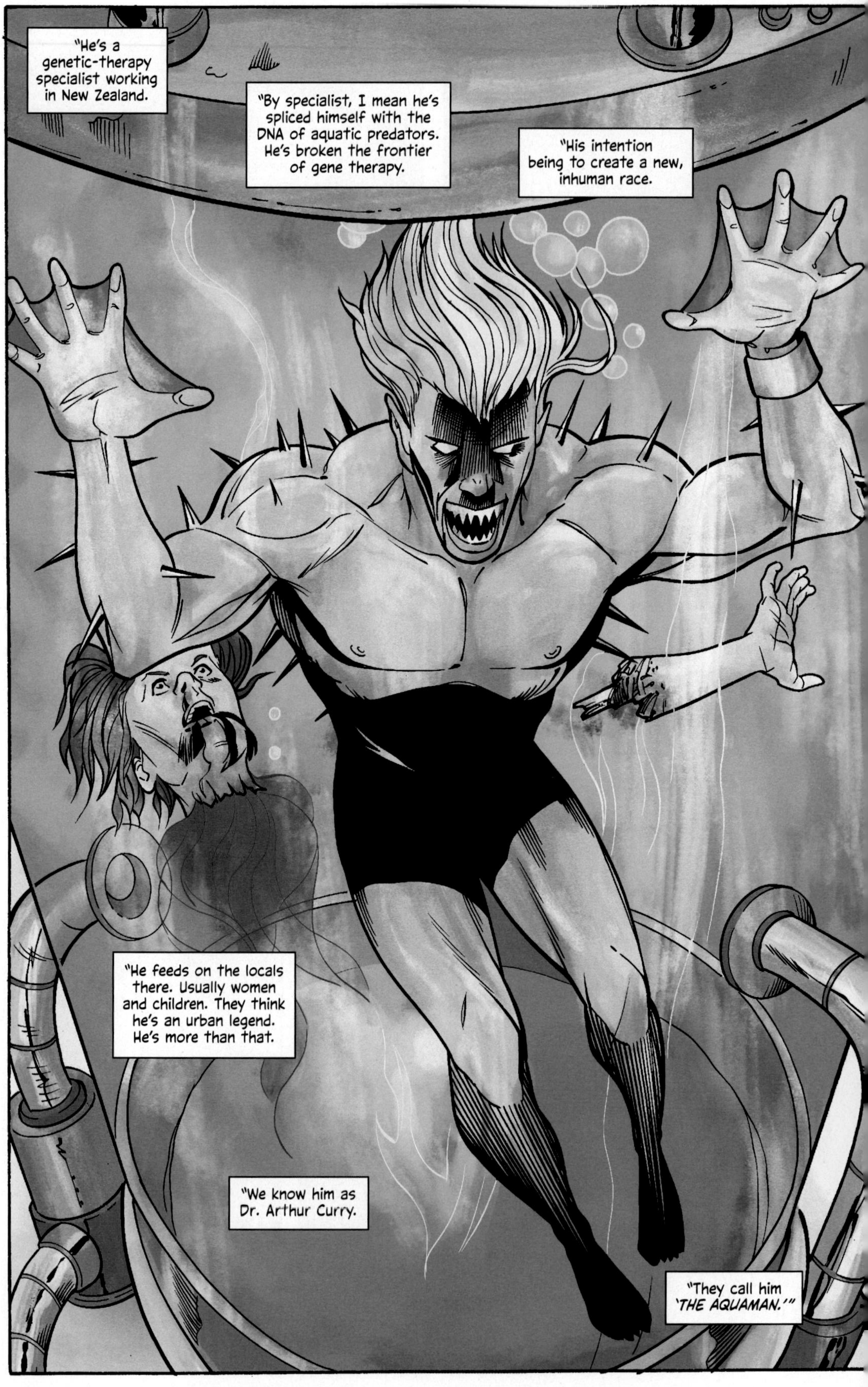
"He's a genetic-therapy specialist working in New Zealand.
"By specialist, I mean he's spliced himself with the DNA of aquatic predators. He's broken the frontier of gene therapy.
"His intention being to create a new, inhuman race.
"He feeds on the locals there. Usually women and children. They think he's an urban legend. He's more than that.
"We know him as Dr. Arthur Curry.
"They call him *'THE AQUAMAN.'"*

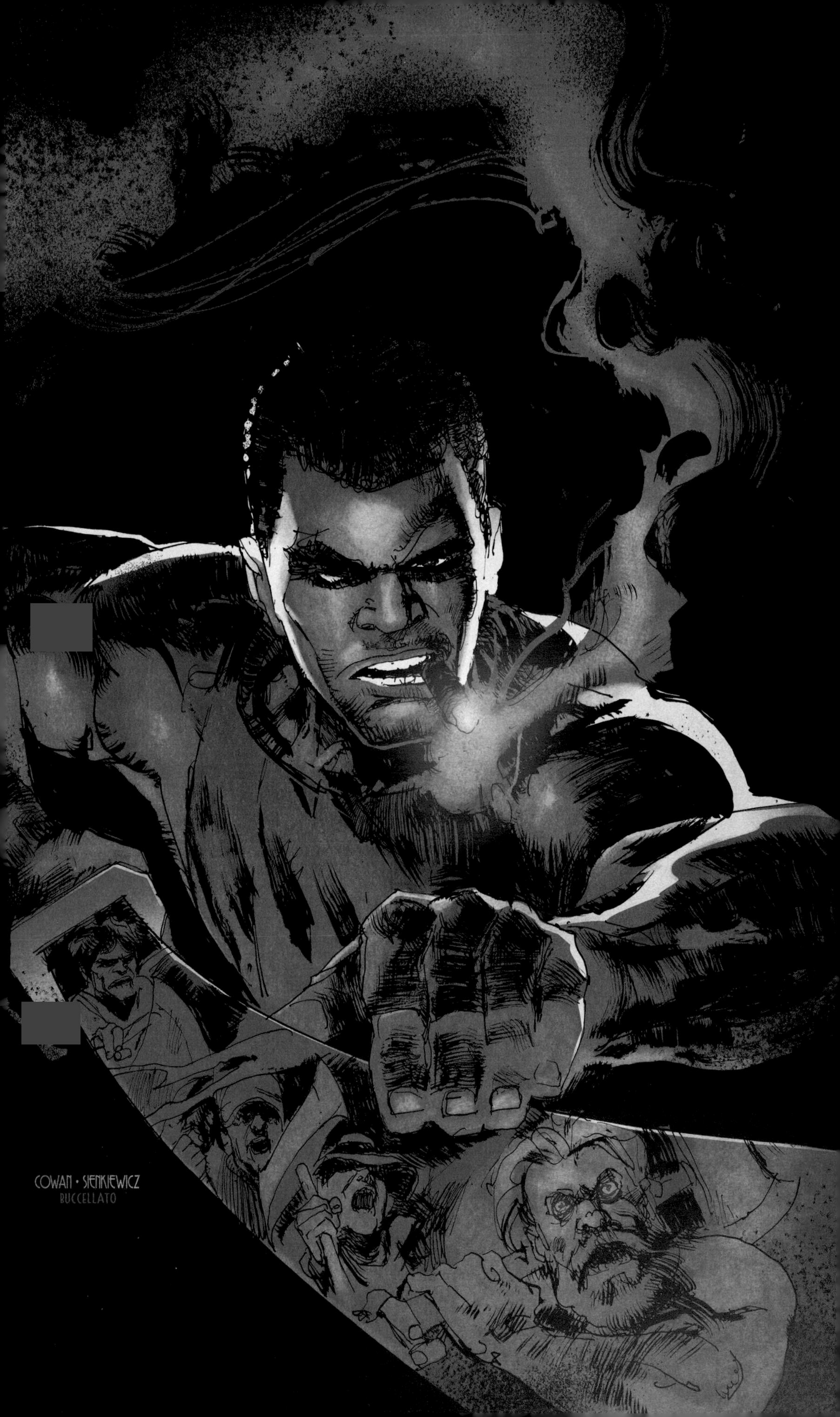
COWAN • SIENKIEWICZ
BUCCELLATO

5

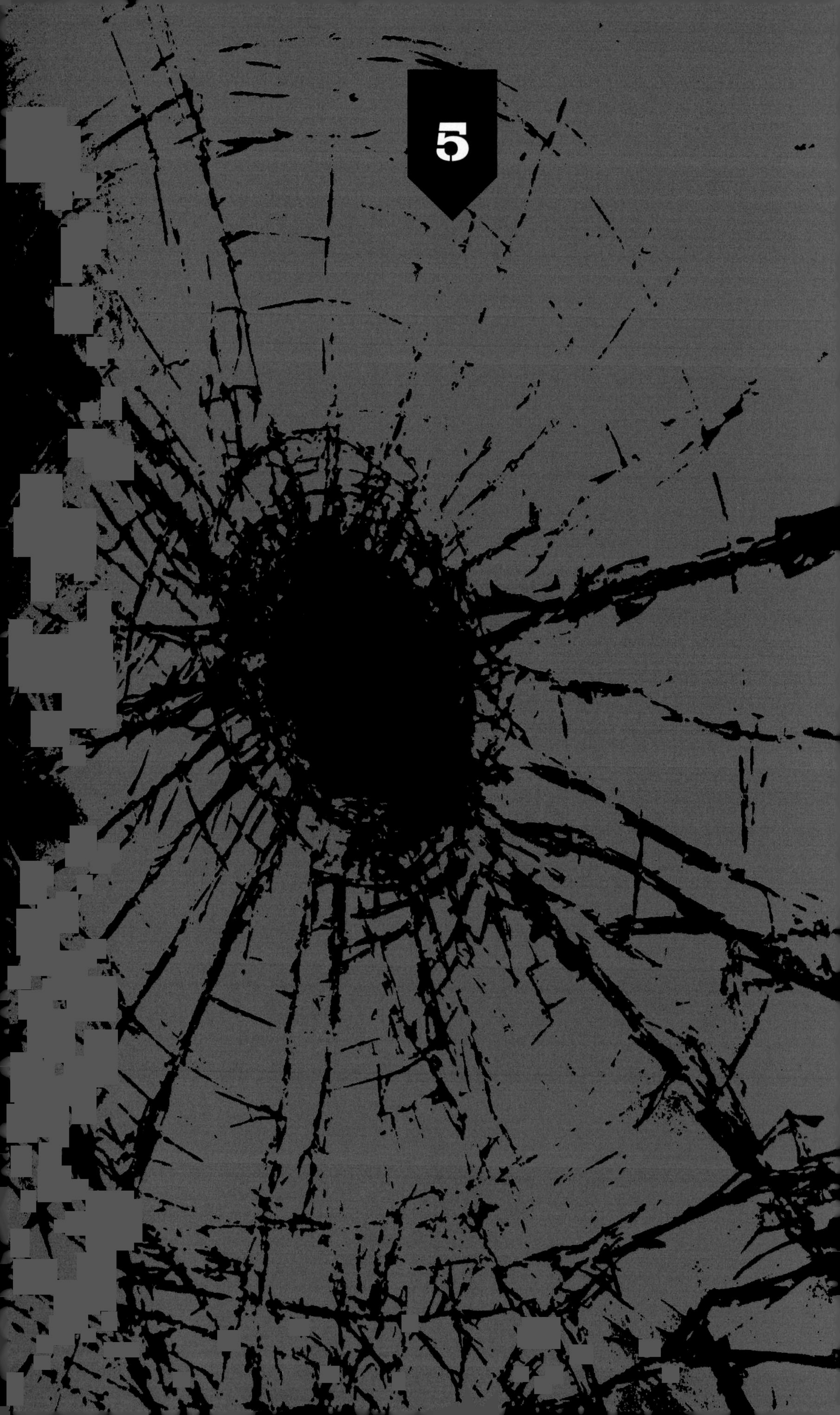

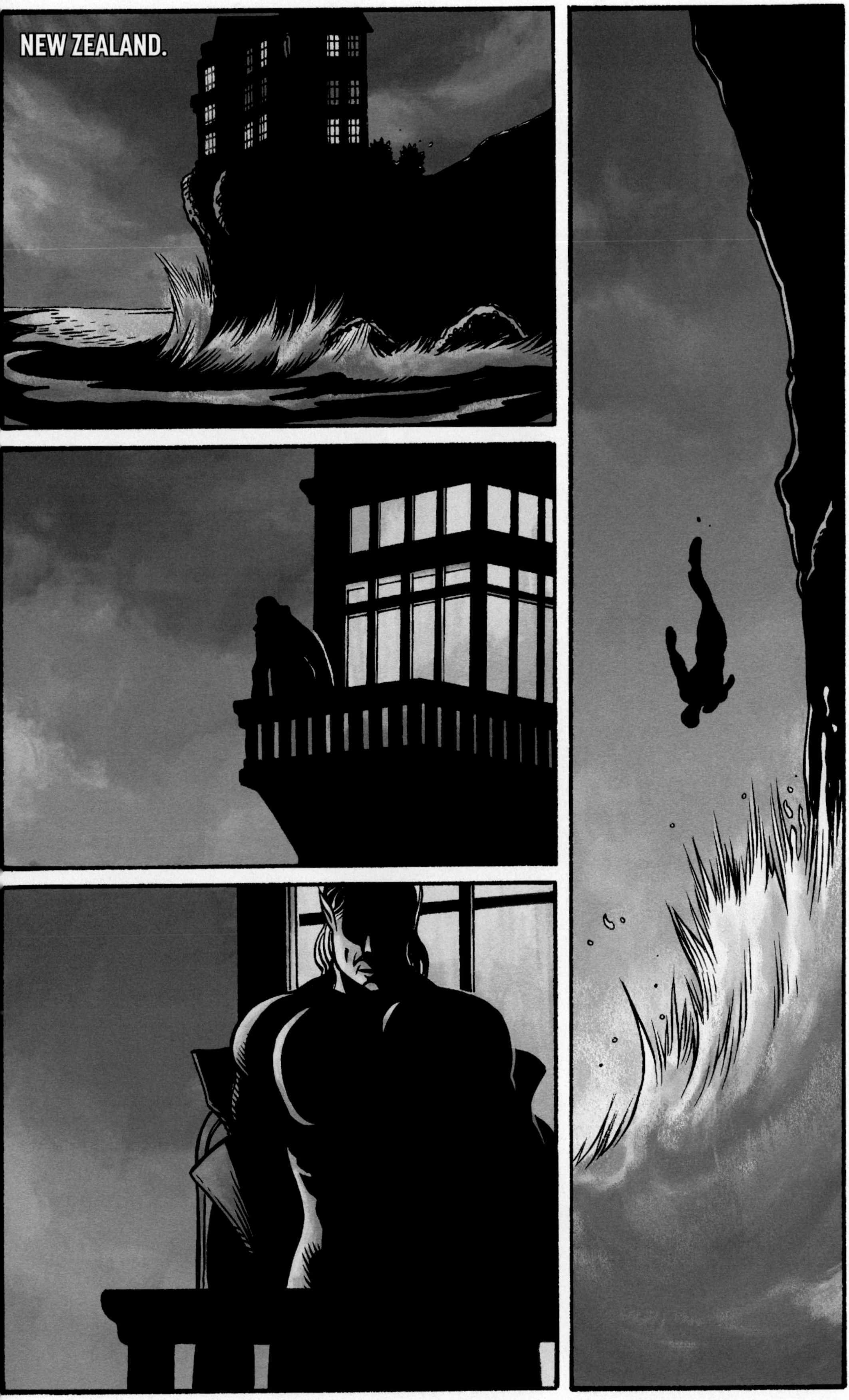
NEW ZEALAND.

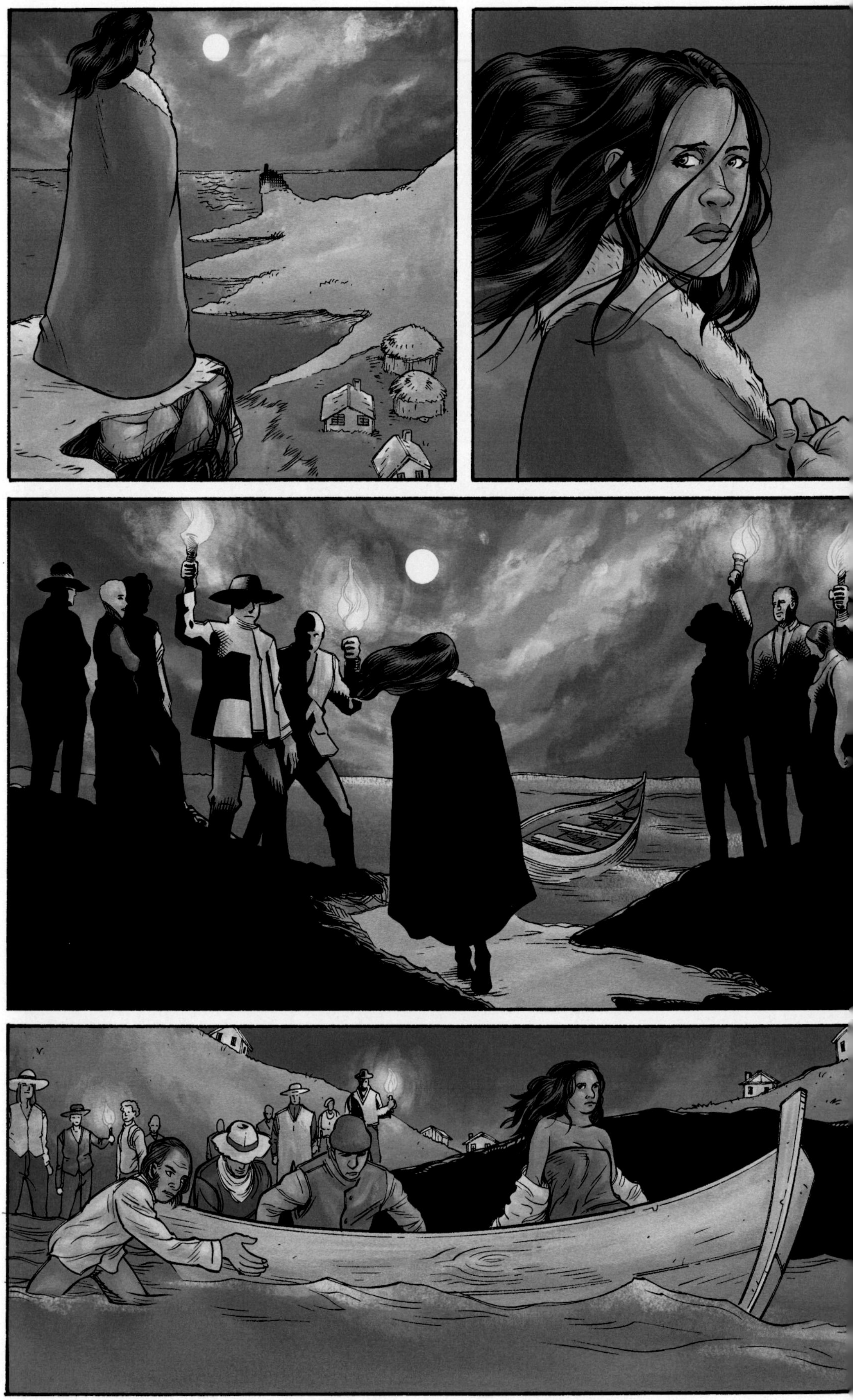

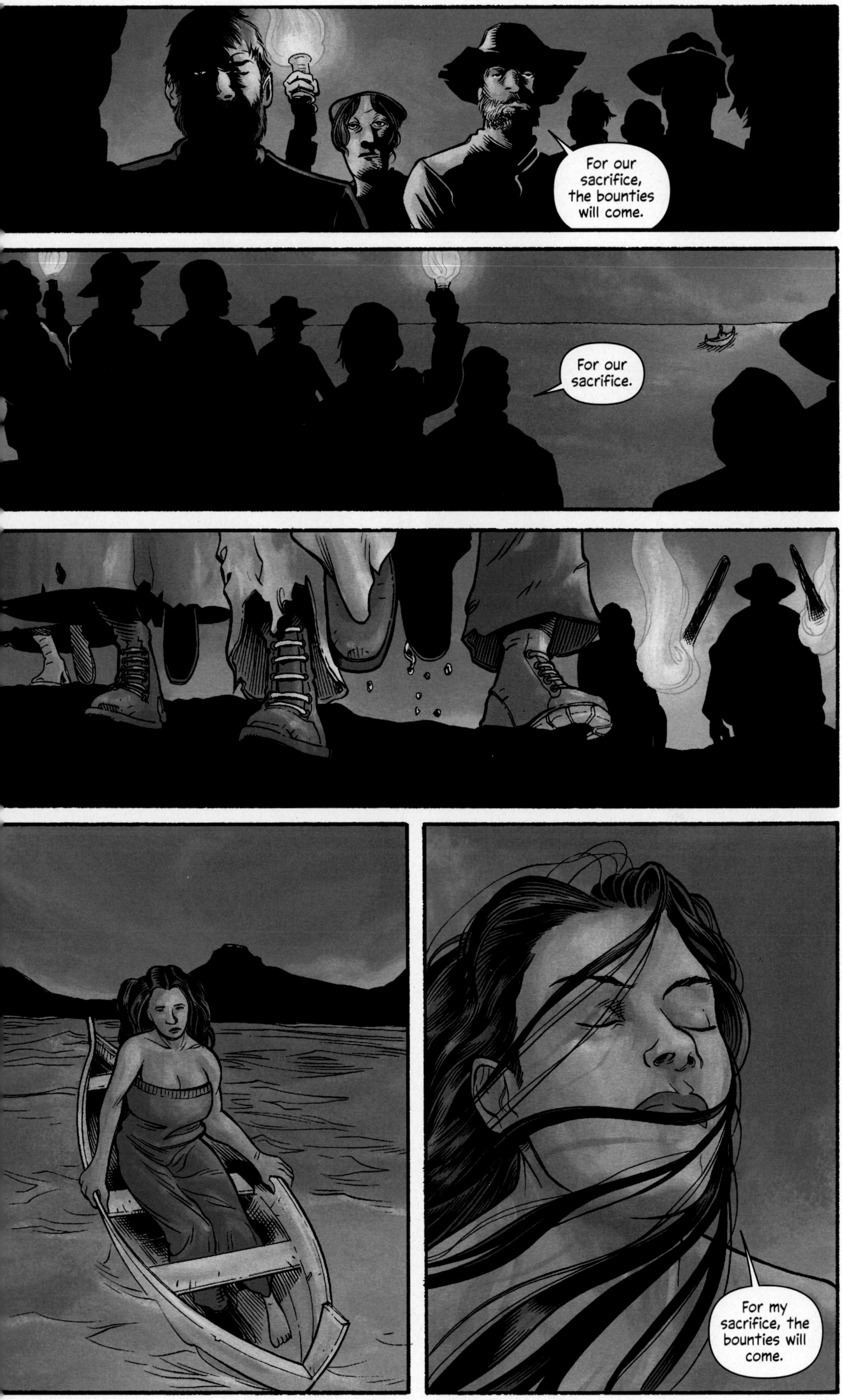
For our sacrifice, the bounties will come.
For our sacrifice.
For my sacrifice, the bounties will come.

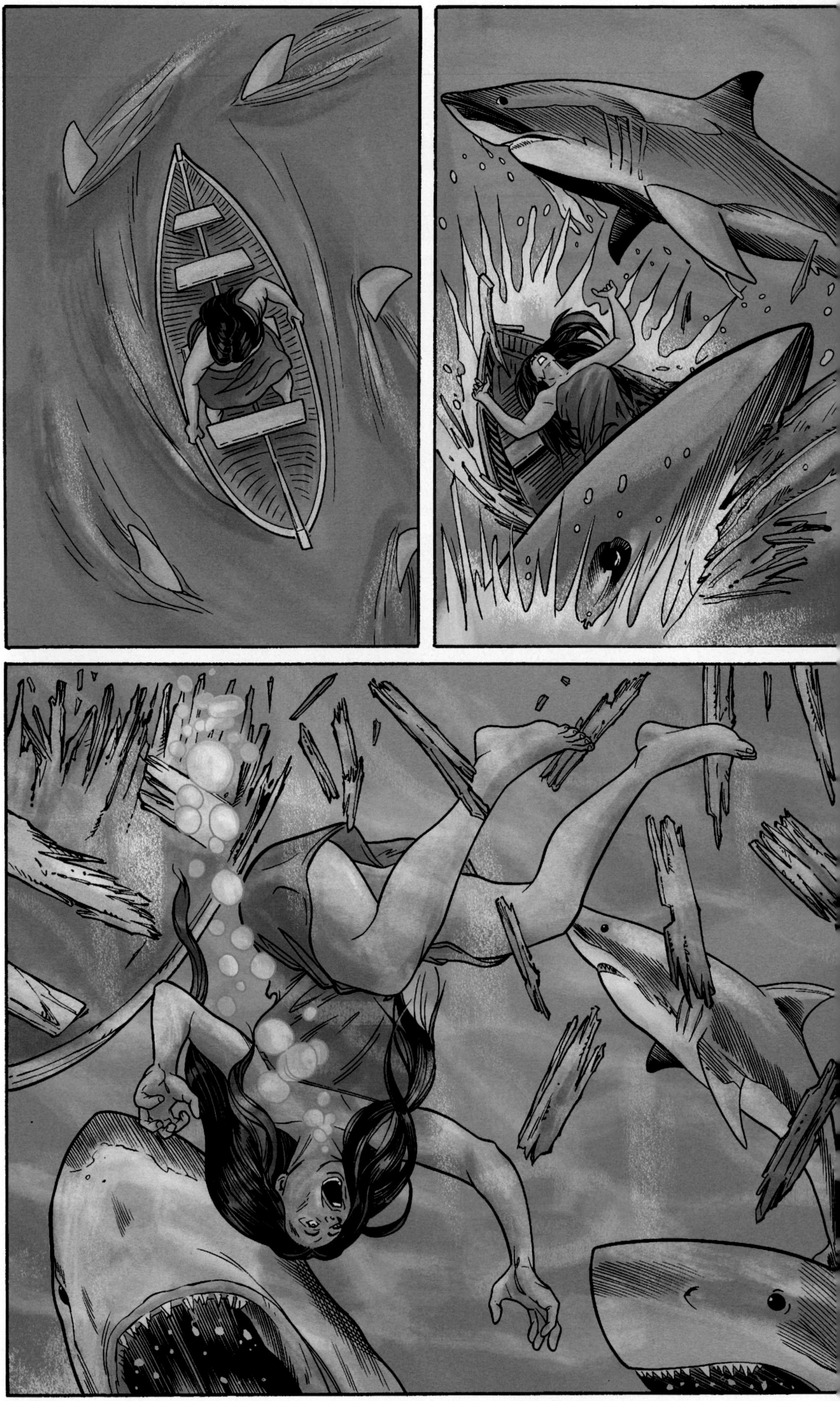

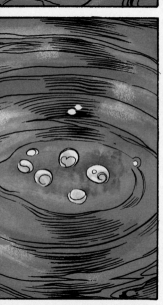

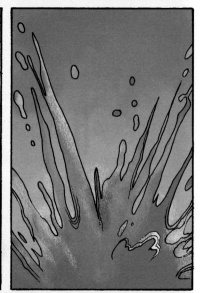

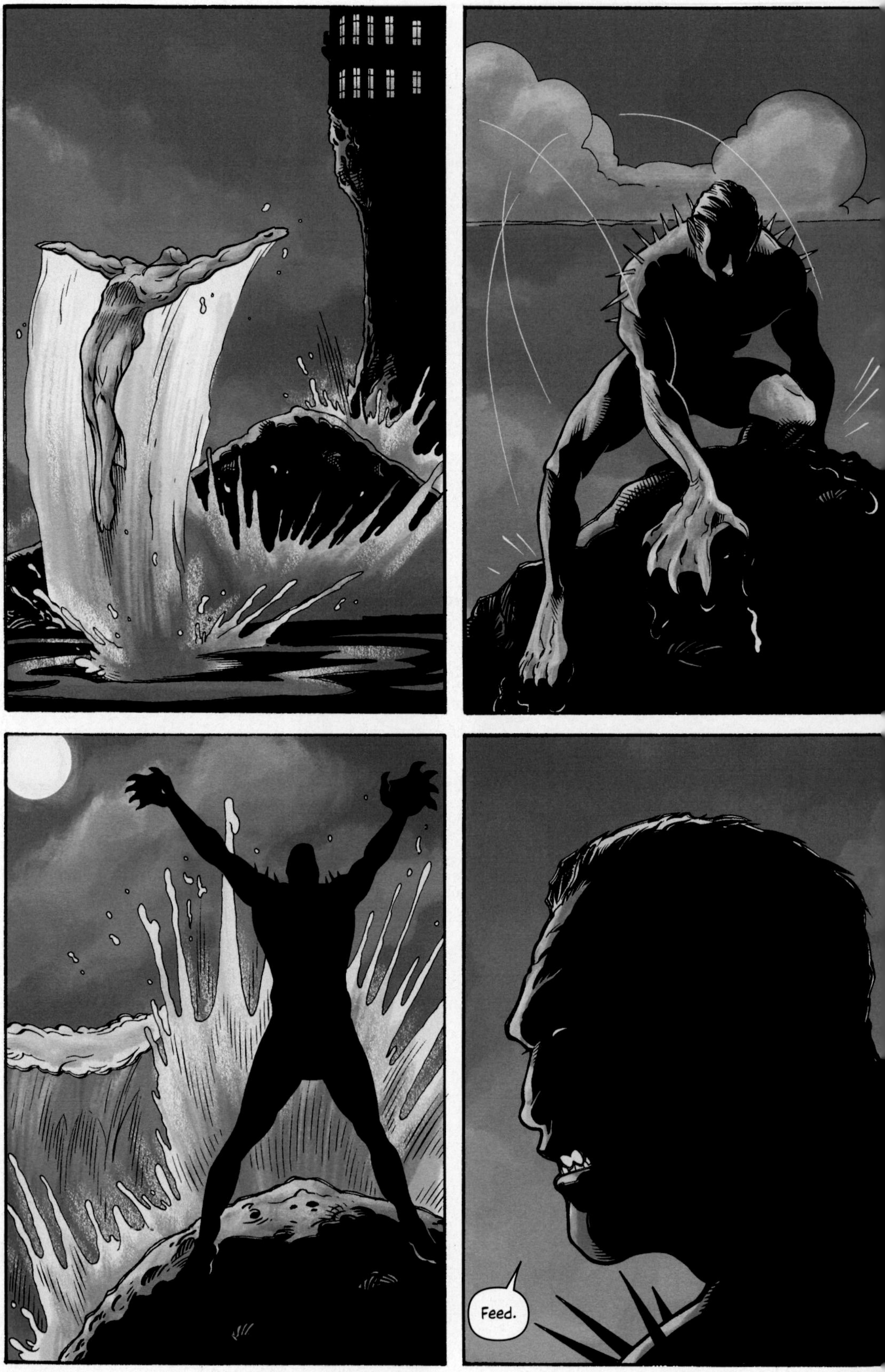
Feed.

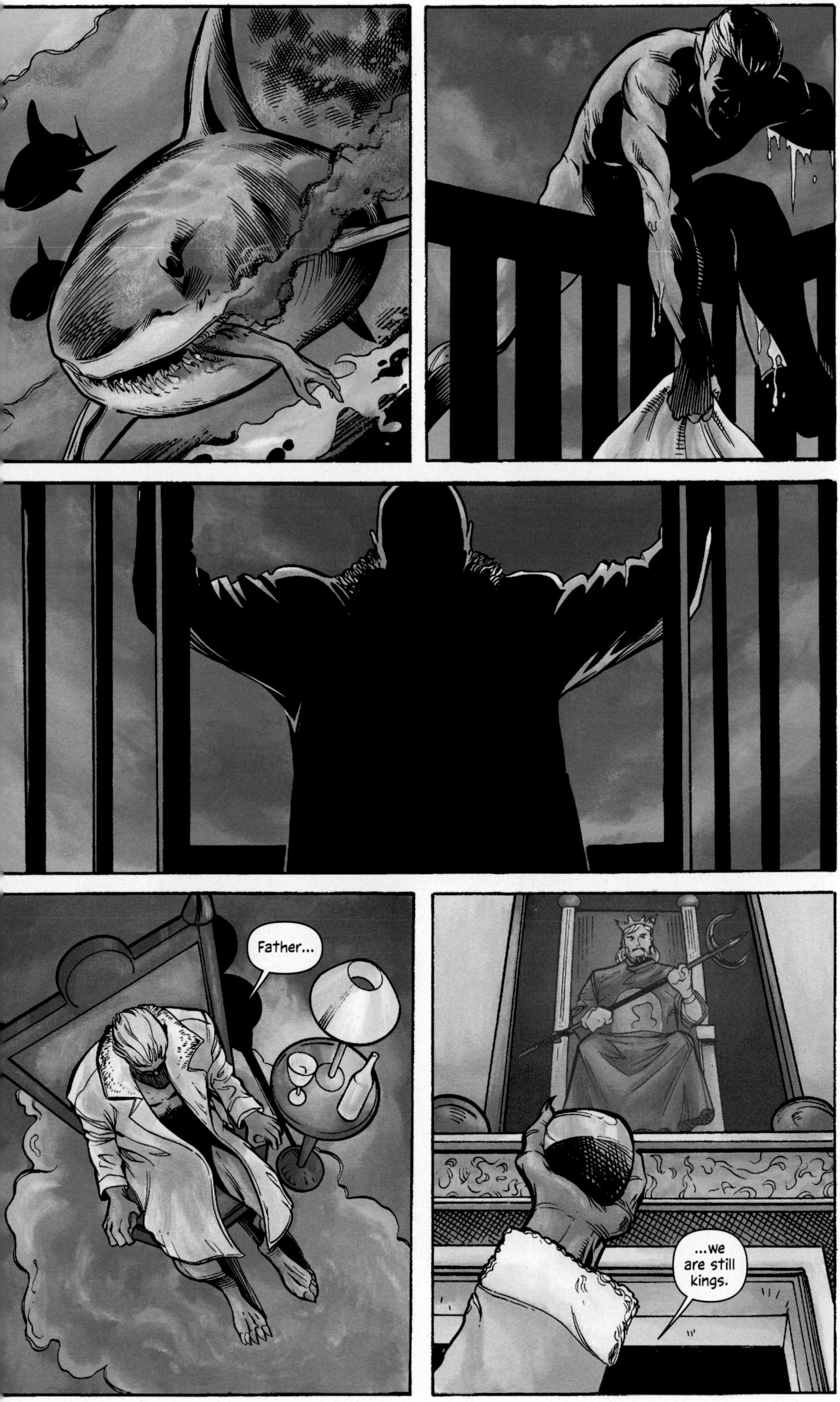
Father...
...we are still kings.

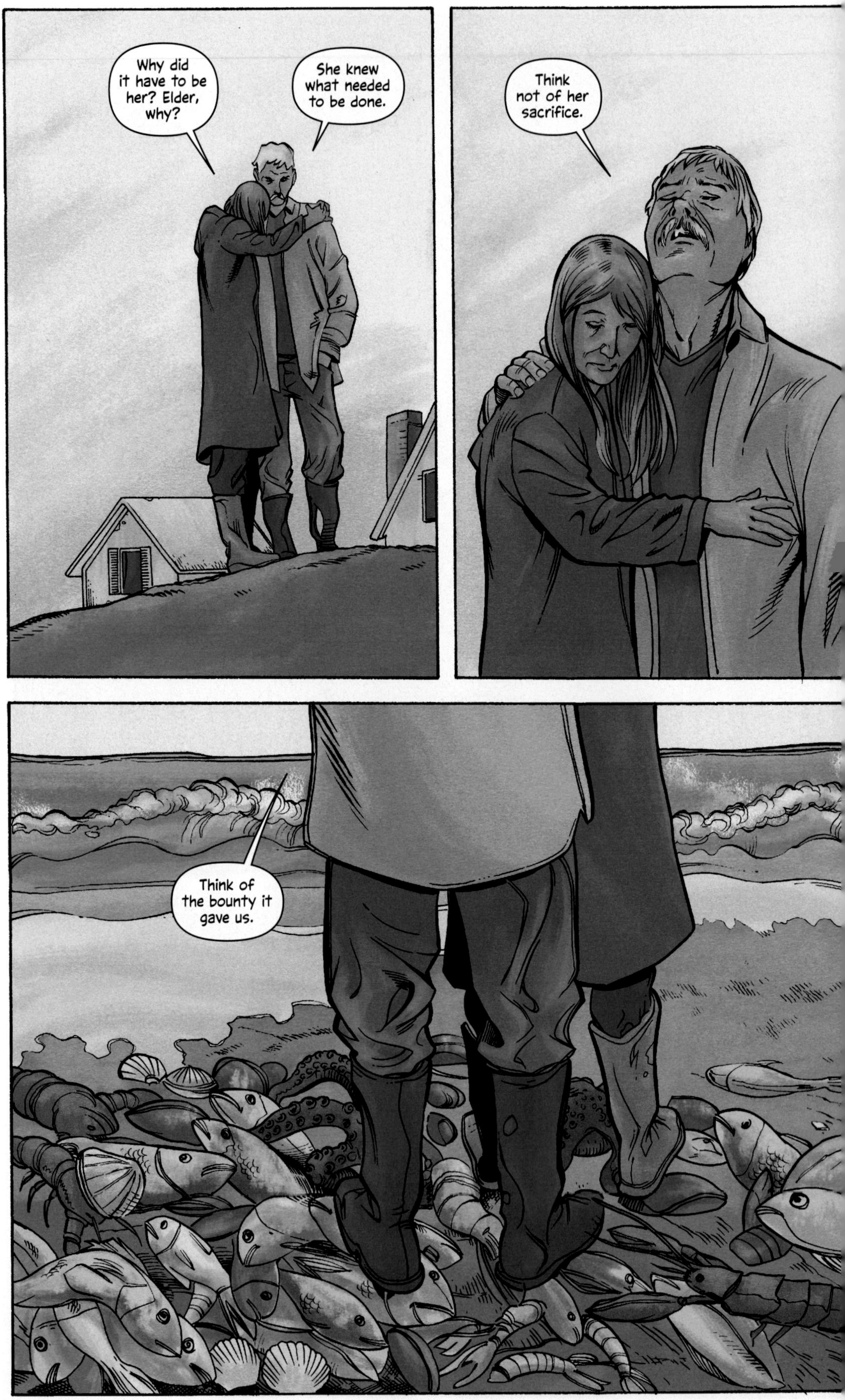
Why did it have to be her? Elder, why?
She knew what needed to be done.
Think not of her sacrifice.
Think of the bounty it gave us.

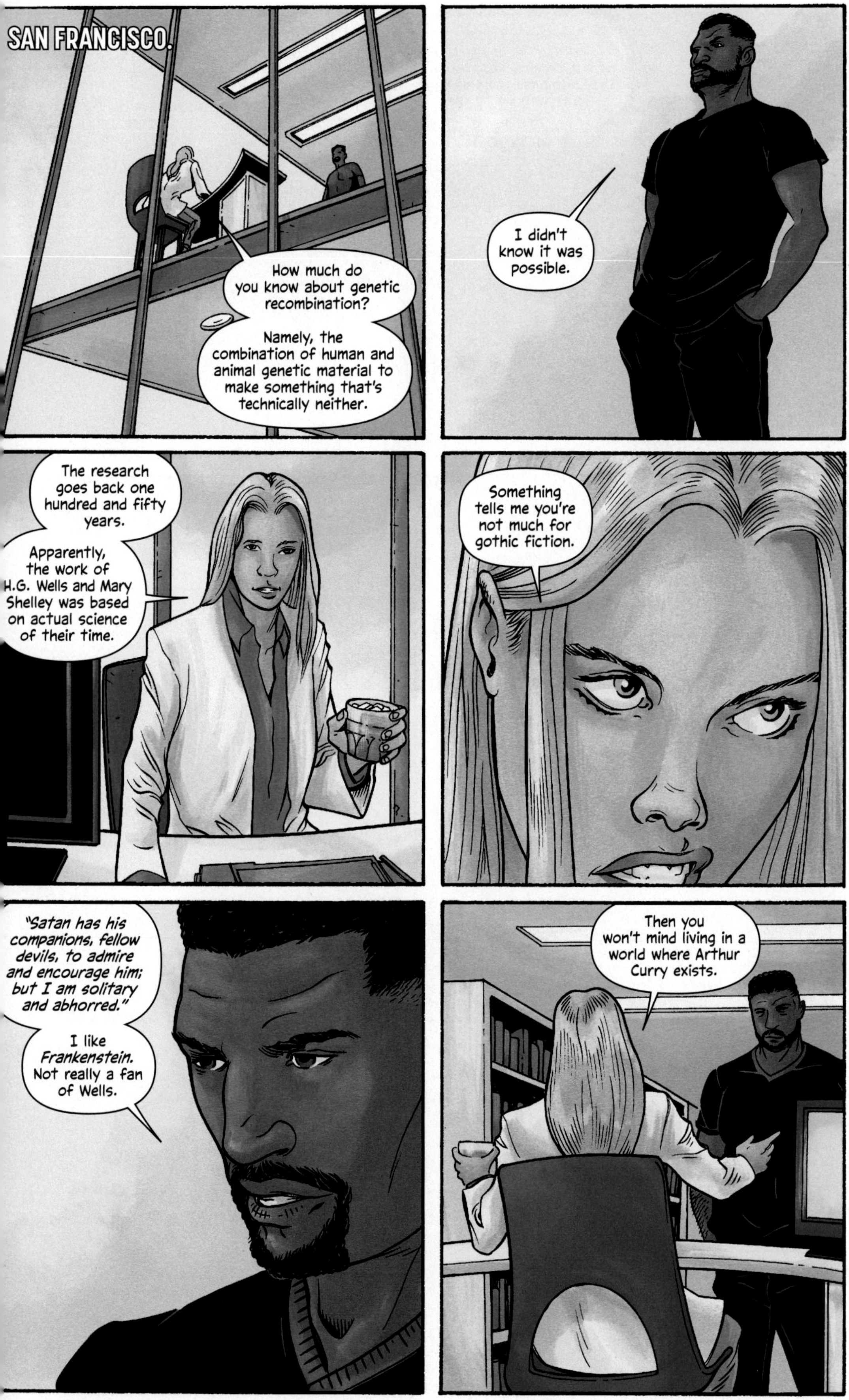

SAN FRANCISCO.
How much do you know about genetic recombination?
Namely, the combination of human and animal genetic material to make something that's technically neither.
I didn't know it was possible.
The research goes back one hundred and fifty years.
Apparently, the work of H.G. Wells and Mary Shelley was based on actual science of their time.
Something tells me you're not much for gothic fiction.
"Satan has his companions, fellow devils, to admire and encourage him; but I am solitary and abhorred."
I like *Frankenstein.* Not really a fan of Wells.
Then you won't mind living in a world where Arthur Curry exists.

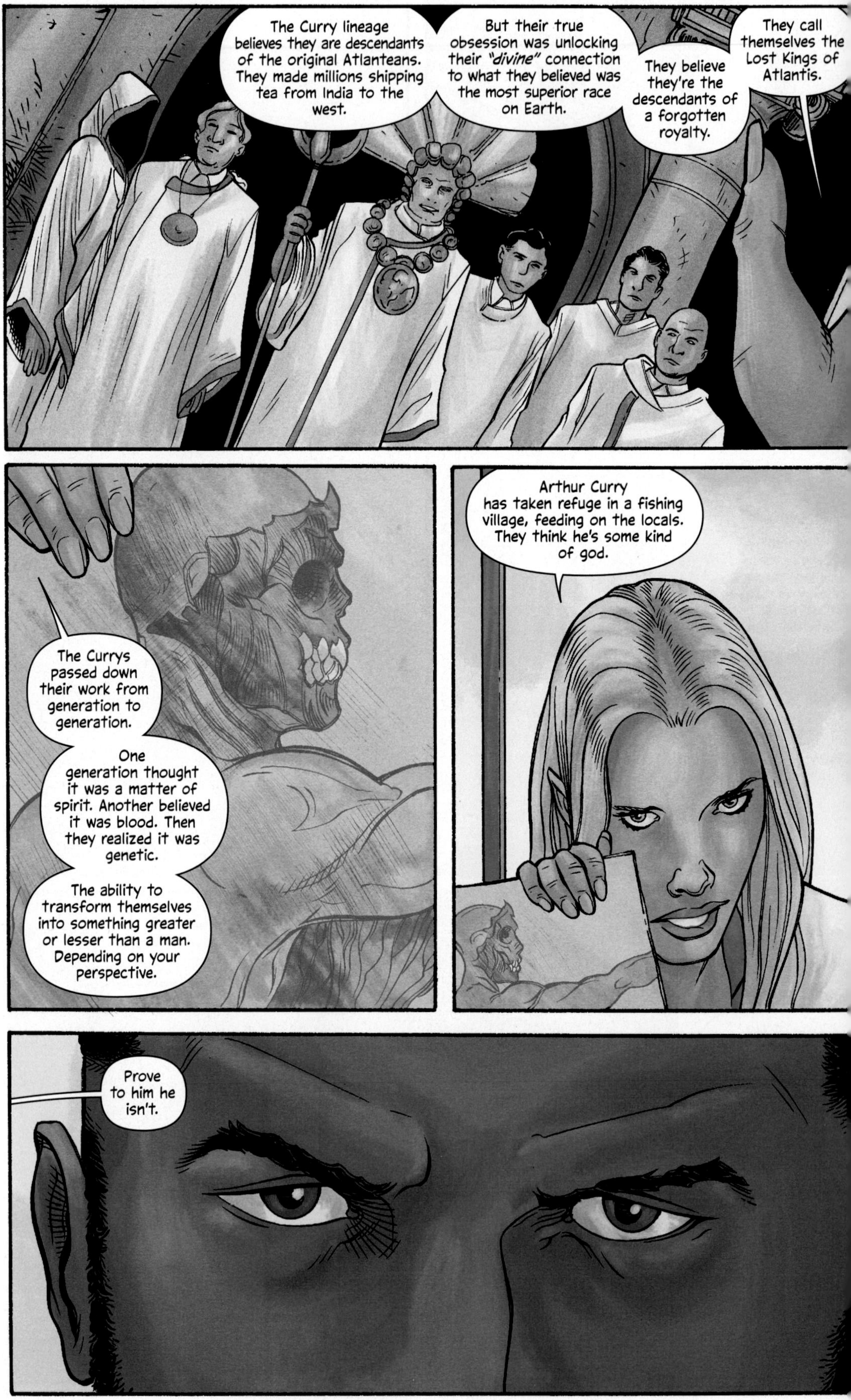

The Curry lineage believes they are descendants of the original Atlanteans. They made millions shipping tea from India to the west.
But their true obsession was unlocking their *"divine"* connection to what they believed was the most superior race on Earth.
They believe they're the descendants of a forgotten royalty.
They call themselves the Lost Kings of Atlantis.
The Currys passed down their work from generation to generation.
One generation thought it was a matter of spirit. Another believed it was blood. Then they realized it was genetic.
The ability to transform themselves into something greater or lesser than a man. Depending on your perspective.
Arthur Curry has taken refuge in a fishing village, feeding on the locals. They think he's some kind of god.
Prove to him he isn't.

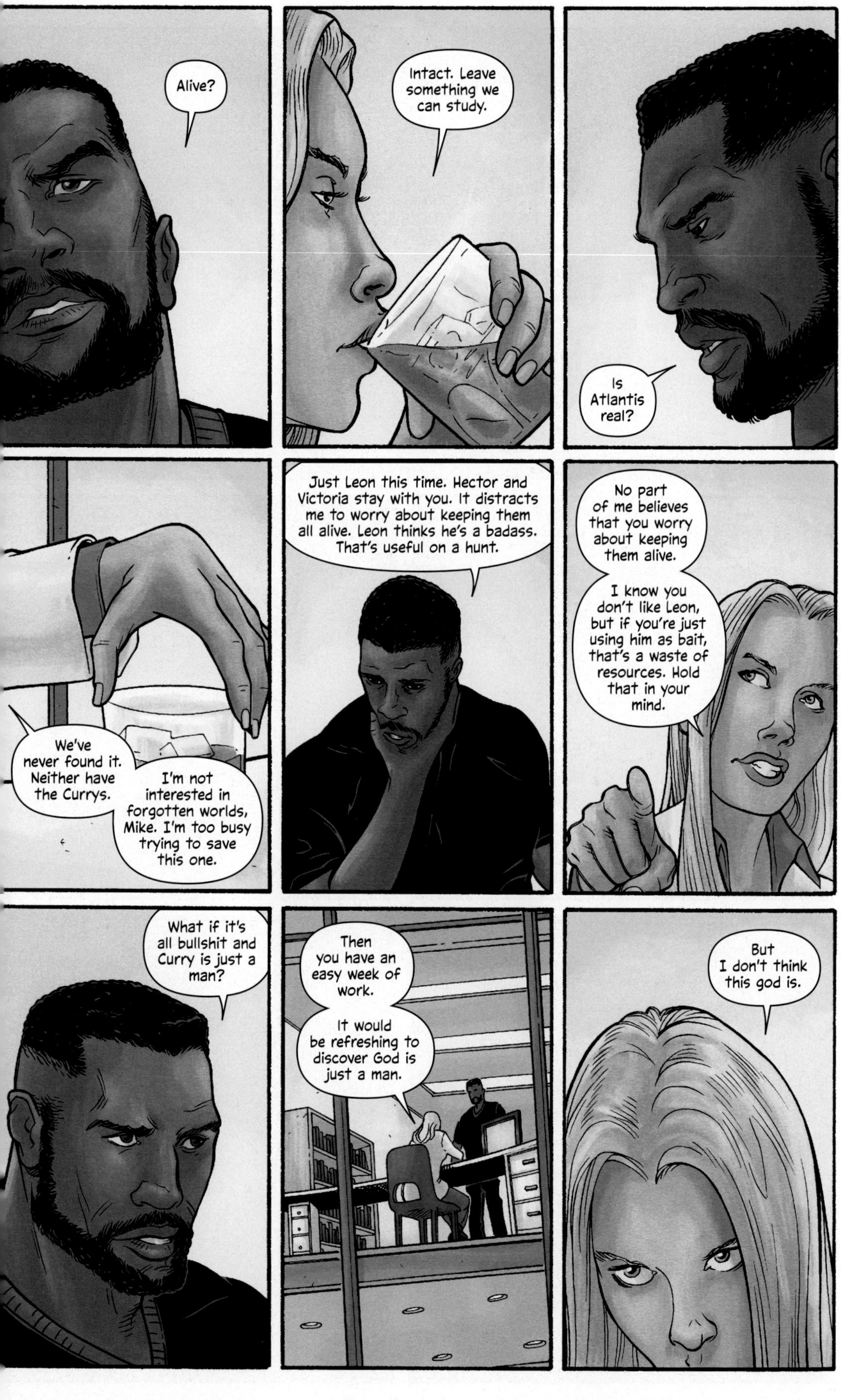
Alive?
Intact. Leave something we can study.
Is Atlantis real?
We've never found it. Neither have the Currys.
I'm not interested in forgotten worlds, Mike. I'm too busy trying to save this one.
Just Leon this time. Hector and Victoria stay with you. It distracts me to worry about keeping them all alive. Leon thinks he's a badass. That's useful on a hunt.
No part of me believes that you worry about keeping them alive.
I know you don't like Leon, but if you're just using him as bait, that's a waste of resources. Hold that in your mind.
What if it's all bullshit and Curry is just a man?
Then you have an easy week of work.
It would be refreshing to discover God is just a man.
But I don't think this god is.

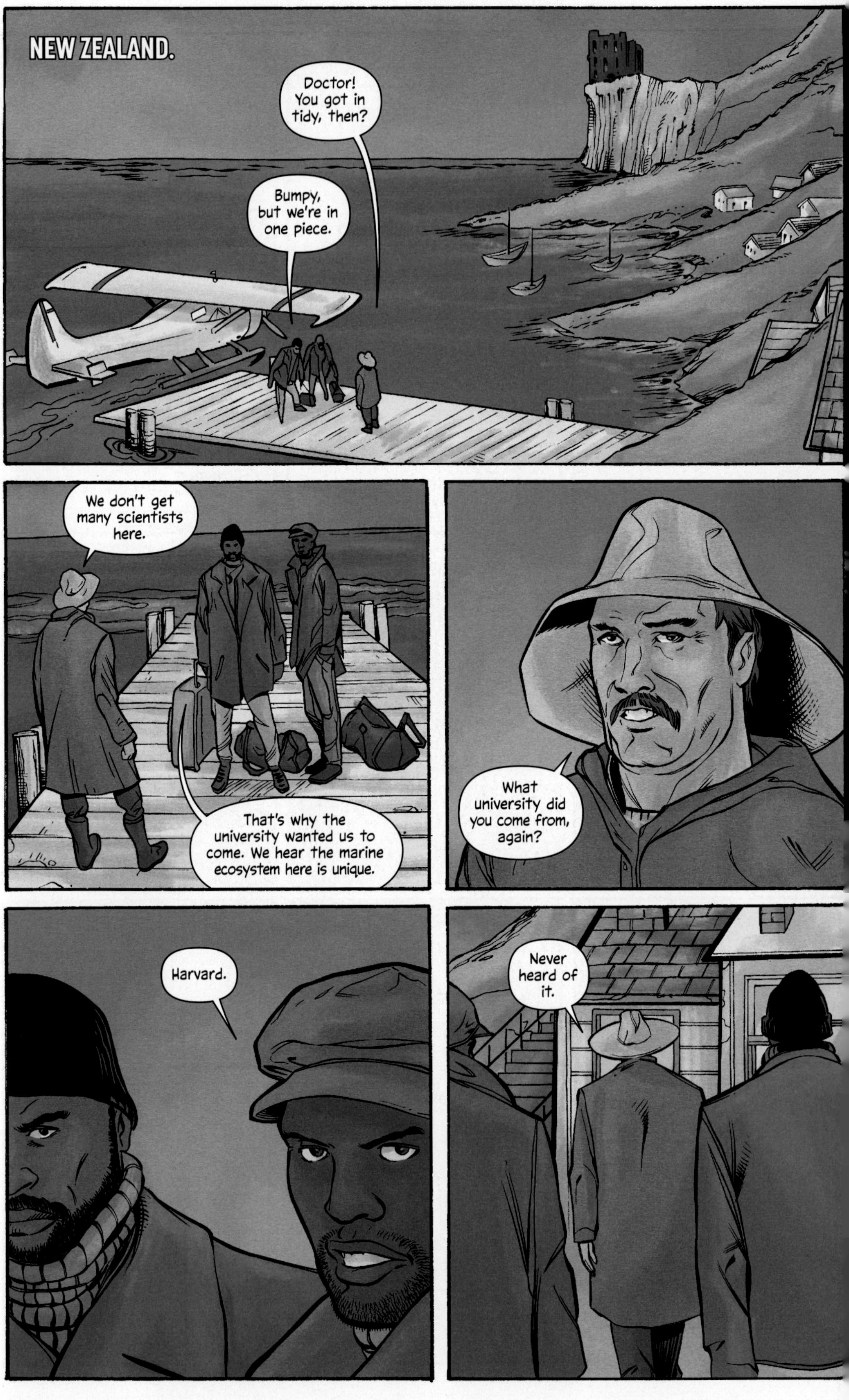
NEW ZEALAND.
Doctor! You got in tidy, then?
Bumpy, but we're in one piece.
We don't get many scientists here.
That's why the university wanted us to come. We hear the marine ecosystem here is unique.
What university did you come from, again?
Harvard.
Never heard of it.

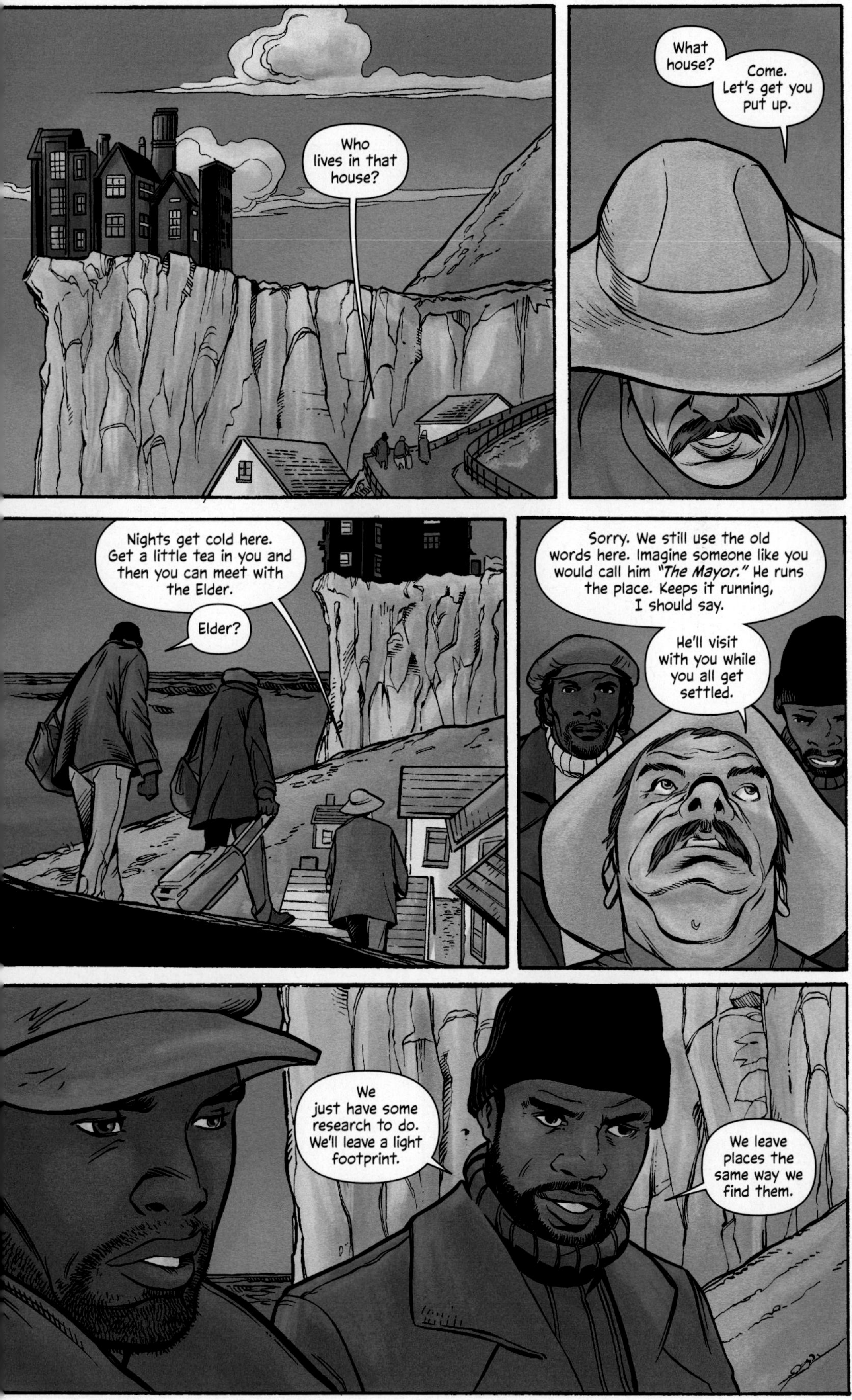
Who lives in that house?
What house?
Come. Let's get you put up.
Nights get cold here. Get a little tea in you and then you can meet with the Elder.
Elder?
Sorry. We still use the old words here. Imagine someone like you would call him *"The Mayor."* He runs the place. Keeps it running, I should say.
He'll visit with you while you all get settled.
We just have some research to do. We'll leave a light footprint.
We leave places the same way we find them.

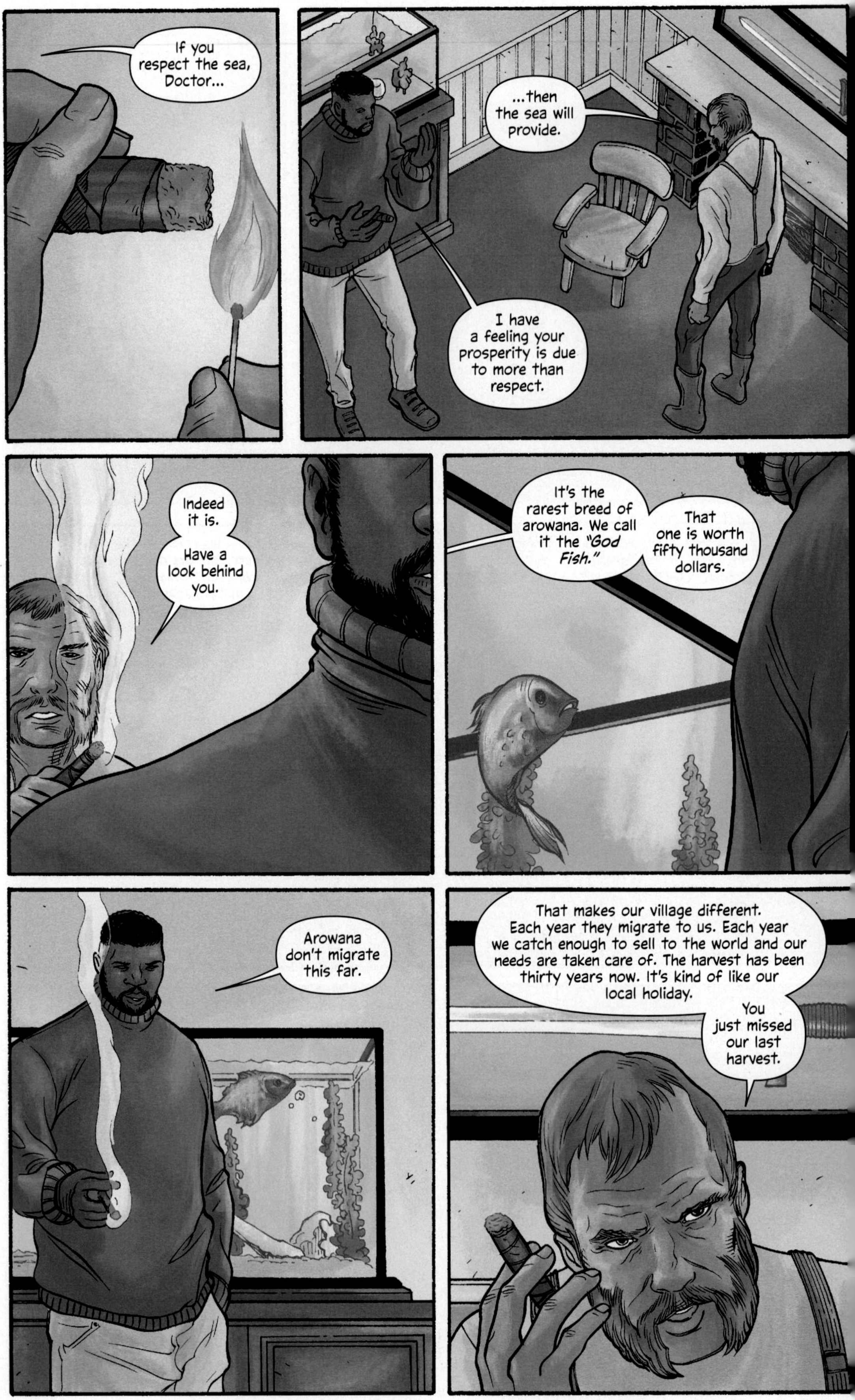
If you respect the sea, Doctor...
...then the sea will provide.
I have a feeling your prosperity is due to more than respect.
Indeed it is.
Have a look behind you.
It's the rarest breed of arowana. We call it the *"God Fish."*
That one is worth fifty thousand dollars.
Arowana don't migrate this far.
That makes our village different. Each year they migrate to us. Each year we catch enough to sell to the world and our needs are taken care of. The harvest has been thirty years now. It's kind of like our local holiday.
You just missed our last harvest.

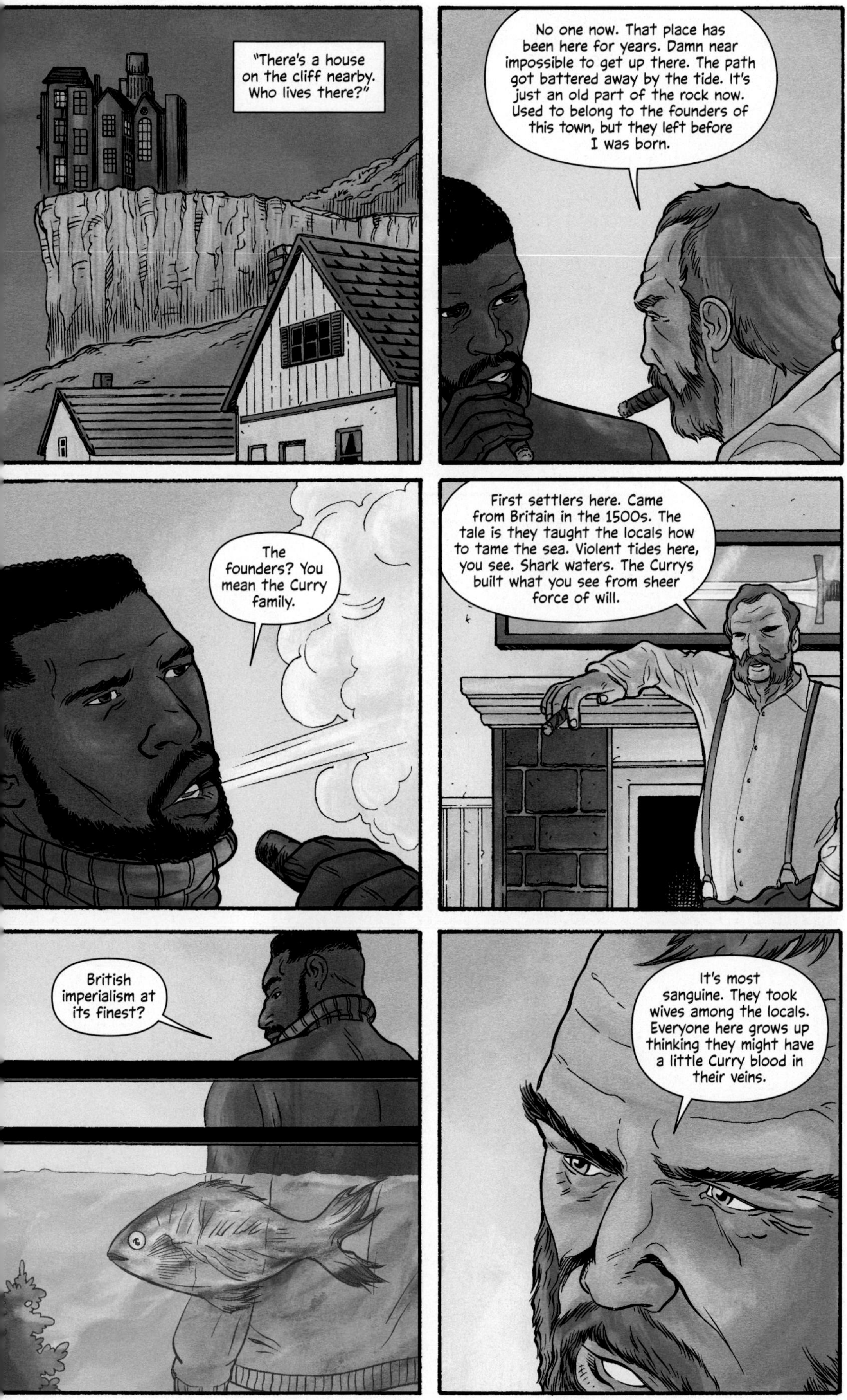
"There's a house on the cliff nearby. Who lives there?"
No one now. That place has been here for years. Damn near impossible to get up there. The path got battered away by the tide. It's just an old part of the rock now. Used to belong to the founders of this town, but they left before I was born.
The founders? You mean the Curry family.
First settlers here. Came from Britain in the 1500s. The tale is they taught the locals how to tame the sea. Violent tides here, you see. Shark waters. The Currys built what you see from sheer force of will.
British imperialism at its finest?
It's most sanguine. They took wives among the locals. Everyone here grows up thinking they might have a little Curry blood in their veins.

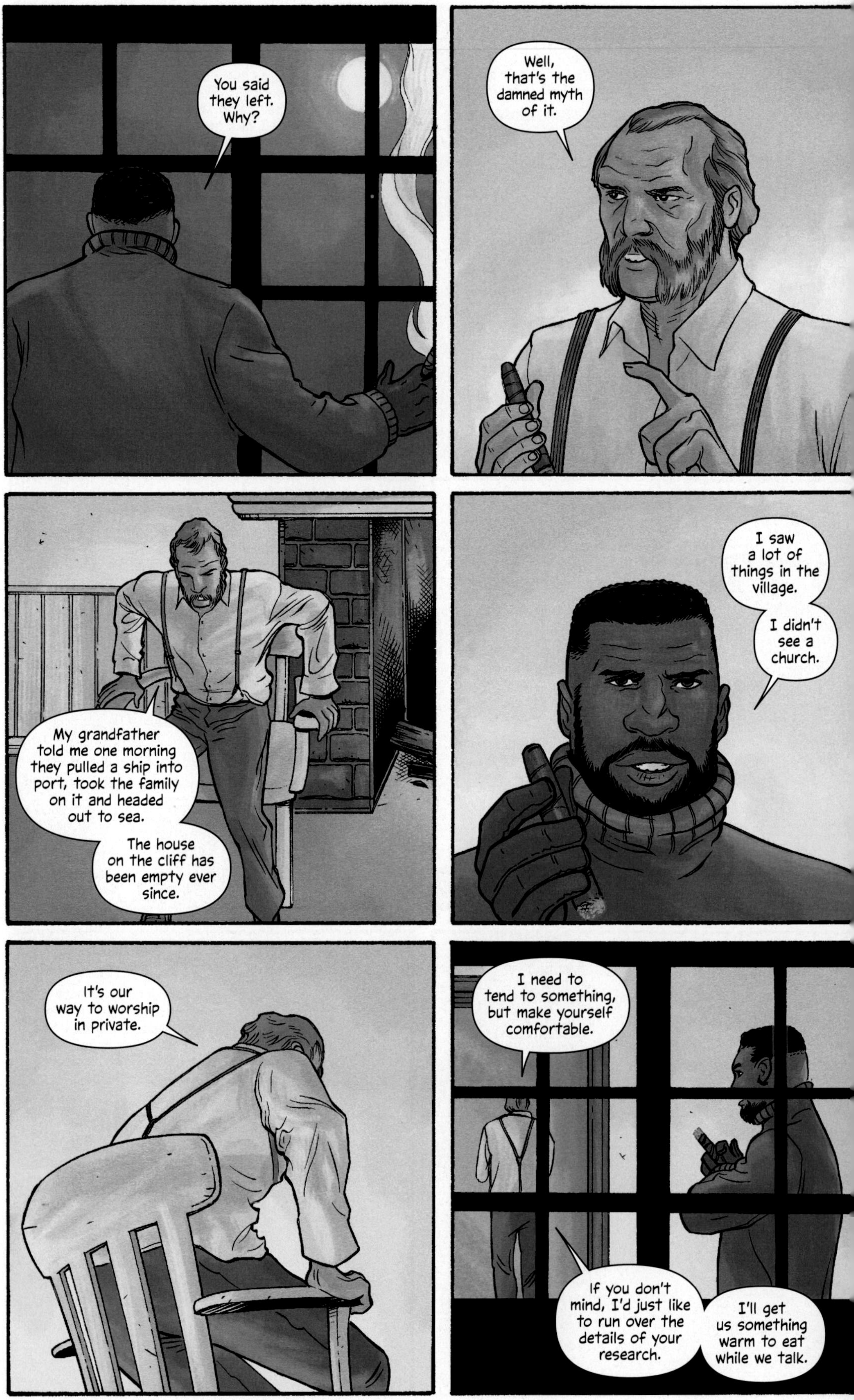

You said they left. Why?
Well, that's the damned myth of it.
My grandfather told me one morning they pulled a ship into port, took the family on it and headed out to sea.
The house on the cliff has been empty ever since.
I saw a lot of things in the village.
I didn't see a church.
It's our way to worship in private.
I need to tend to something, but make yourself comfortable.
I'll get us something warm to eat while we talk.
If you don't mind, I'd just like to run over the details of your research.

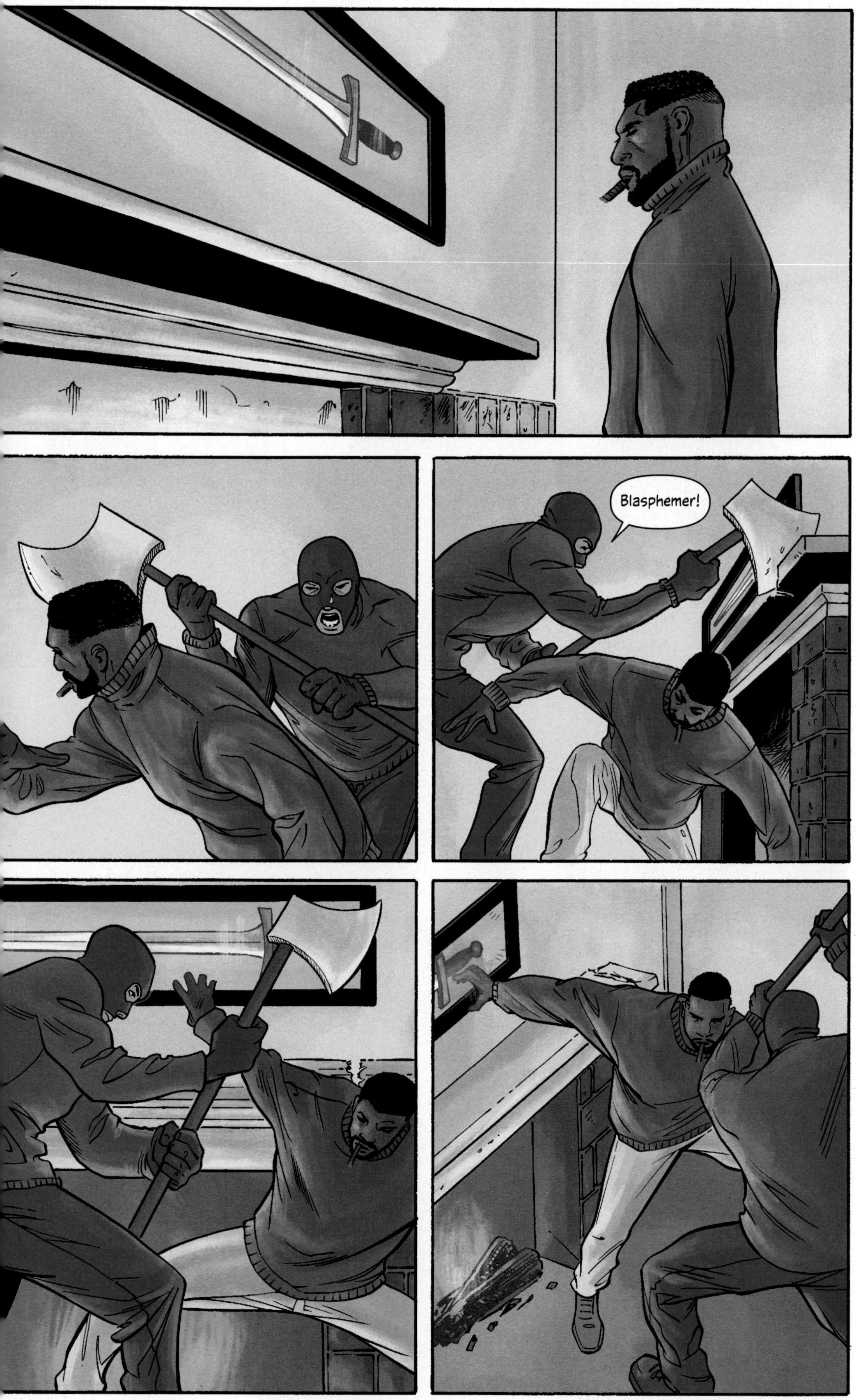
Blasphemer!

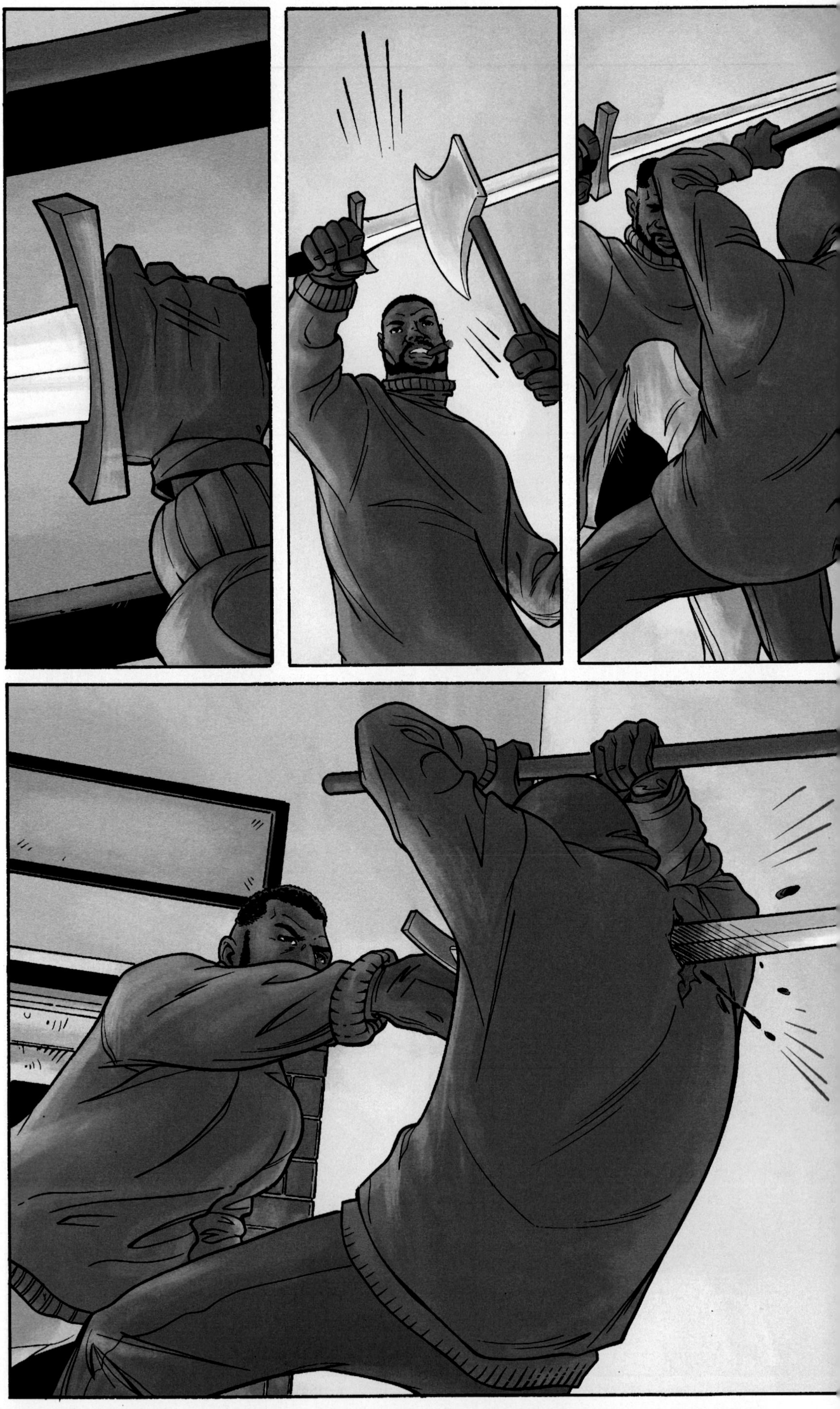

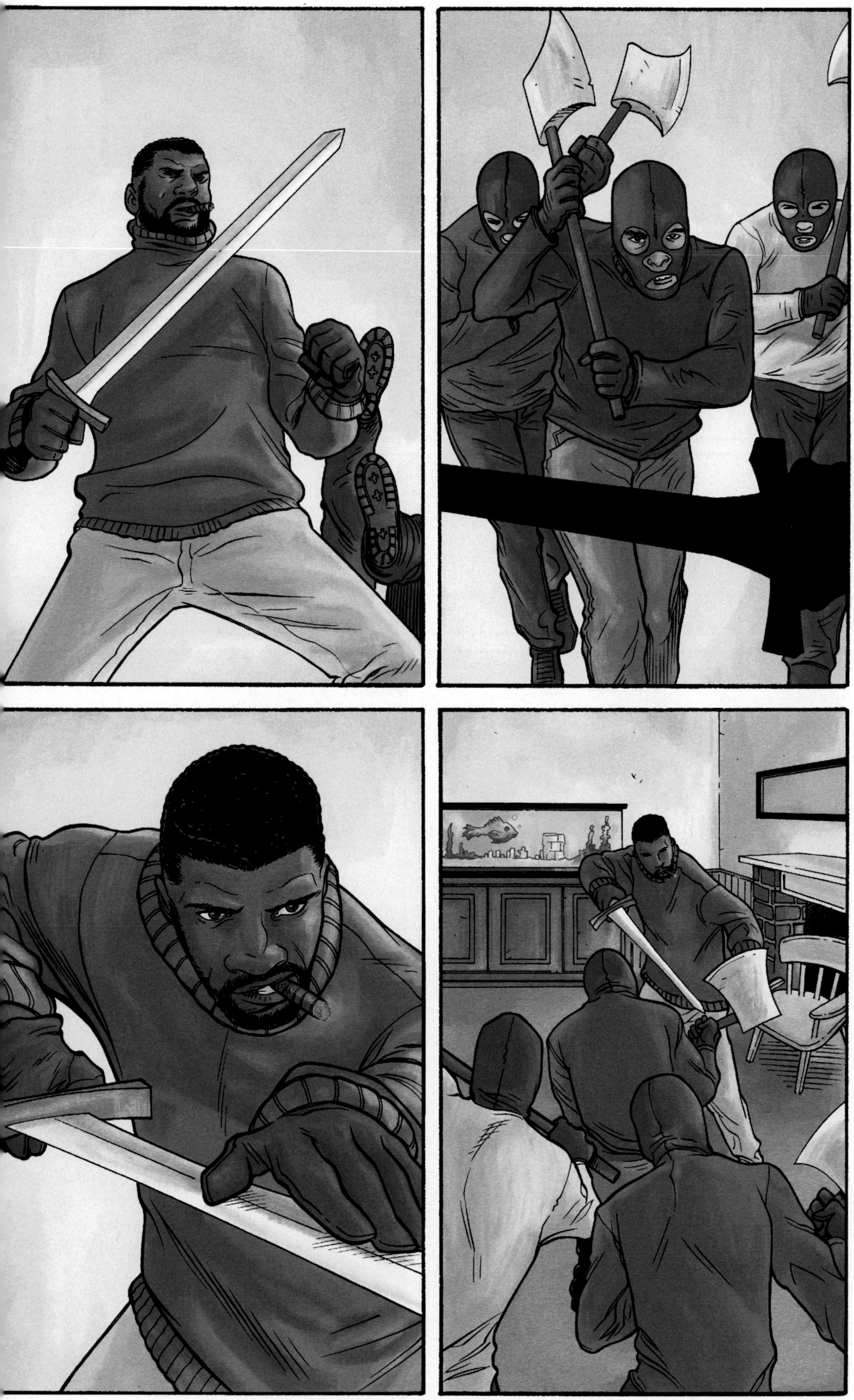

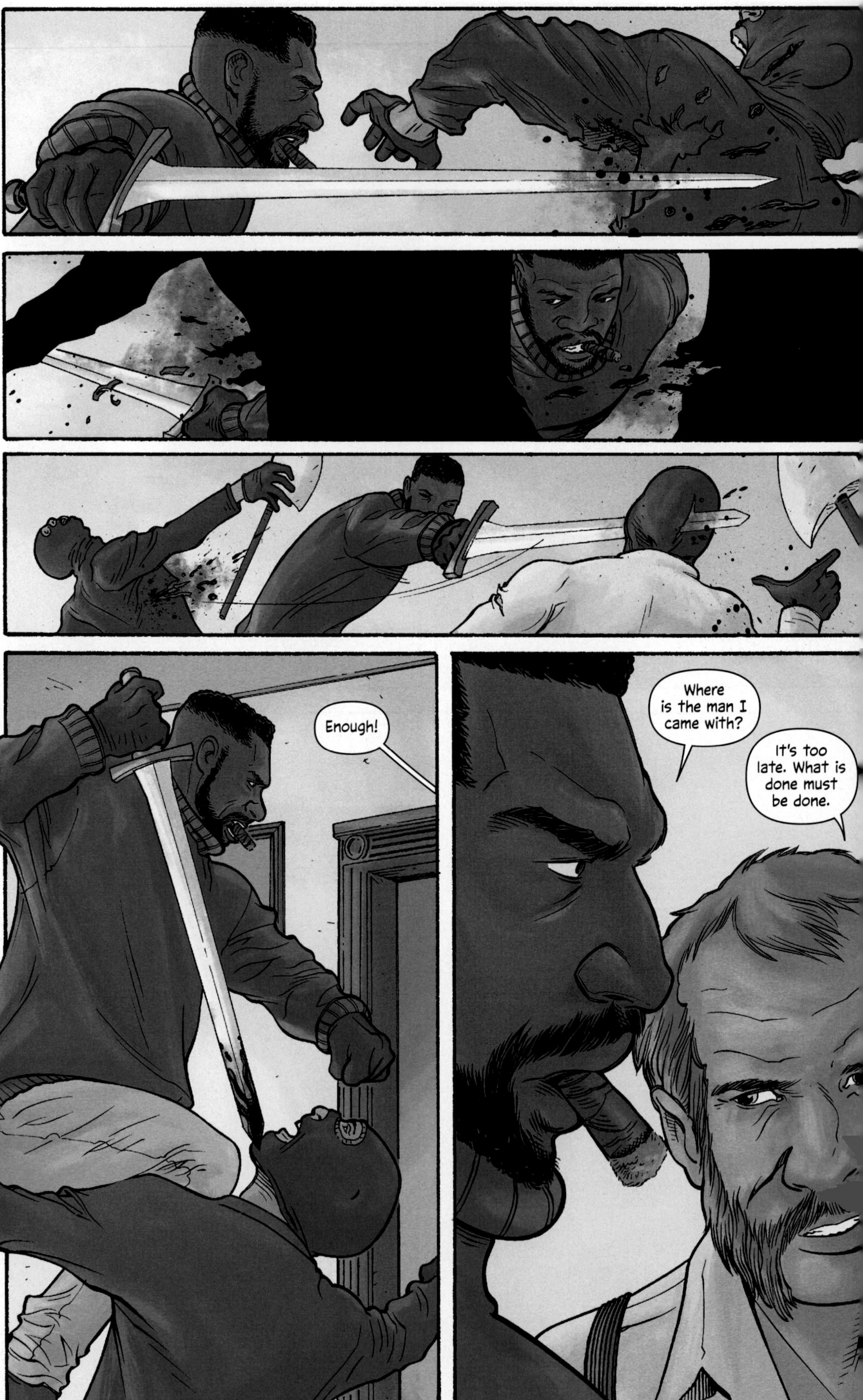
Enough!
Where is the man I came with?
It's too late. What is done must be done.

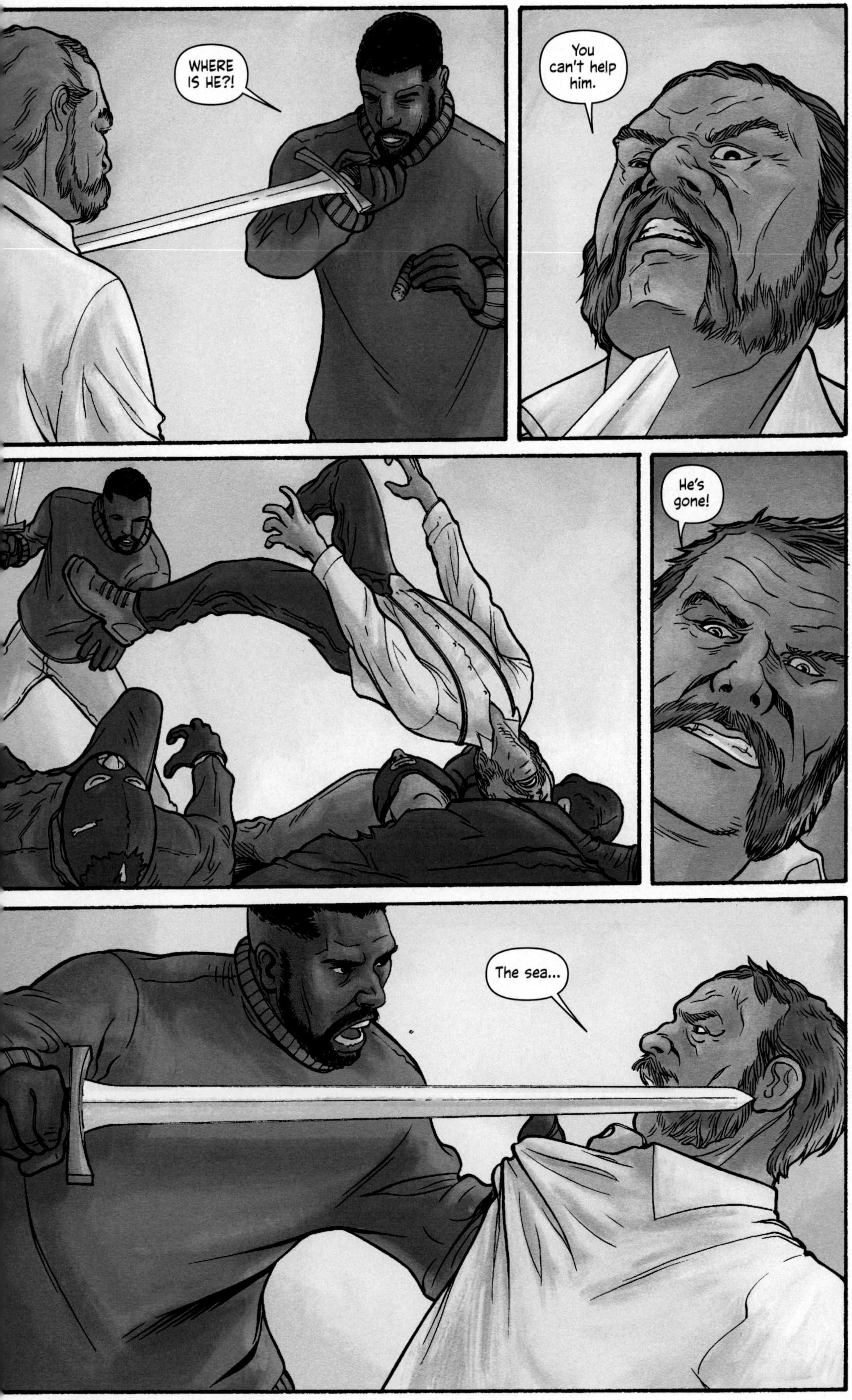
WHERE IS HE?!
You can't help him.
He's gone!
The sea...

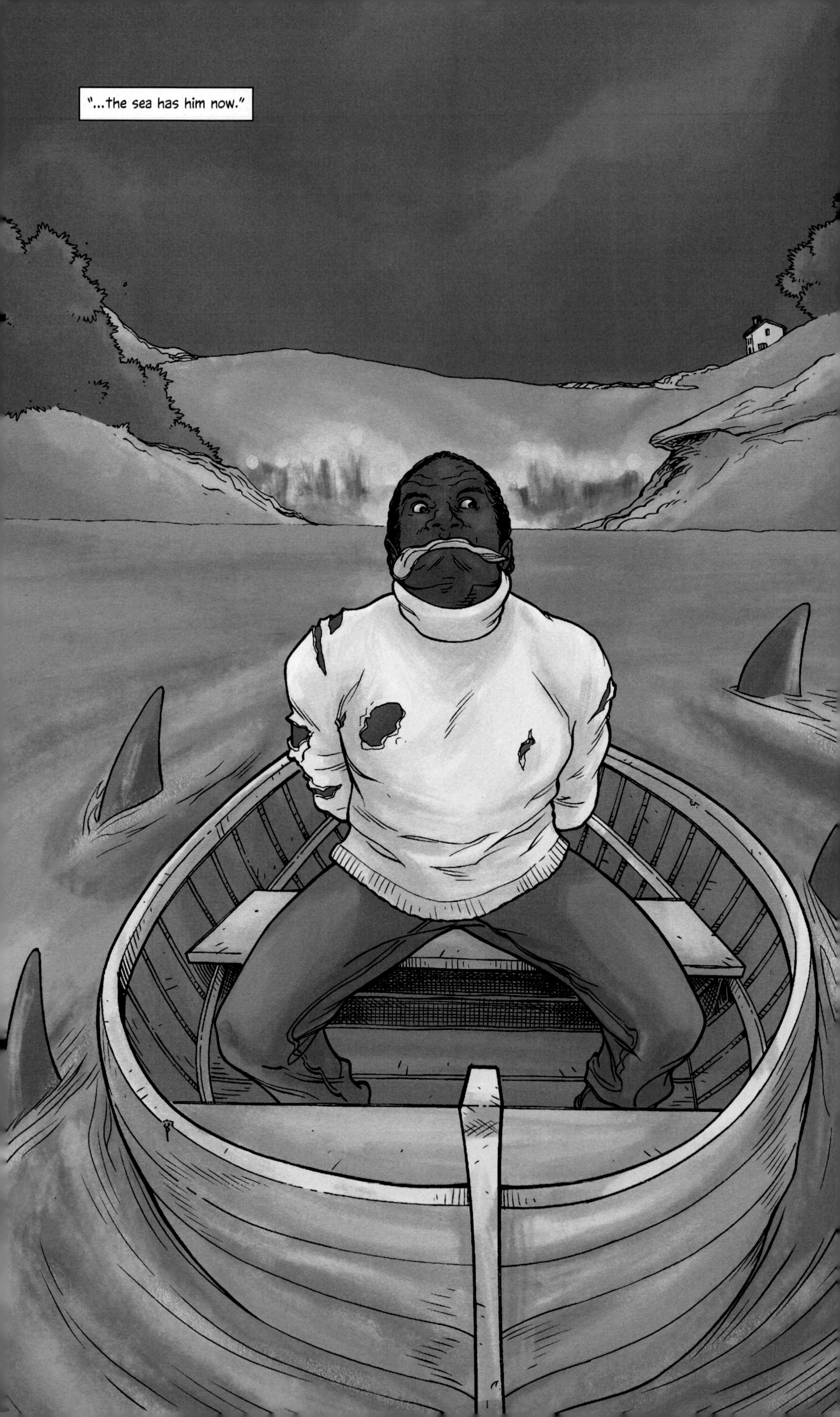
"...the sea has him now."

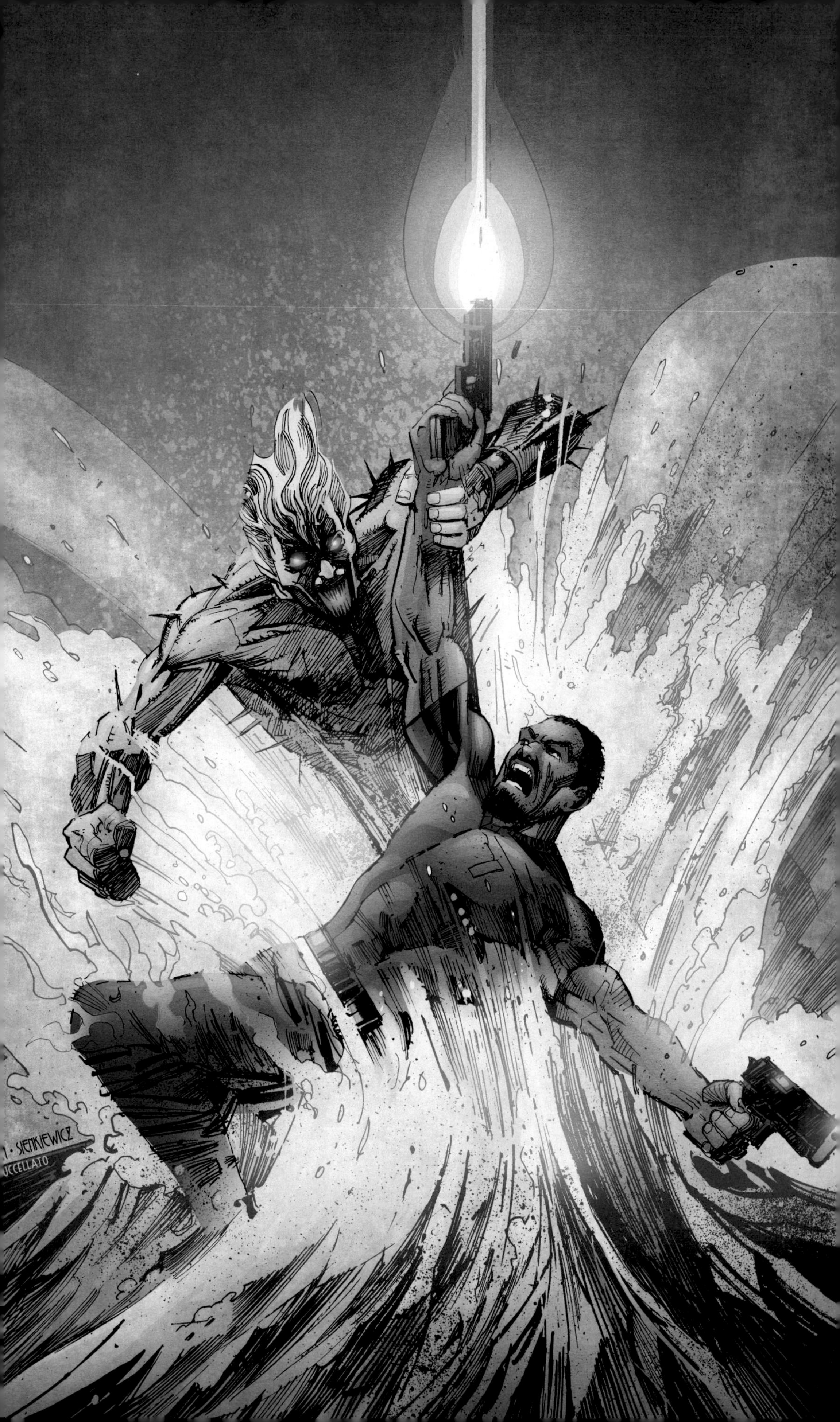
SIENKIEWICZ

6

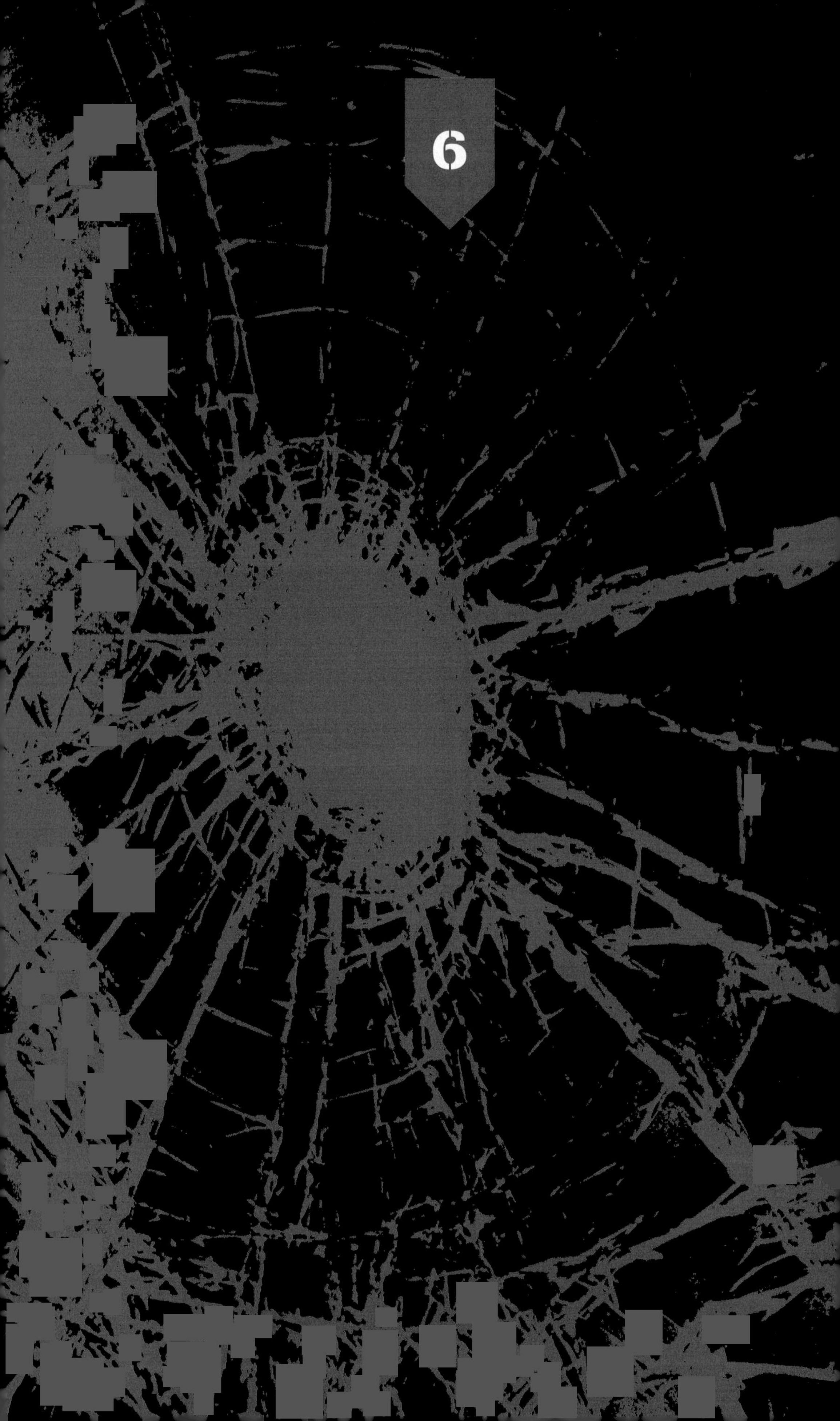

A little conversation about death, Michael.
That's all I want.
Death is a necessity, Michael.
It's not an enemy.
When the stars were born...
...the darkness died.
Didn't it?
Death is change, Michael.
Anything that changes kills something.
So you're dying, Michael.
Changing.
So tell me.
What are you becoming?

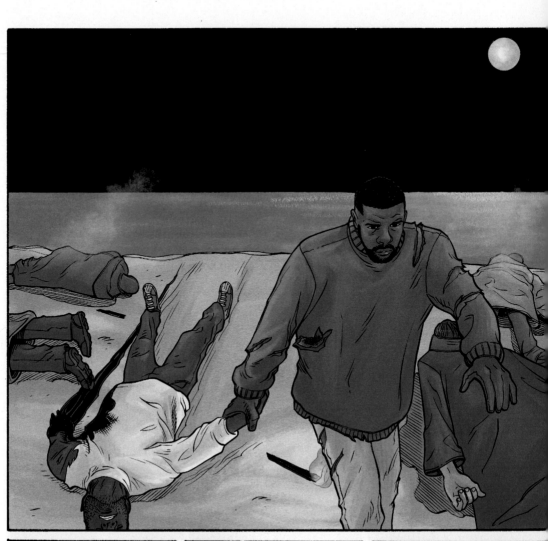

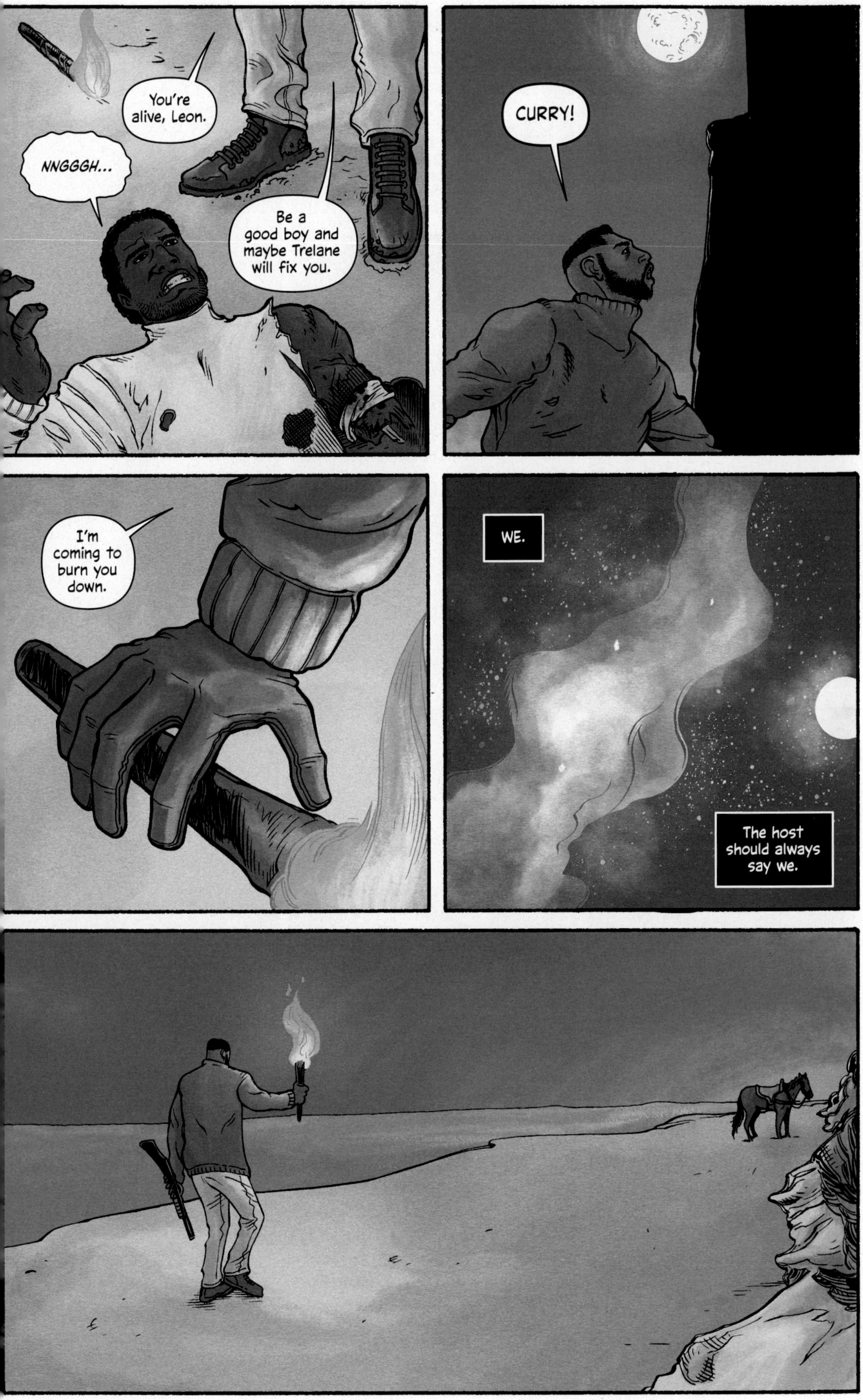
NNGGGH...
You're alive, Leon.
Be a good boy and maybe Trelane will fix you.
CURRY!
I'm coming to burn you down.
WE.
The host should always say we.

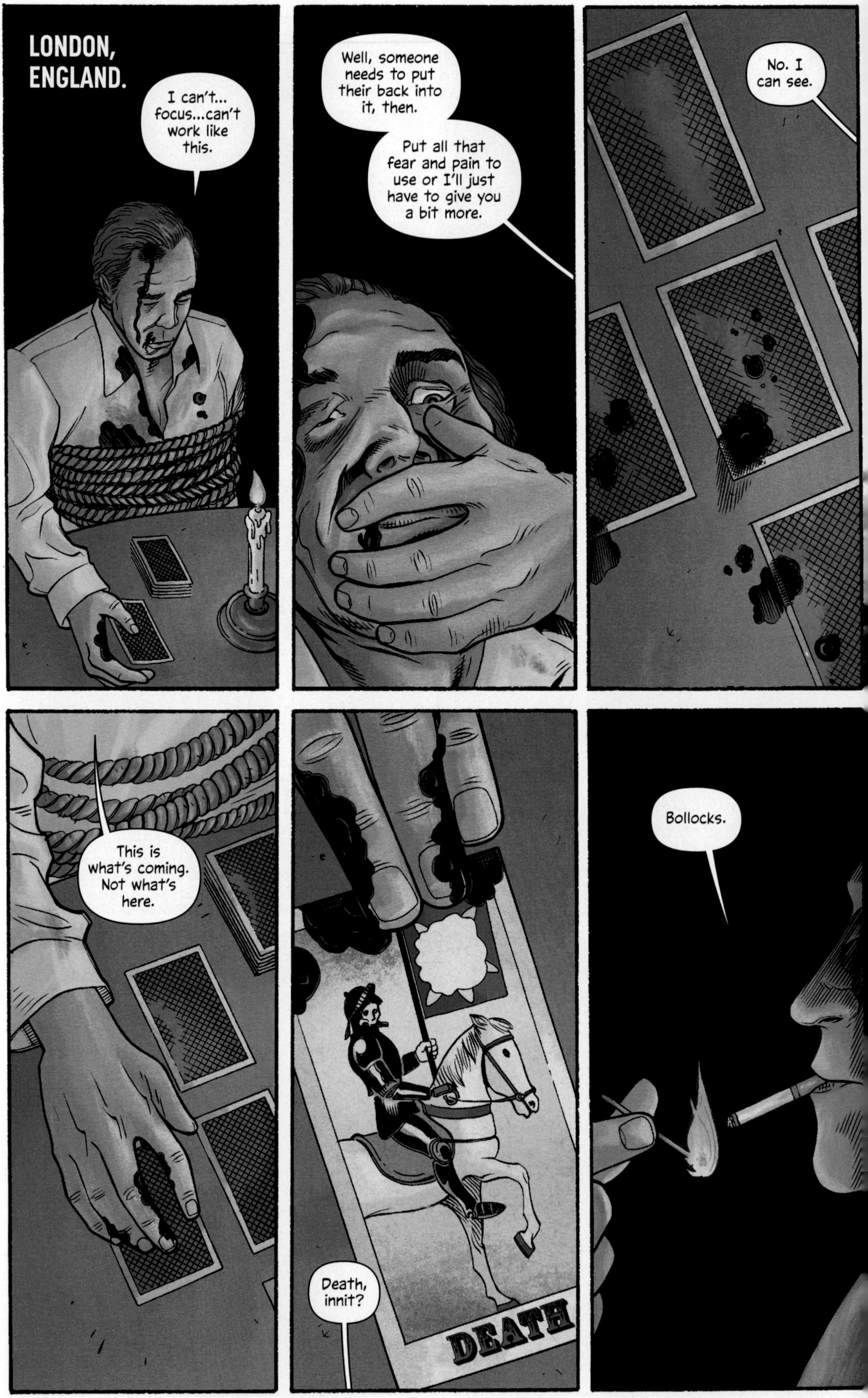
LONDON, ENGLAND.
I can't... focus...can't work like this.
Well, someone needs to put their back into it, then.
Put all that fear and pain to use or I'll just have to give you a bit more.
No. I can see.
This is what's coming. Not what's here.
Death, innit?
DEATH
Bollocks.

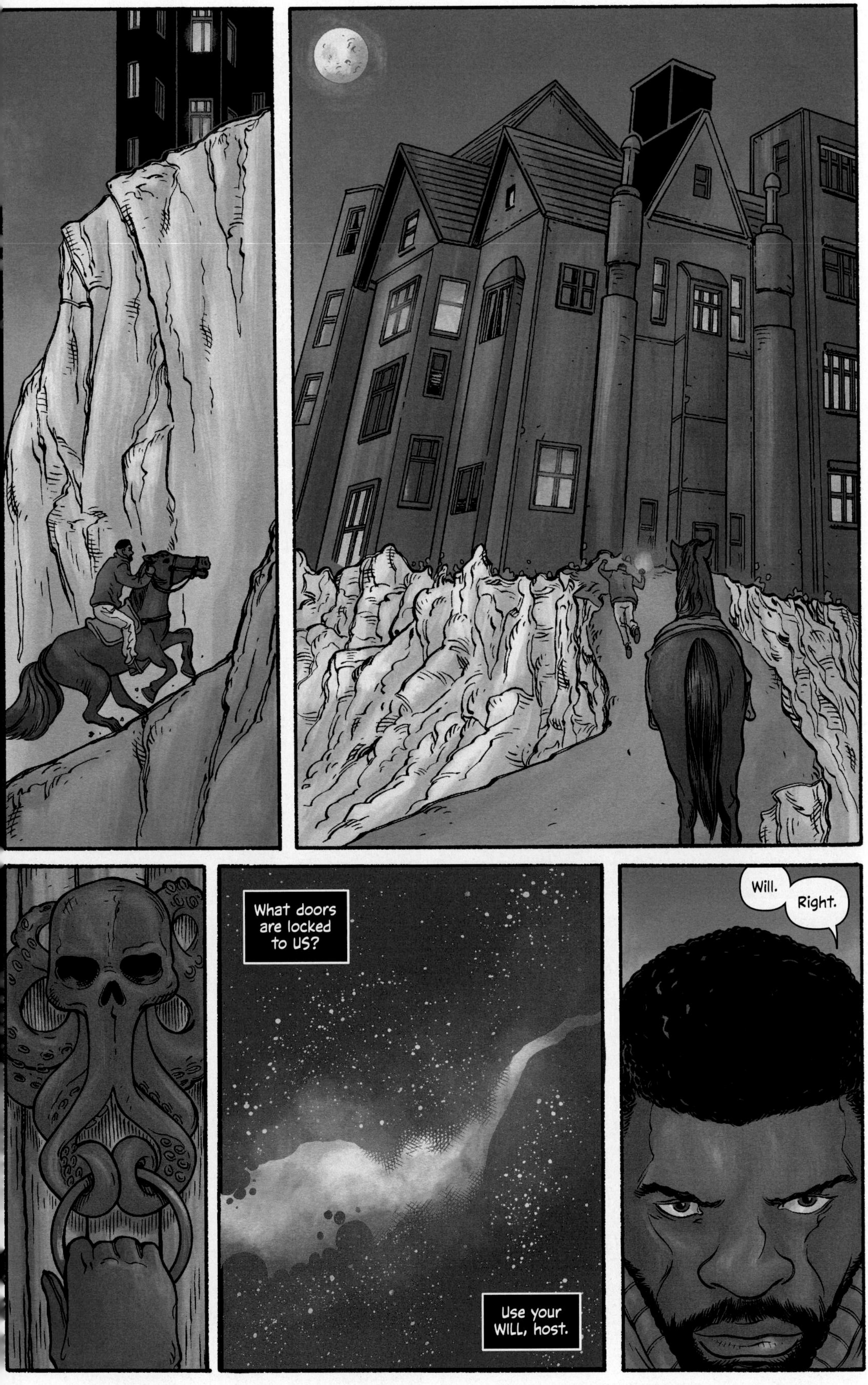
What doors are locked to US?
Use your WILL, host.
Will.
Right.

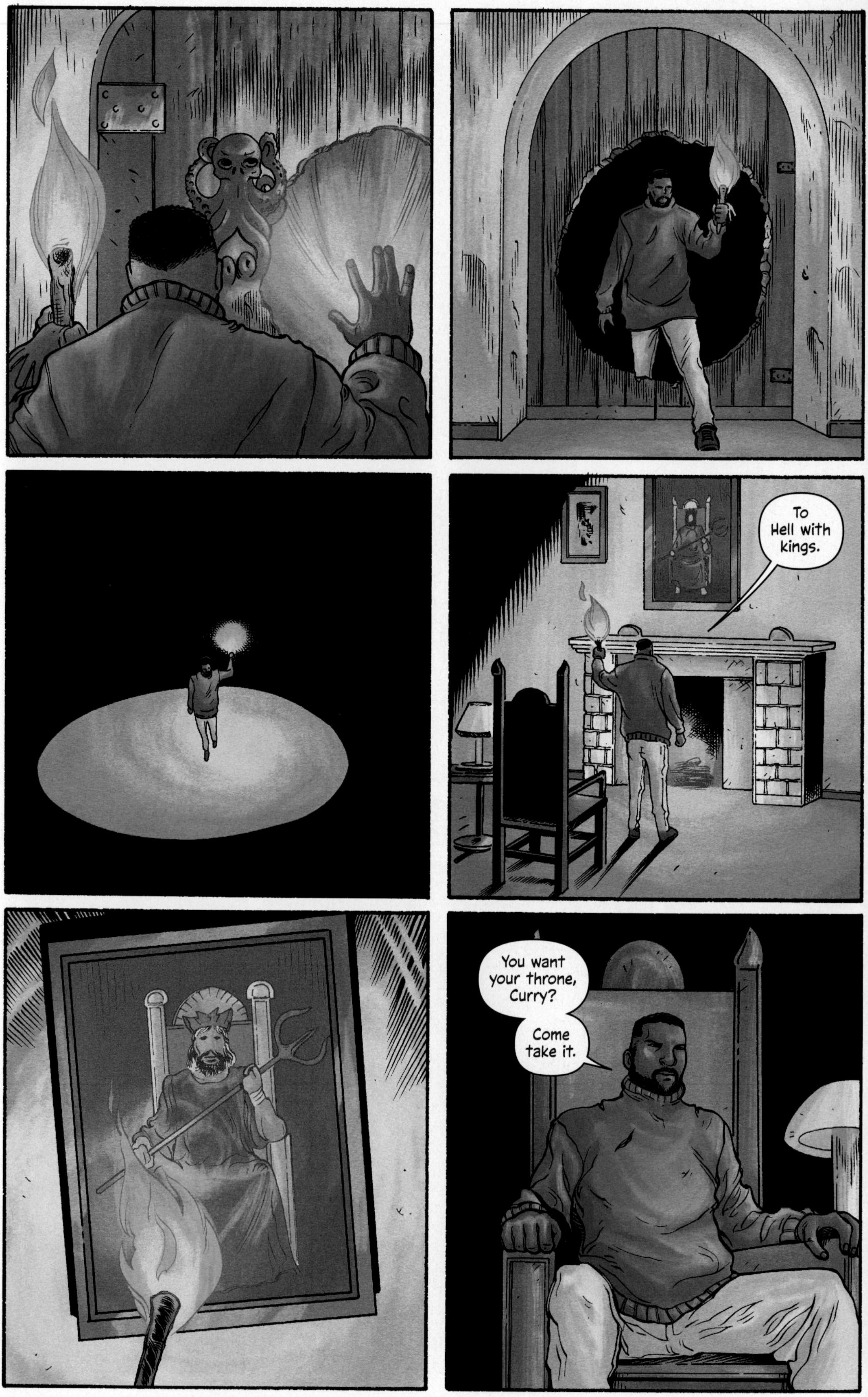
To Hell with kings.
You want your throne, Curry?
Come take it.

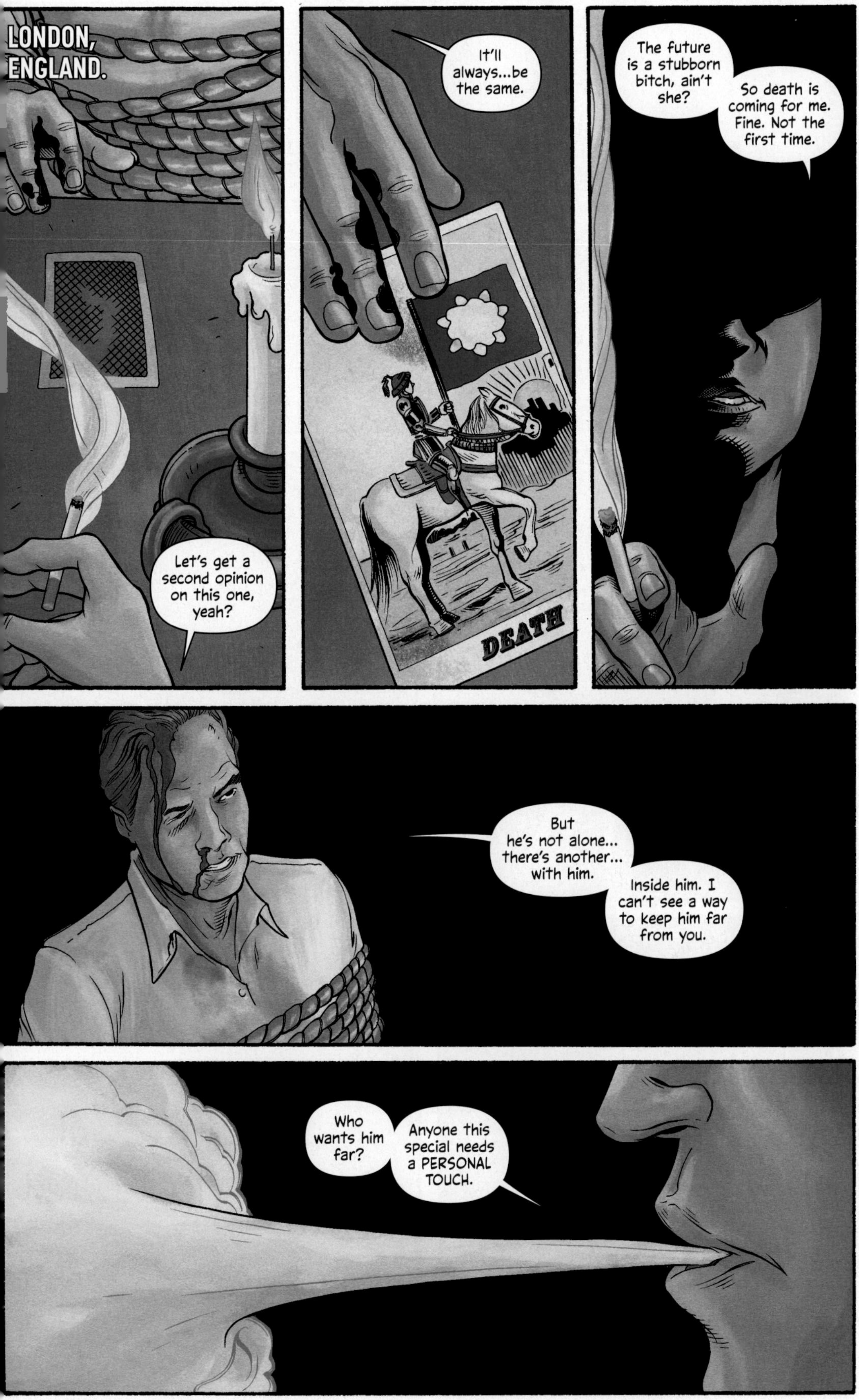
LONDON, ENGLAND.
Let's get a second opinion on this one, yeah?
It'll always...be the same.
DEATH
The future is a stubborn bitch, ain't she?
So death is coming for me. Fine. Not the first time.
But he's not alone... there's another... with him.
Inside him. I can't see a way to keep him far from you.
Who wants him far?
Anyone this special needs a PERSONAL TOUCH.

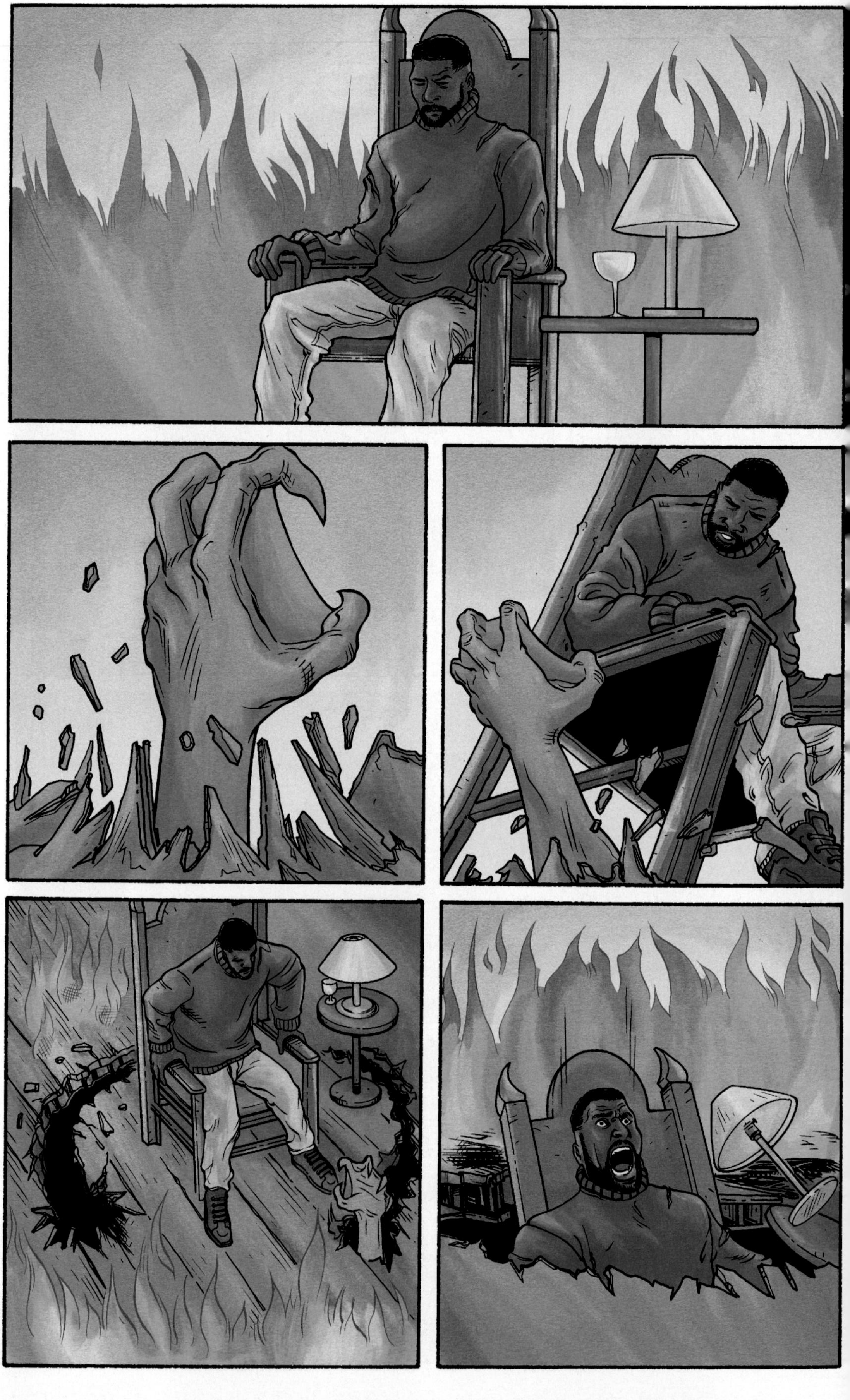

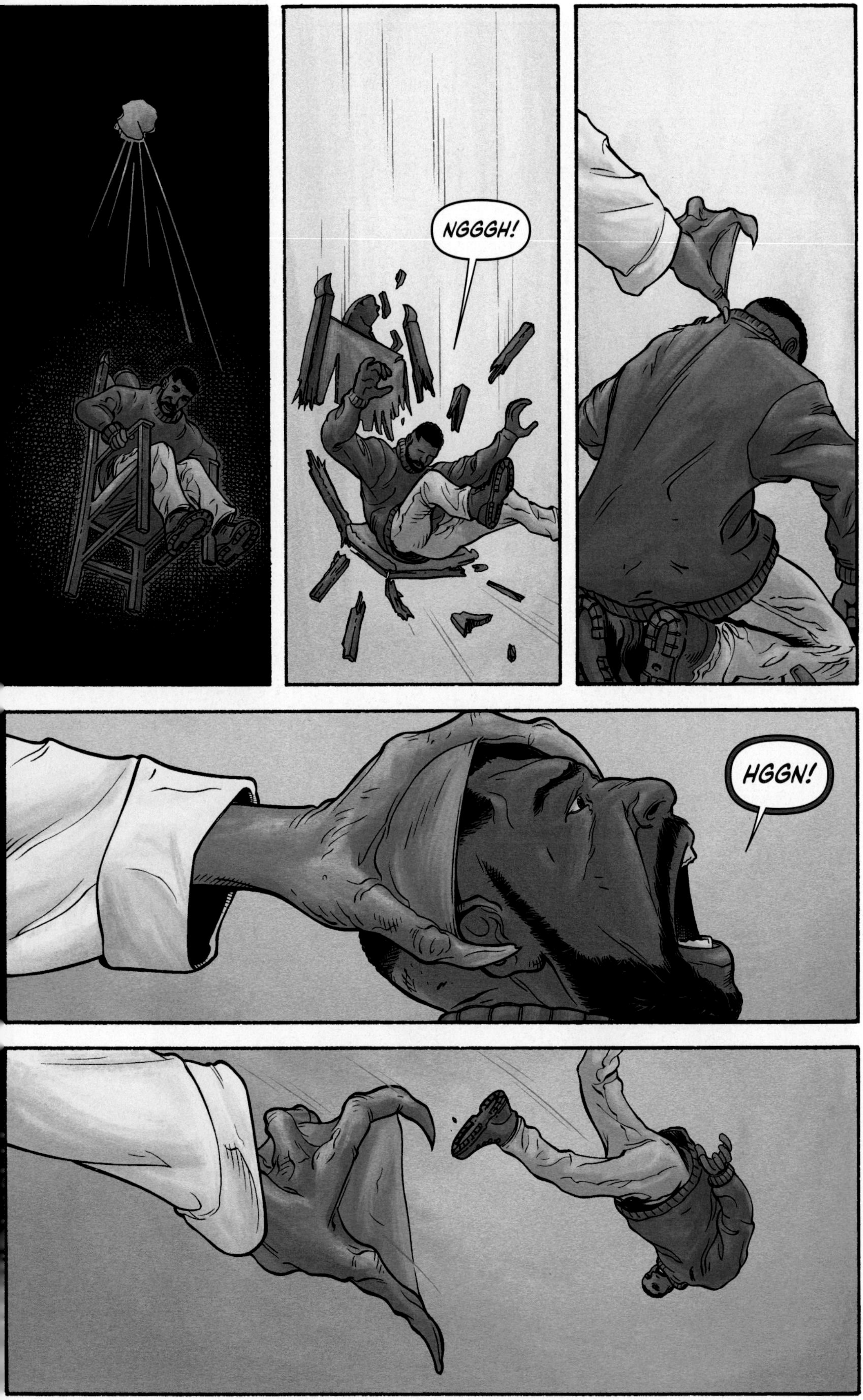
NGGGH!
HGGN!

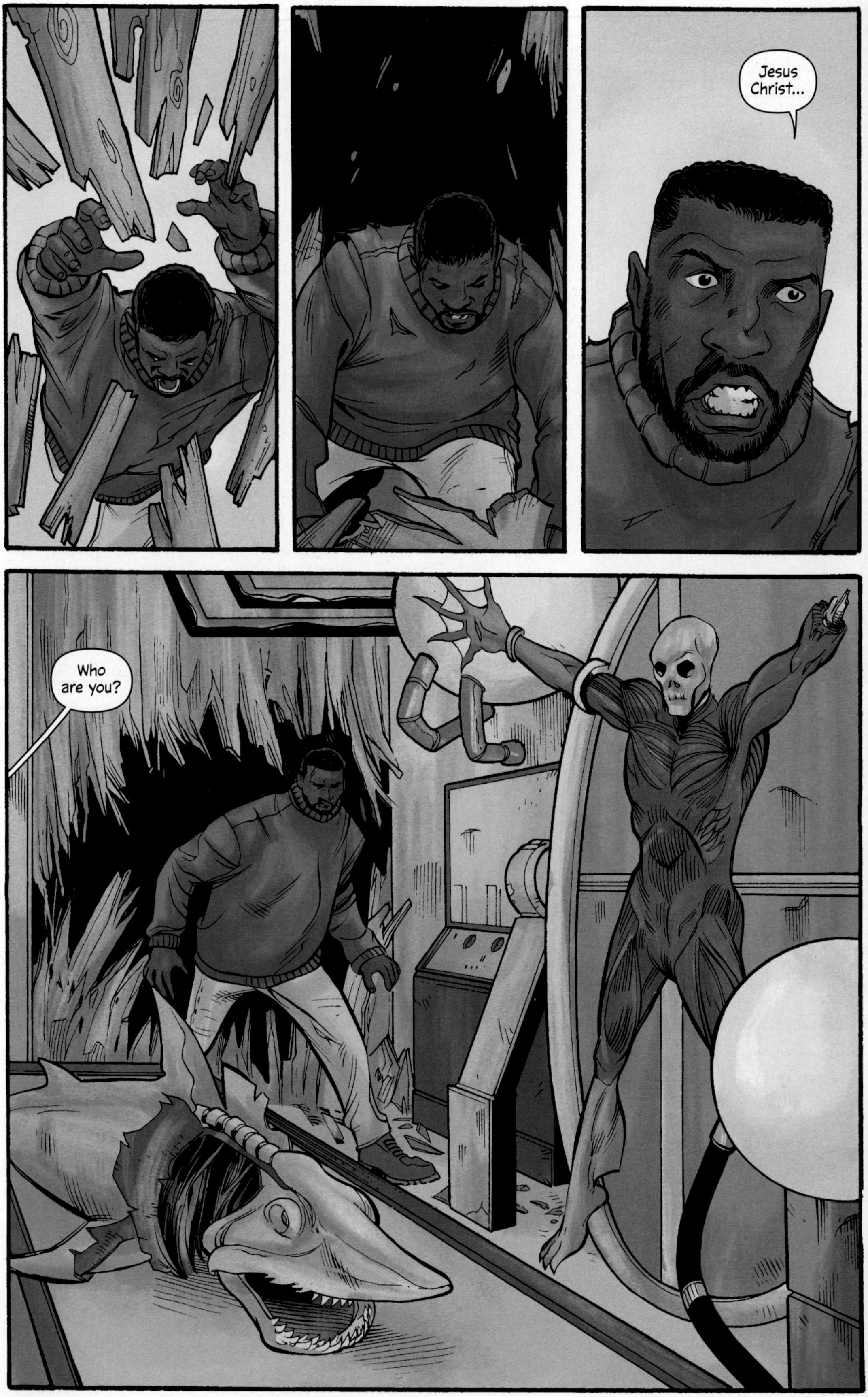

Jesus Christ...
Who are you?

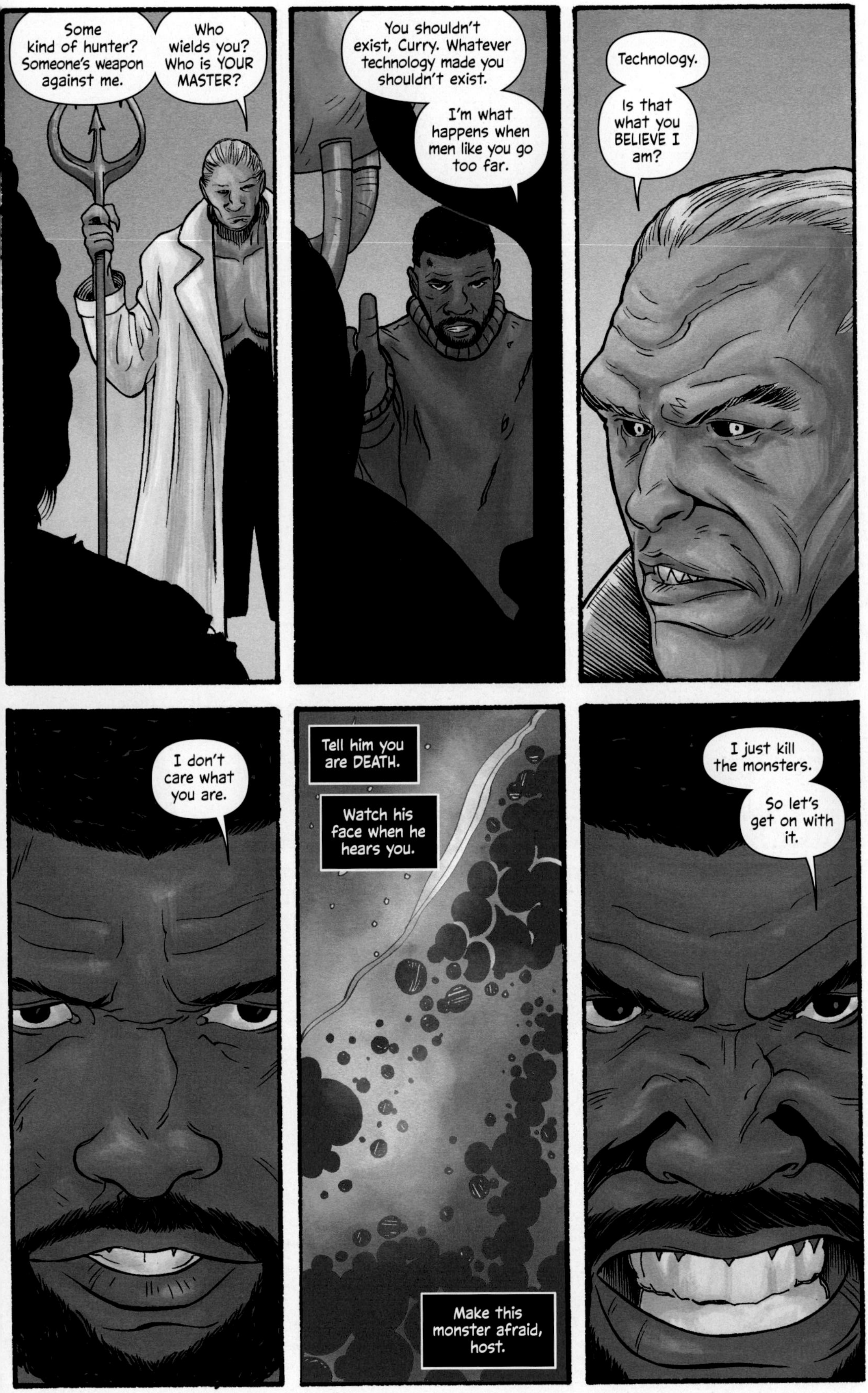
Some kind of hunter? Someone's weapon against me.
Who wields you? Who is YOUR MASTER?
You shouldn't exist, Curry. Whatever technology made you shouldn't exist.
I'm what happens when men like you go too far.
Technology.
Is that what you BELIEVE I am?
I don't care what you are.
Tell him you are DEATH.
Watch his face when he hears you.
Make this monster afraid, host.
I just kill the monsters.
So let's get on with it.

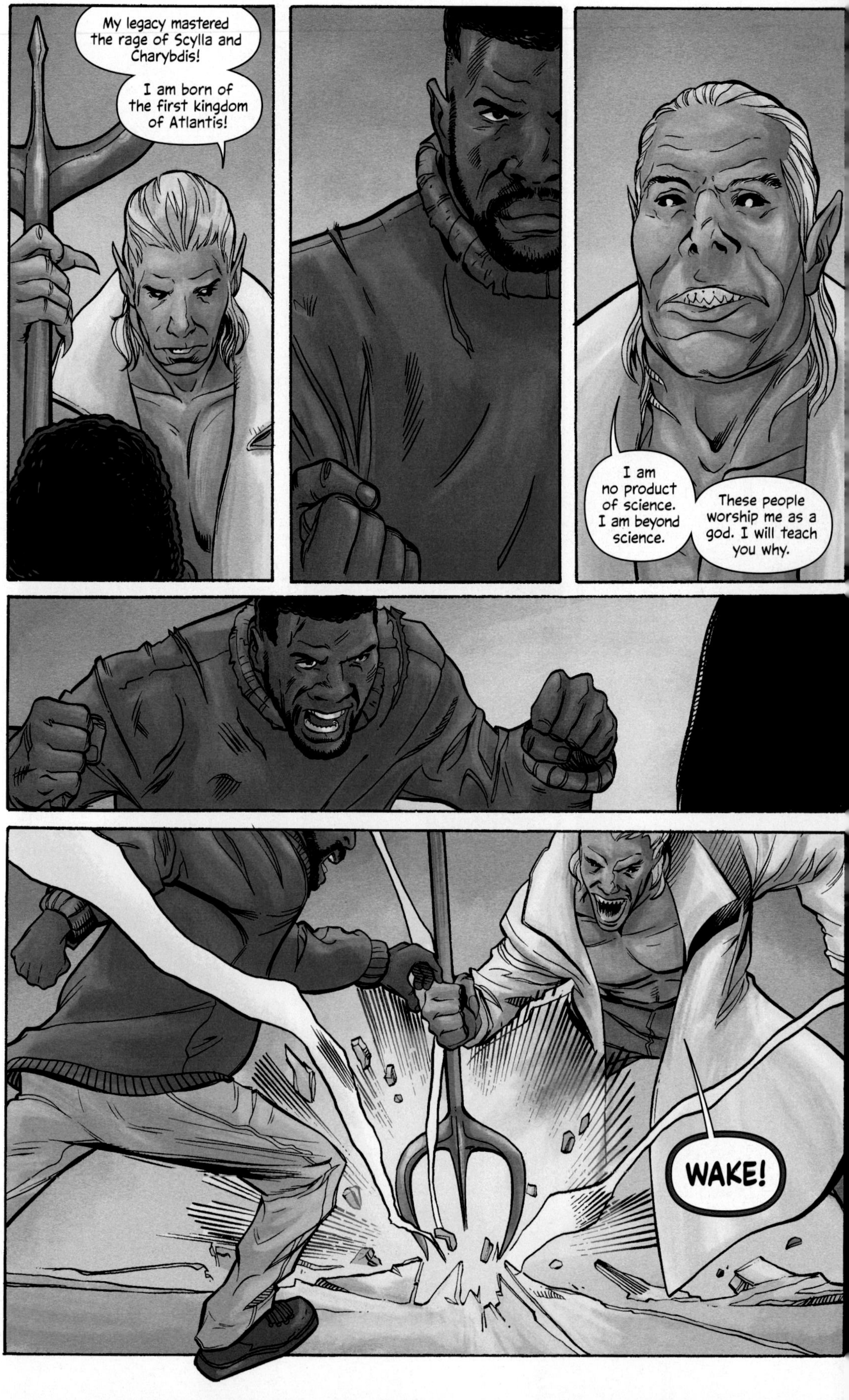
My legacy mastered the rage of Scylla and Charybdis!
I am born of the first kingdom of Atlantis!
I am no product of science. I am beyond science.
These people worship me as a god. I will teach you why.
WAKE!

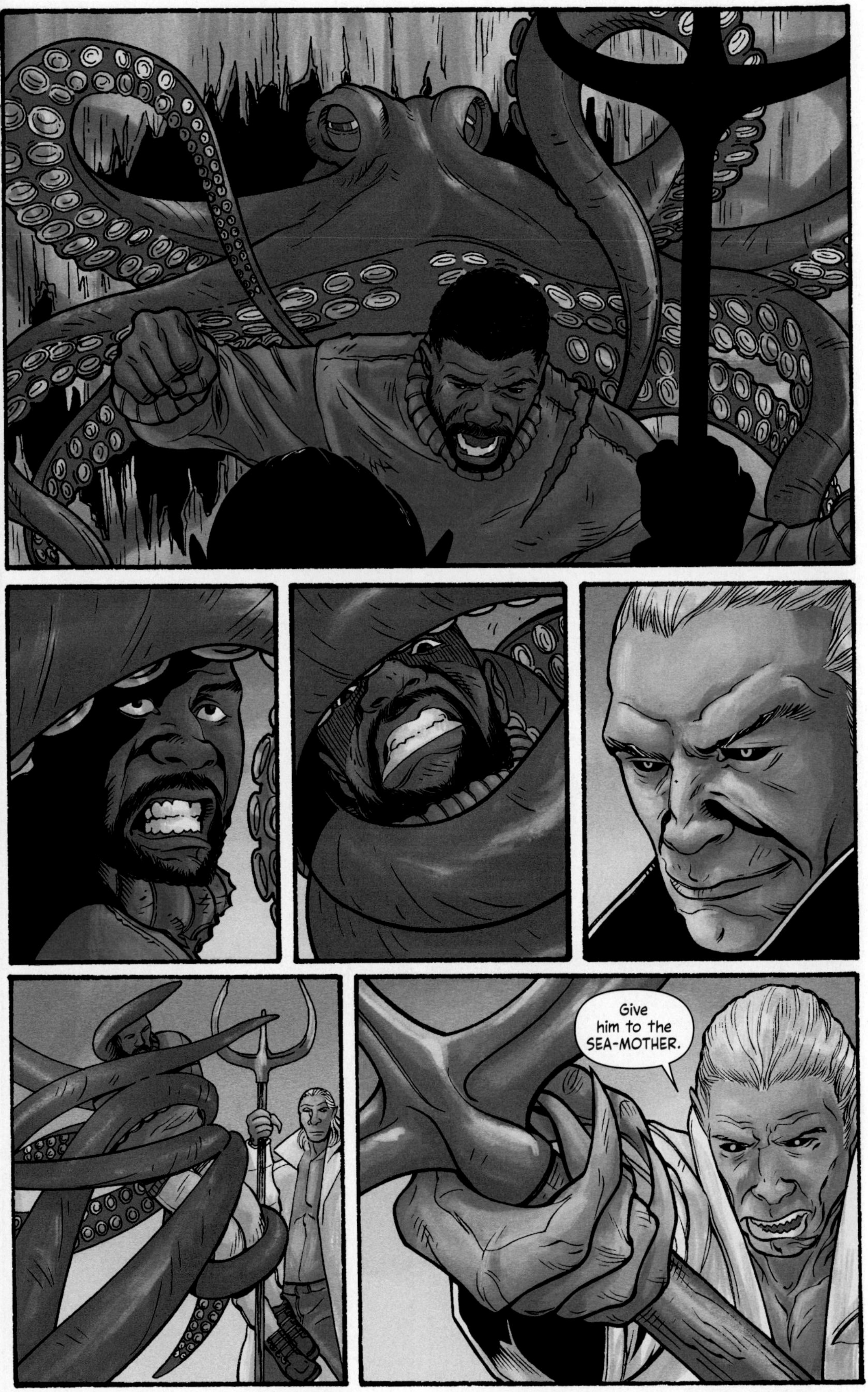
Give him to the SEA-MOTHER.

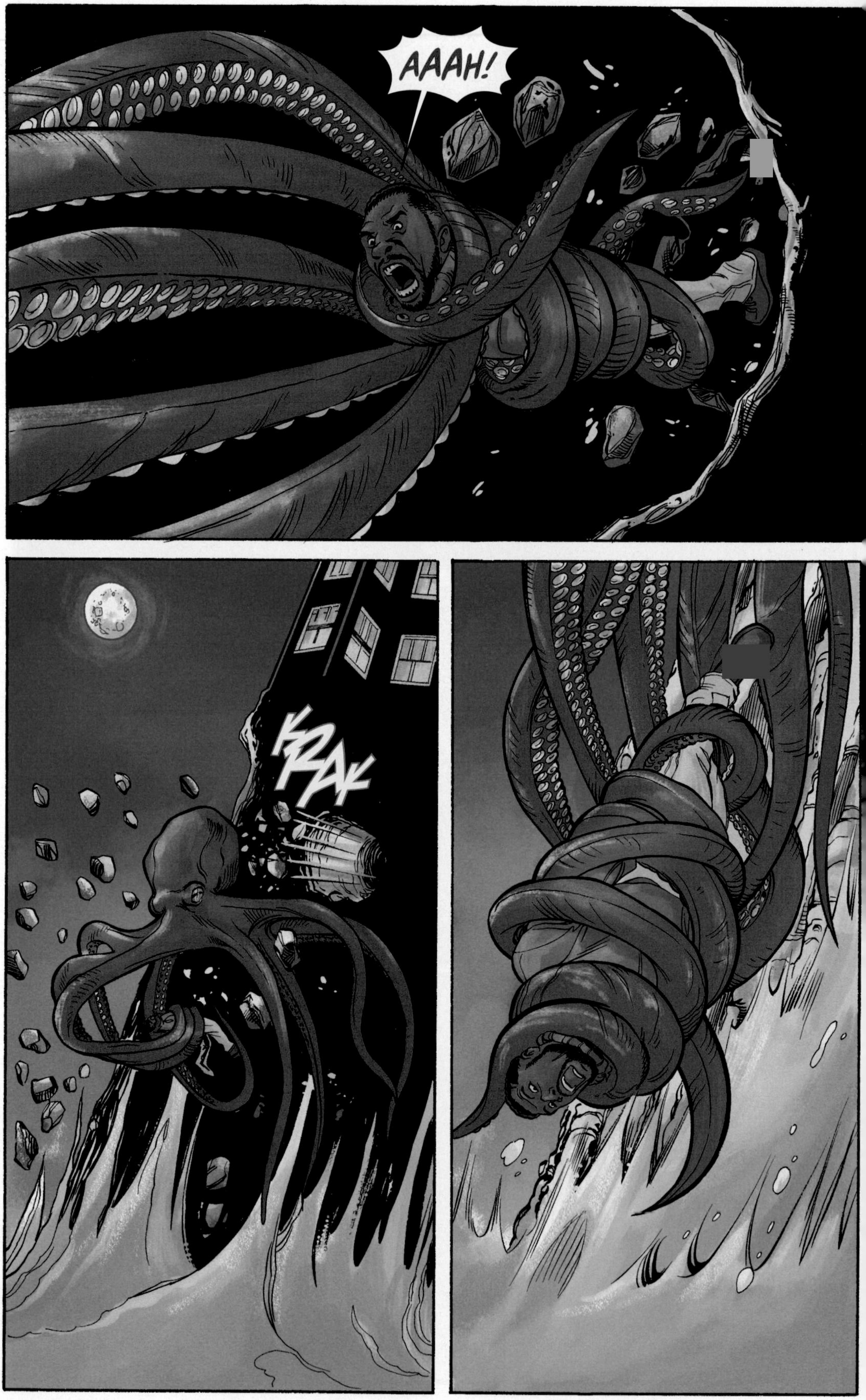
AAAH!
KRAK

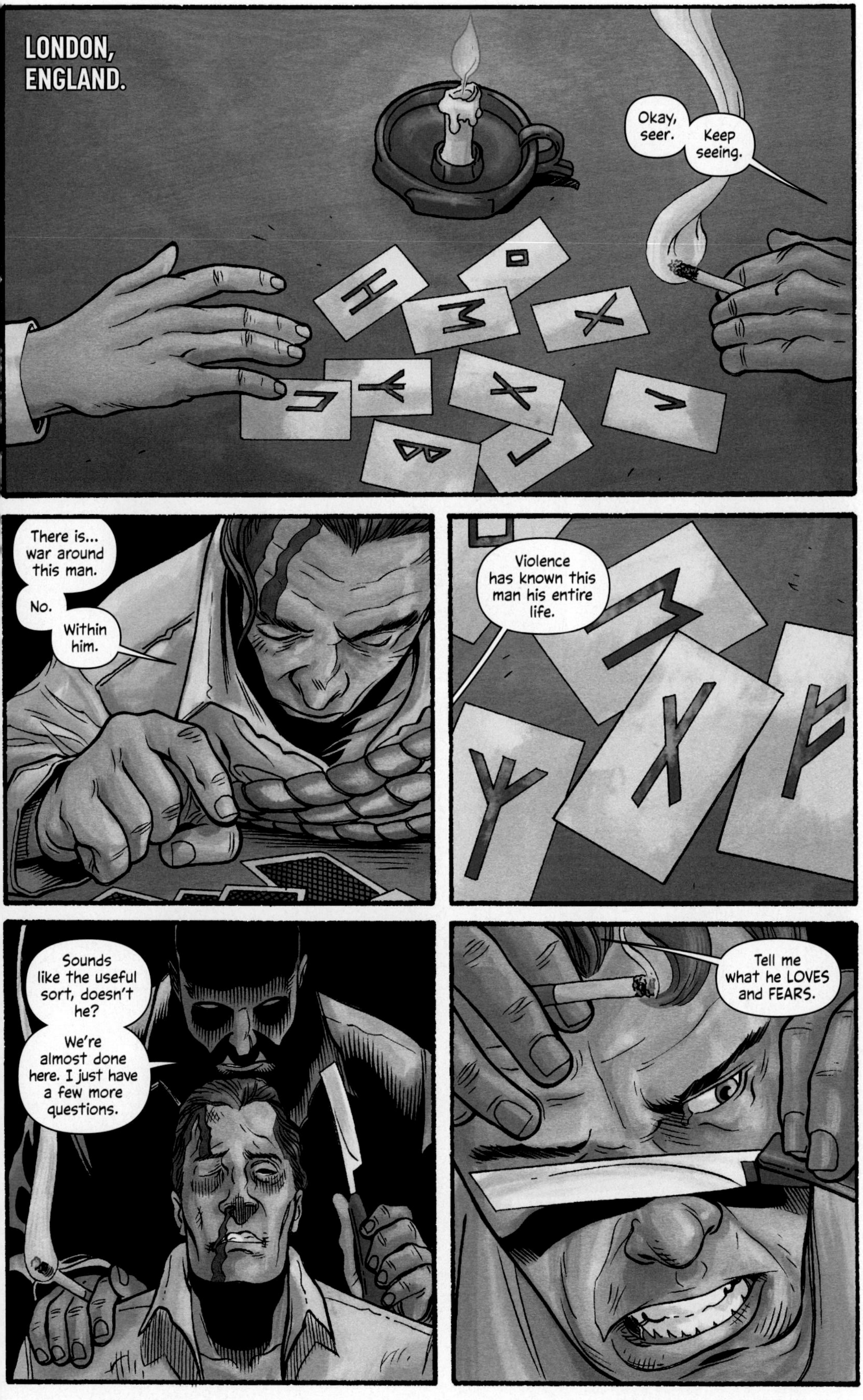
LONDON, ENGLAND.
Okay, seer.
Keep seeing.
There is... war around this man.
No.
Within him.
Violence has known this man his entire life.
Sounds like the useful sort, doesn't he?
We're almost done here. I just have a few more questions.
Tell me what he LOVES and FEARS.

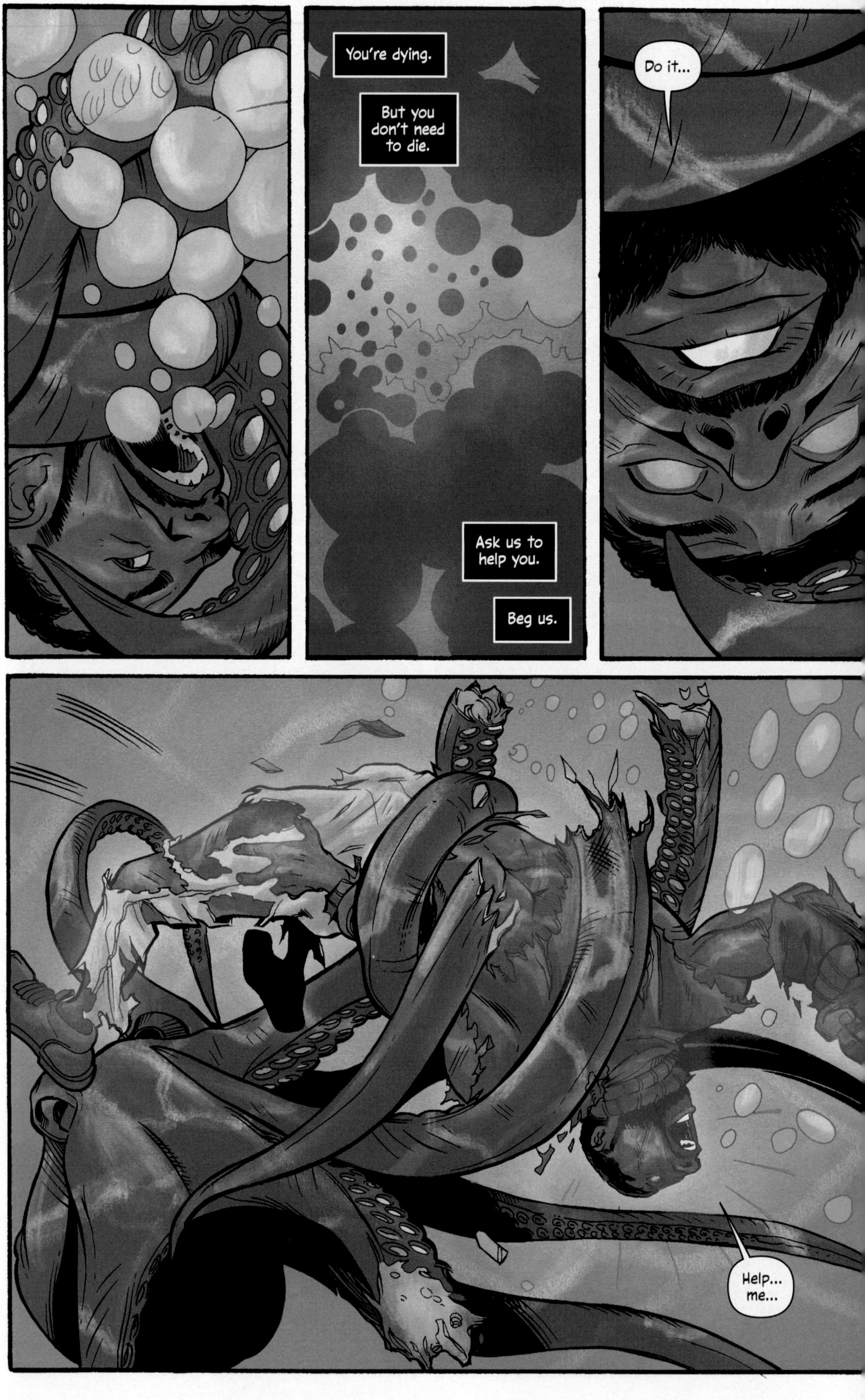
You're dying.
But you don't need to die.
Ask us to help you.
Beg us.
Do it...
Help... me...

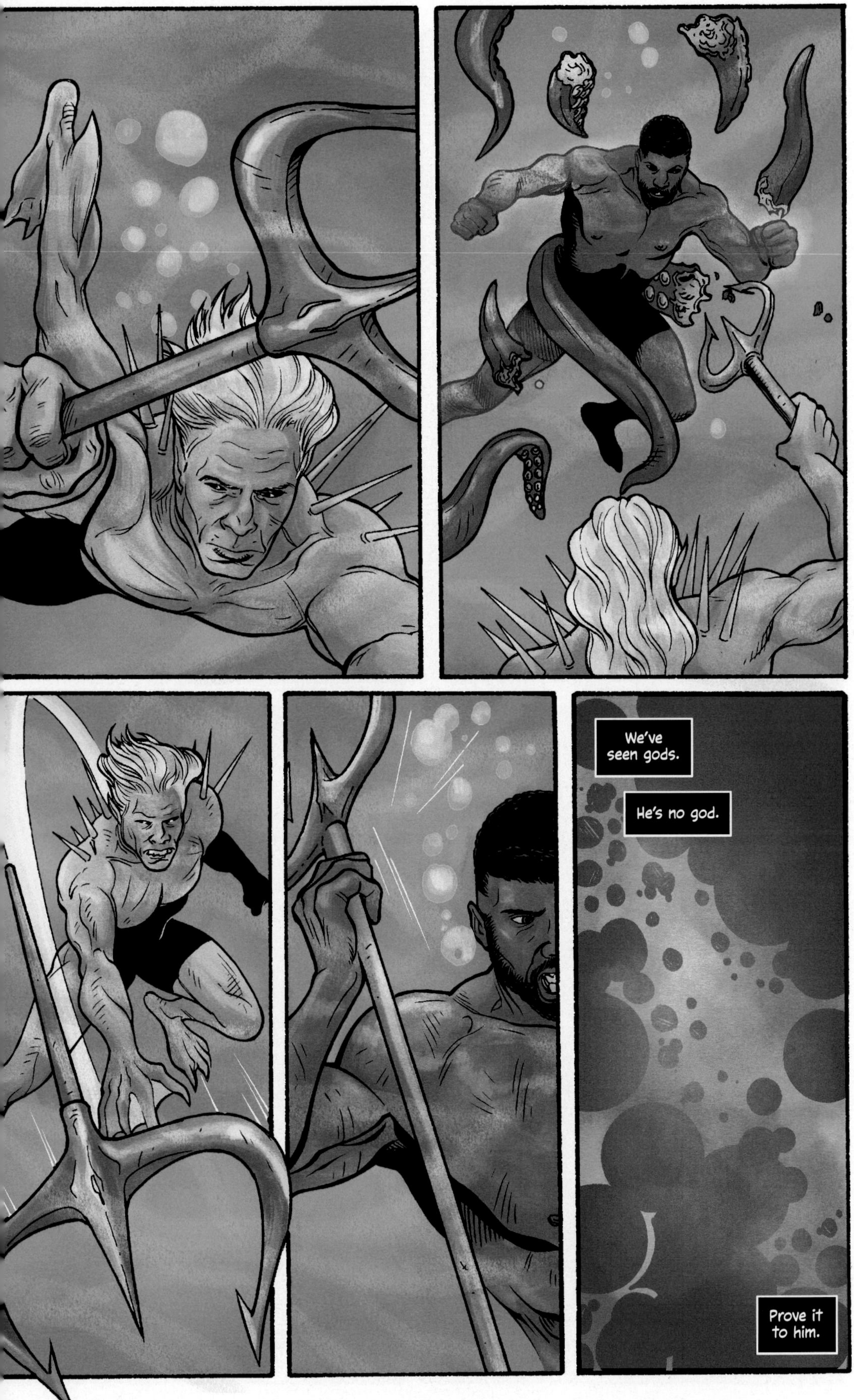
We've seen gods.
He's no god.
Prove it to him.

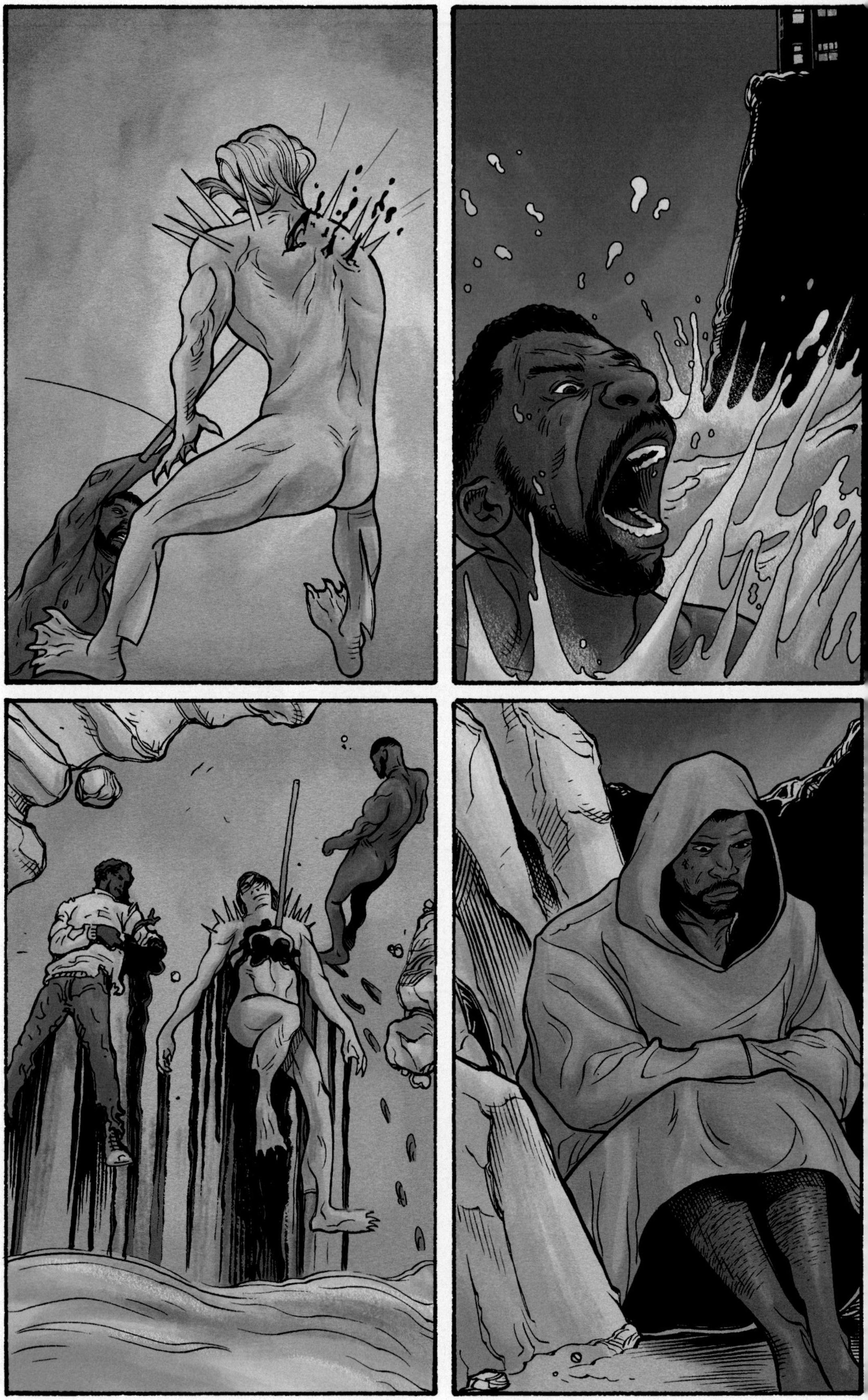

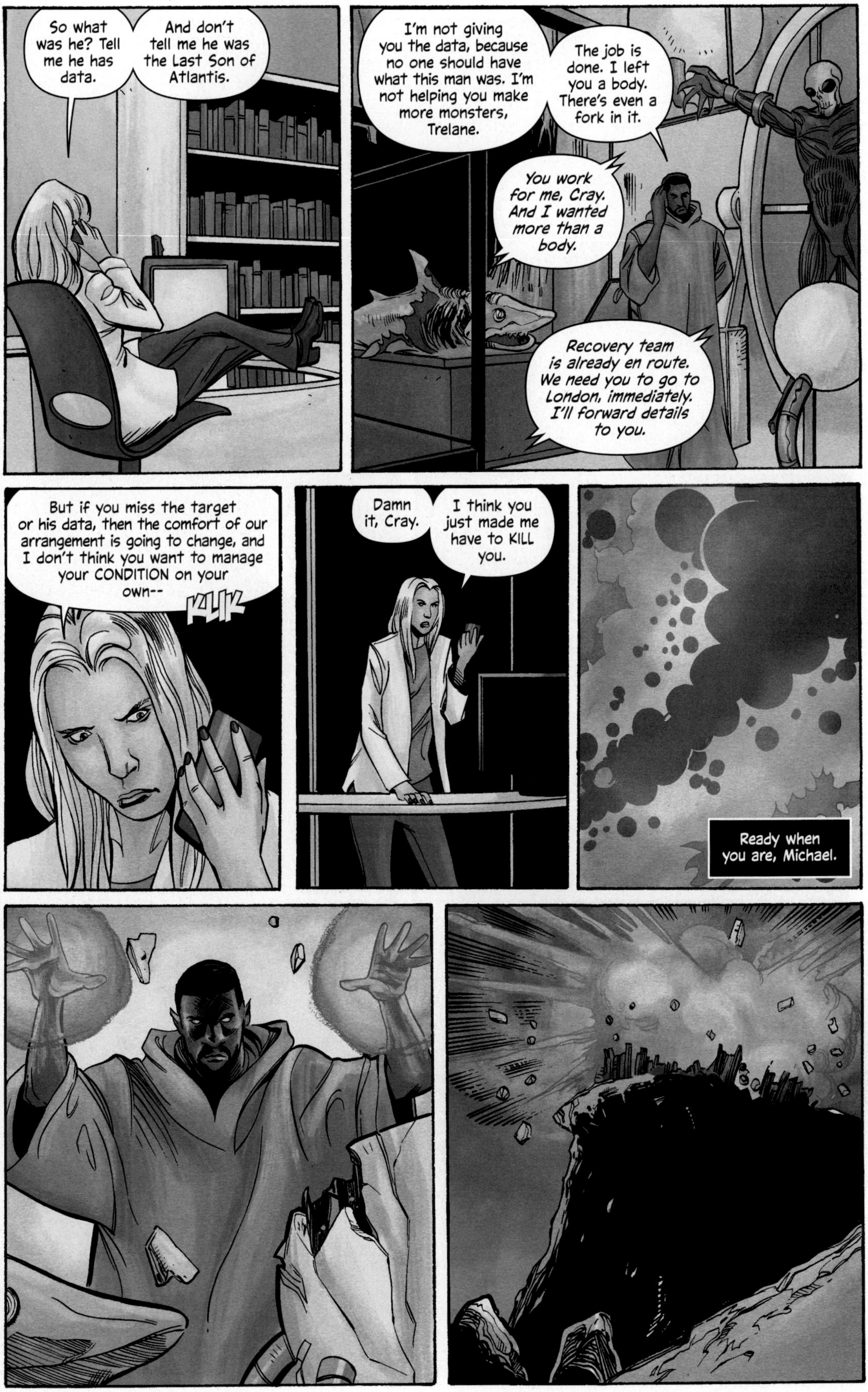

So what was he? Tell me he has data.
And don't tell me he was the Last Son of Atlantis.
I'm not giving you the data, because no one should have what this man was. I'm not helping you make more monsters, Trelane.
The job is done. I left you a body. There's even a fork in it.
You work for me, Cray. And I wanted more than a body.
Recovery team is already en route. We need you to go to London, immediately. I'll forward details to you.
But if you miss the target or his data, then the comfort of our arrangement is going to change, and I don't think you want to manage your CONDITION on your own--
KLIK
Damn it, Cray.
I think you just made me have to KILL you.
Ready when you are, Michael.

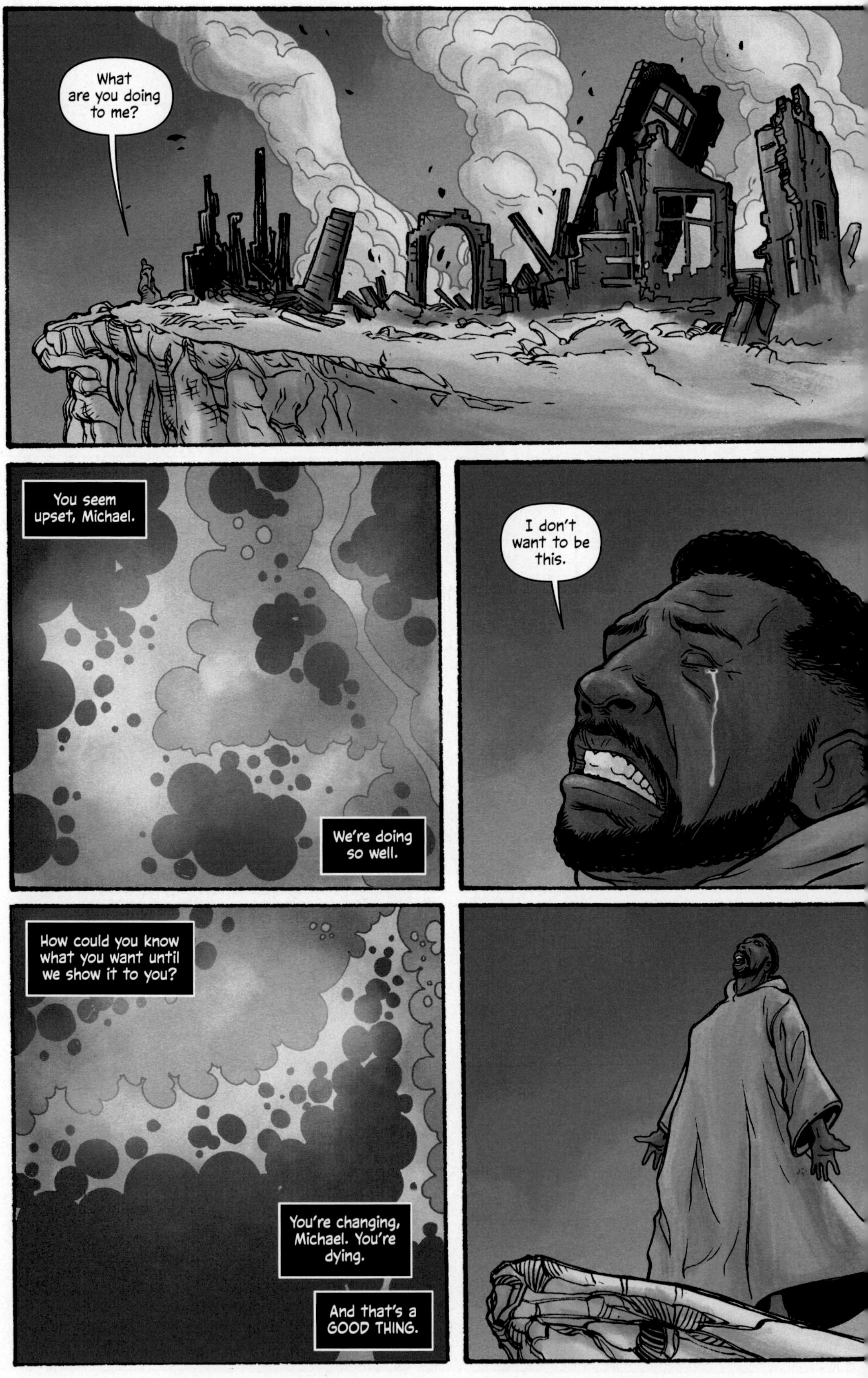
What are you doing to me?
You seem upset, Michael.
We're doing so well.
I don't want to be this.
How could you know what you want until we show it to you?
You're changing, Michael. You're dying.
And that's a GOOD THING.

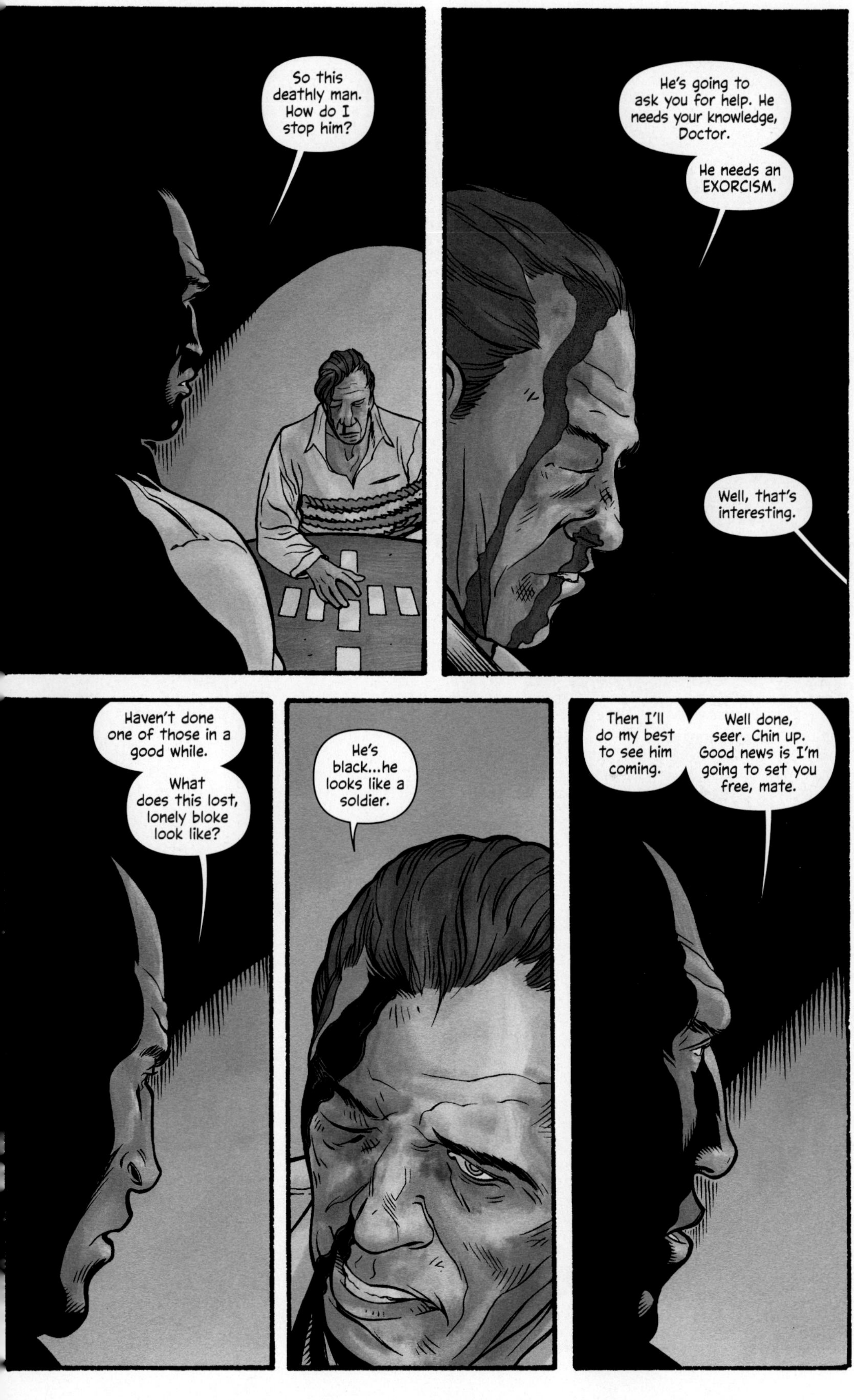
So this deathly man. How do I stop him?
He's going to ask you for help. He needs your knowledge, Doctor.
He needs an EXORCISM.
Well, that's interesting.
Haven't done one of those in a good while.
What does this lost, lonely bloke look like?
He's black...he looks like a soldier.
Then I'll do my best to see him coming.
Well done, seer. Chin up. Good news is I'm going to set you free, mate.

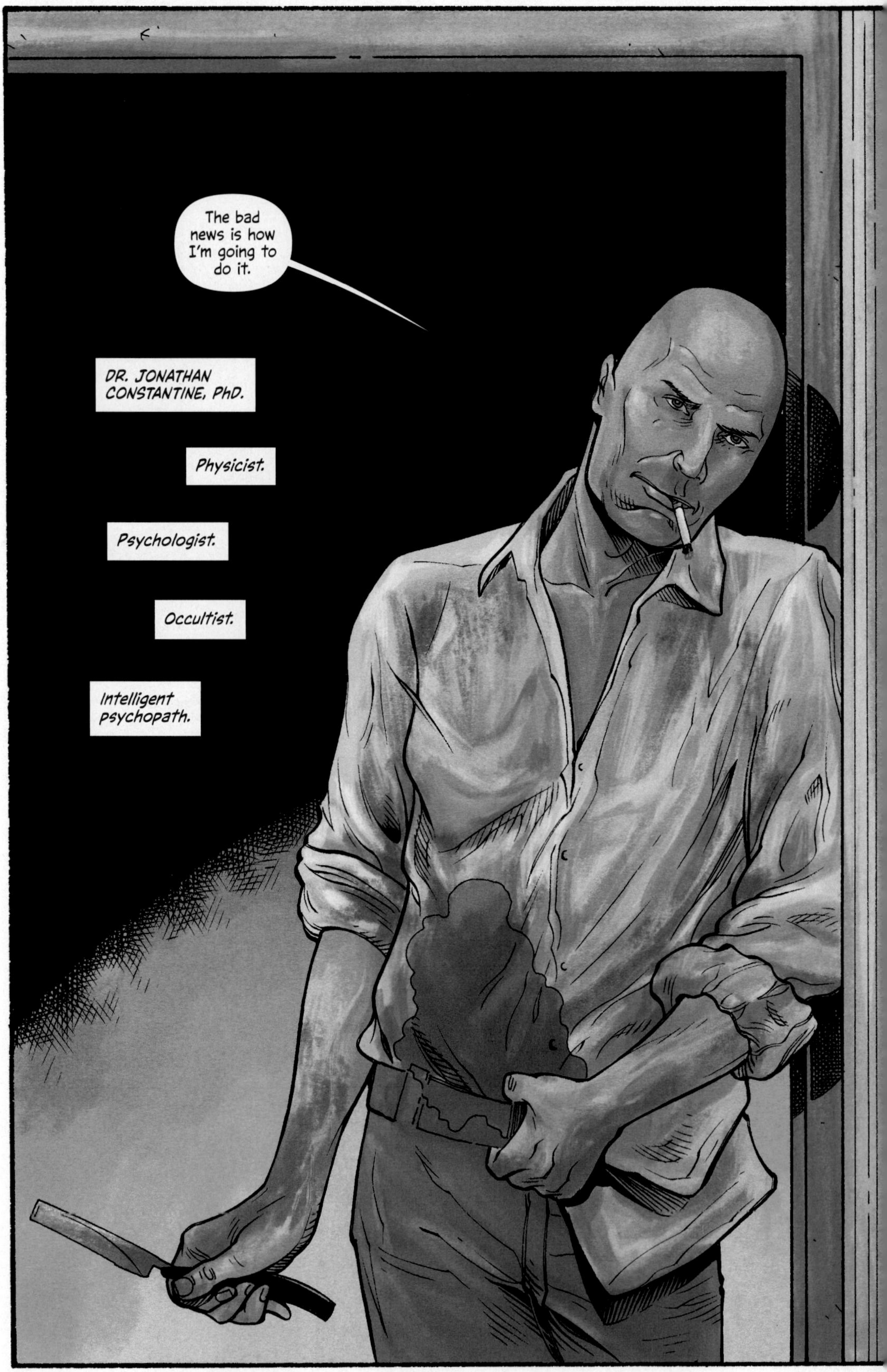
The bad news is how I'm going to do it.
DR. JONATHAN CONSTANTINE, PhD.
Physicist.
Psychologist.
Occultist.
Intelligent psychopath.

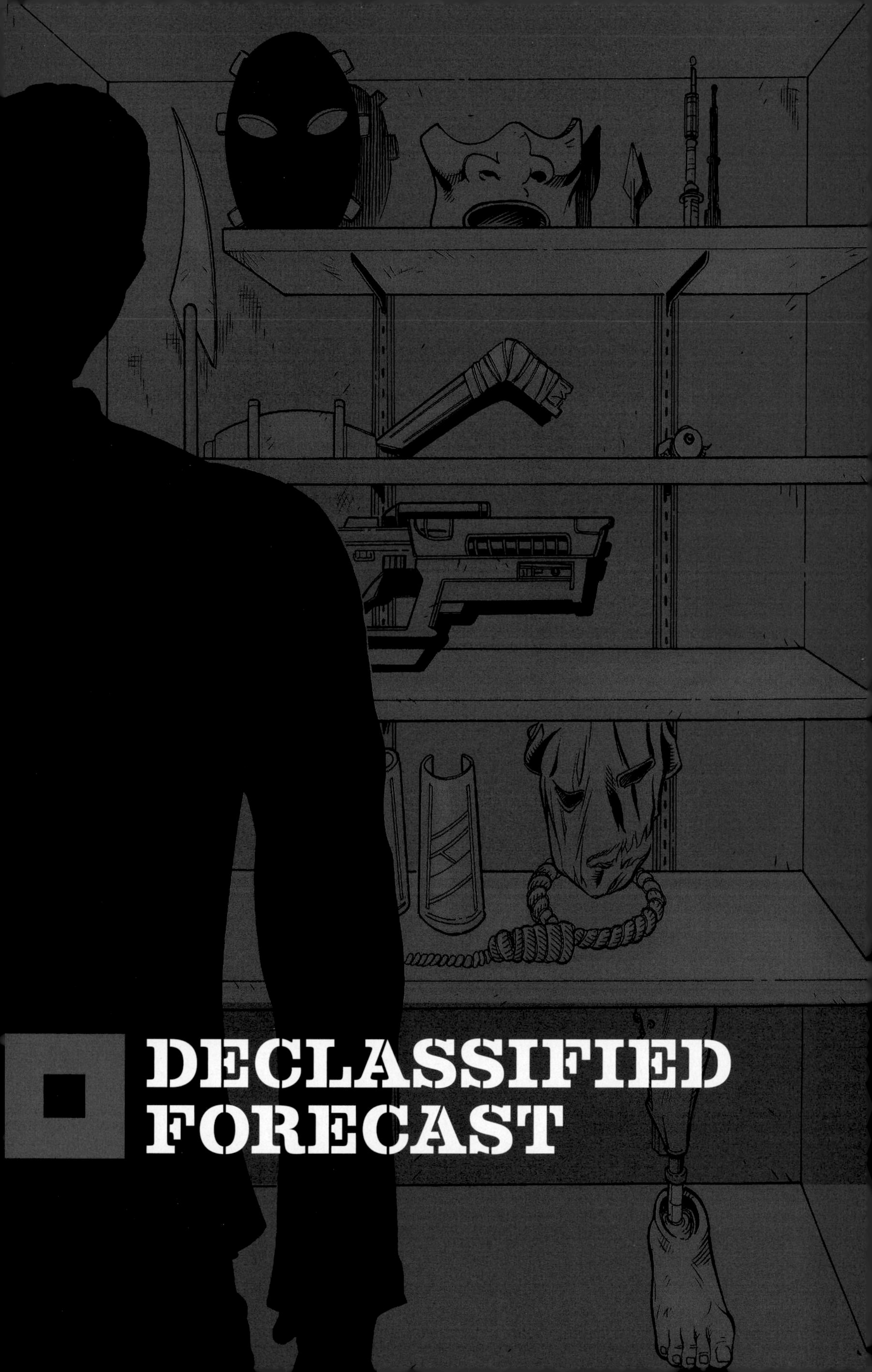
DECLASSIFIED
FORECAST

WILDSTORM: **MICHAEL CRAY #1**
Variant Cover by Gene Ha

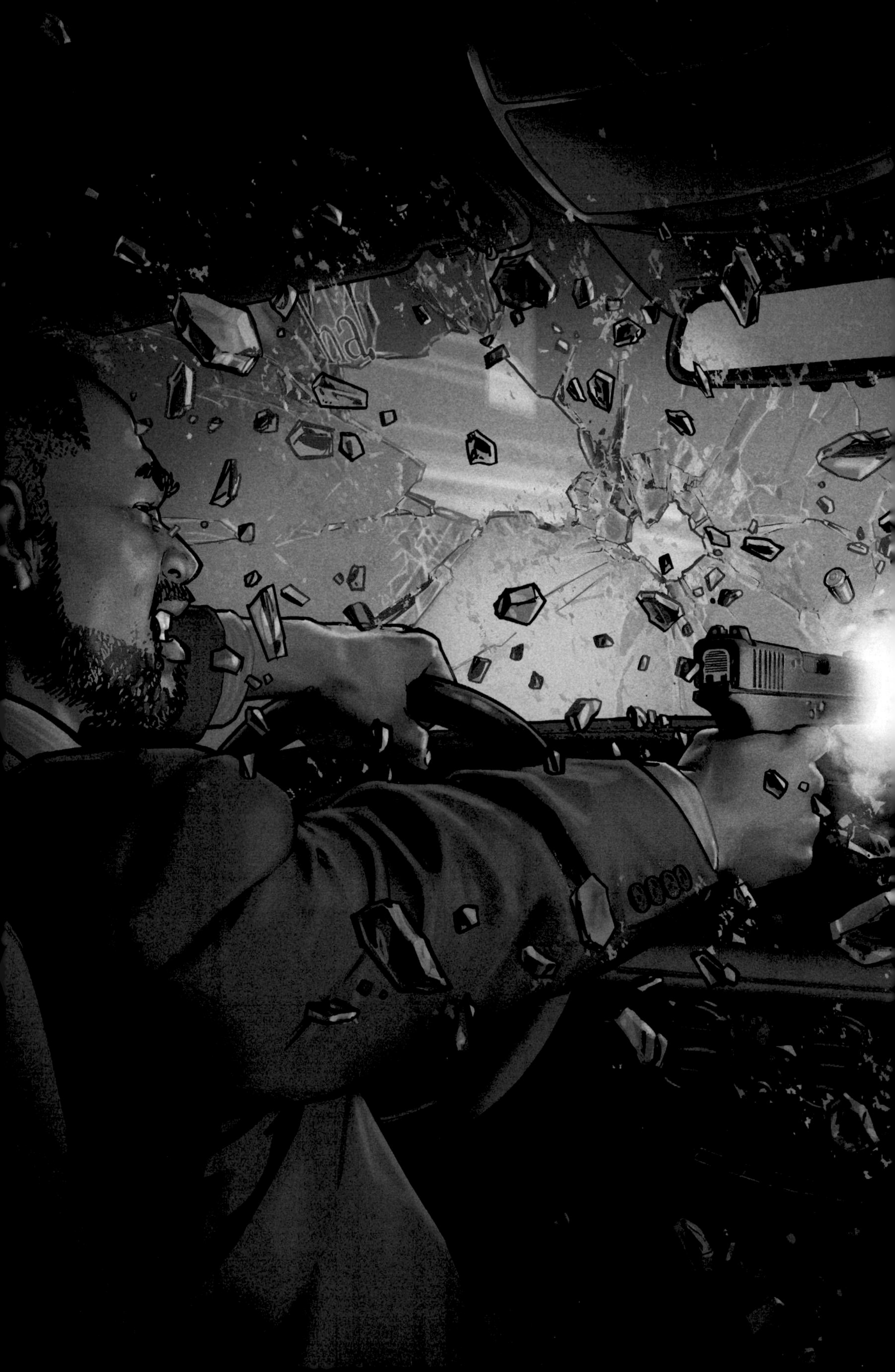

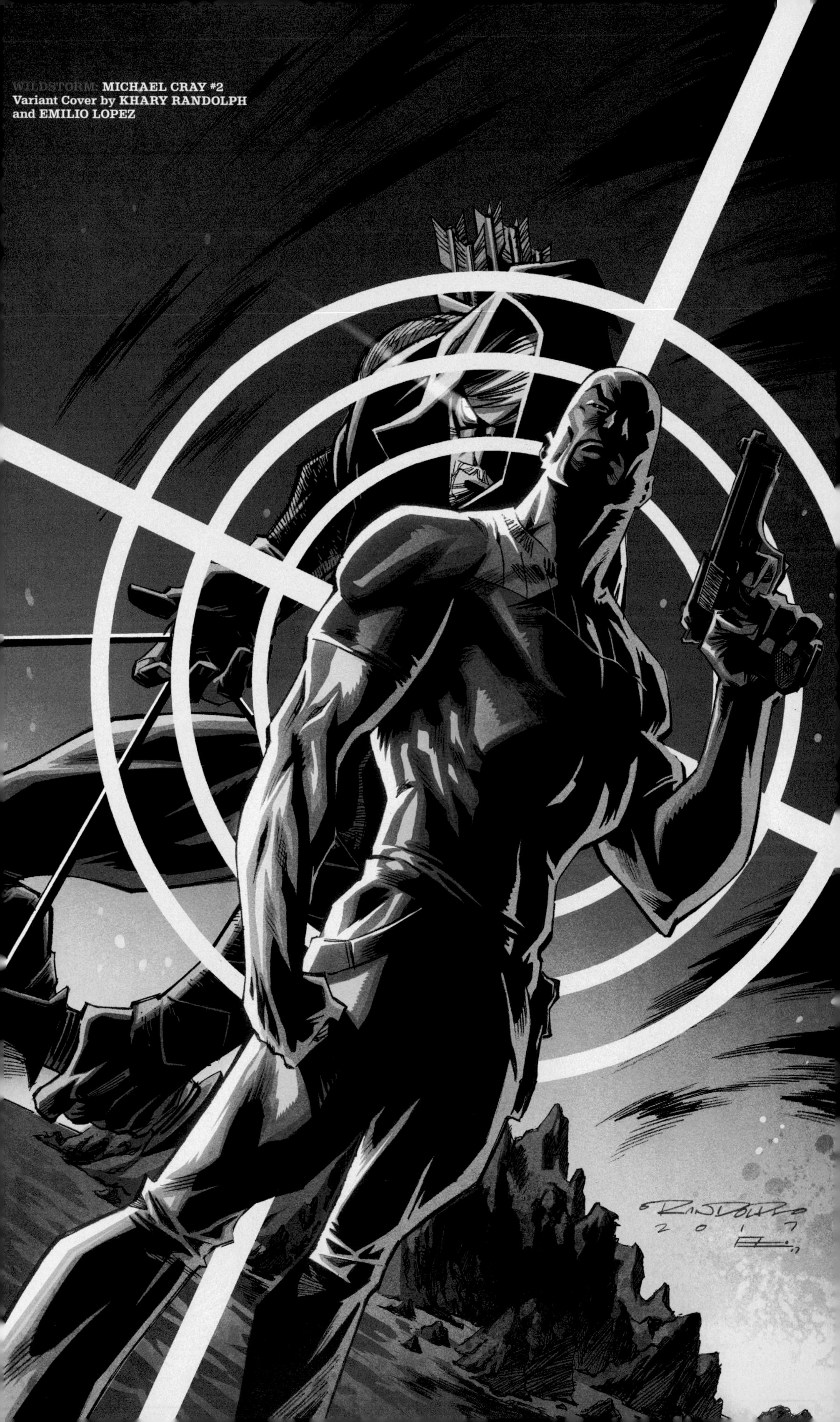

WILDSTORM: MICHAEL CRAY #2
Variant Cover by KHARY RANDOLPH
and EMILIO LOPEZ

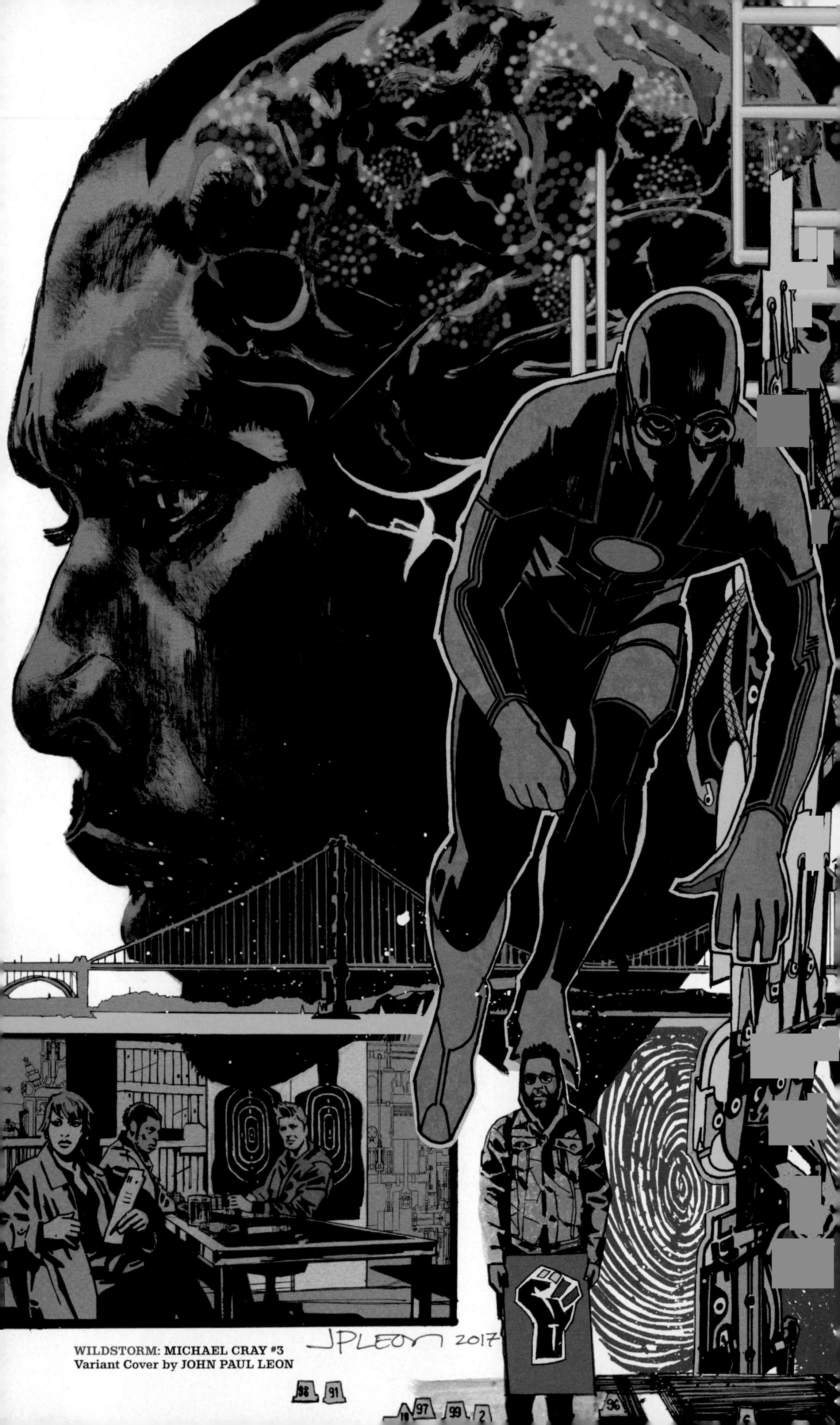
JPLEON 2017

WILDSTORM: MICHAEL CRAY #3
Variant Cover by **JOHN PAUL LEON**

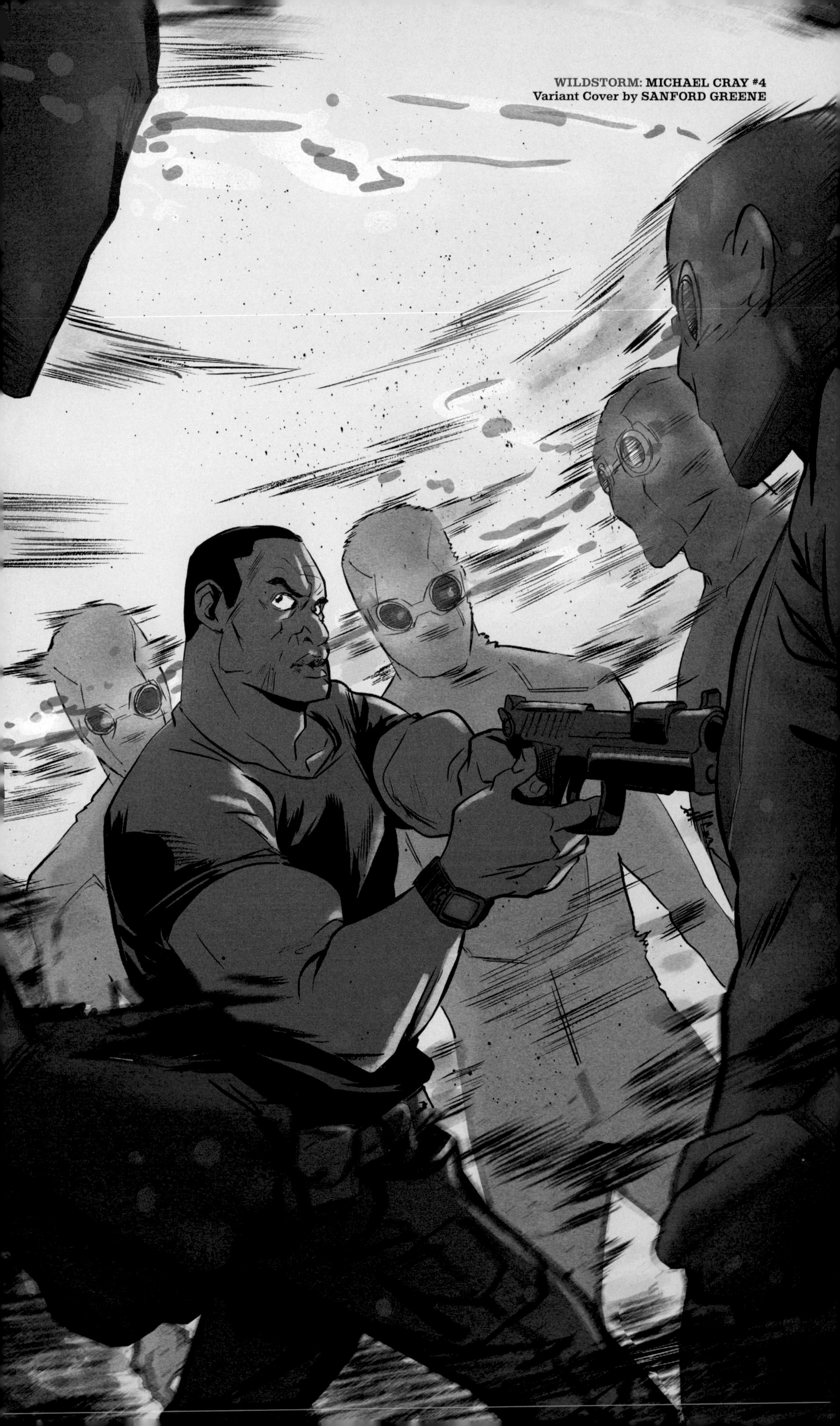

WILDSTORM: MICHAEL CRAY #4
Variant Cover by SANFORD GREENE

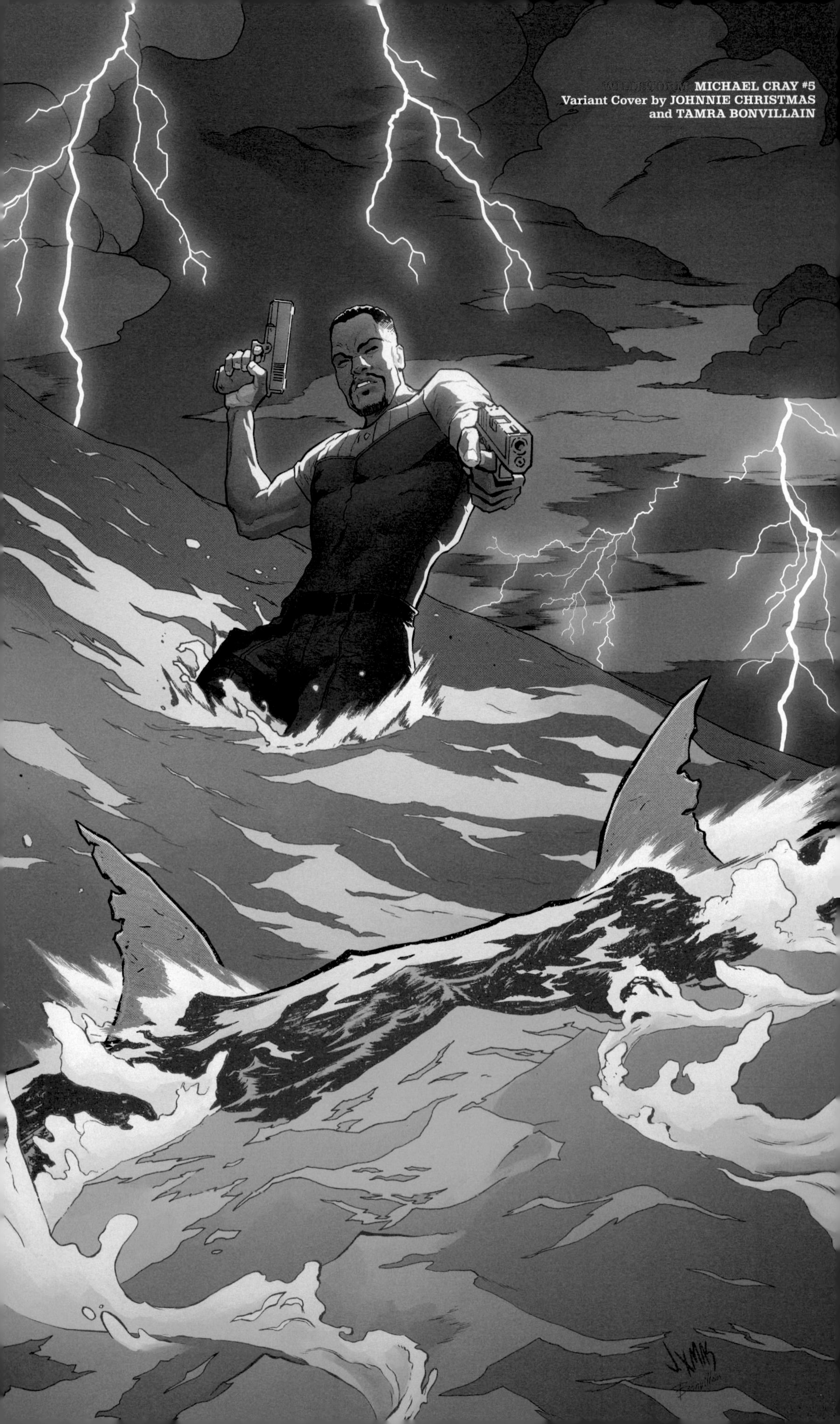

MICHAEL CRAY #5
Variant Cover by JOHNNIE CHRISTMAS
and TAMRA BONVILLAIN

MICHAEL CRAY #6
Variant Cover by LARRY STROMAN,
MARK MORALES and HI-FI

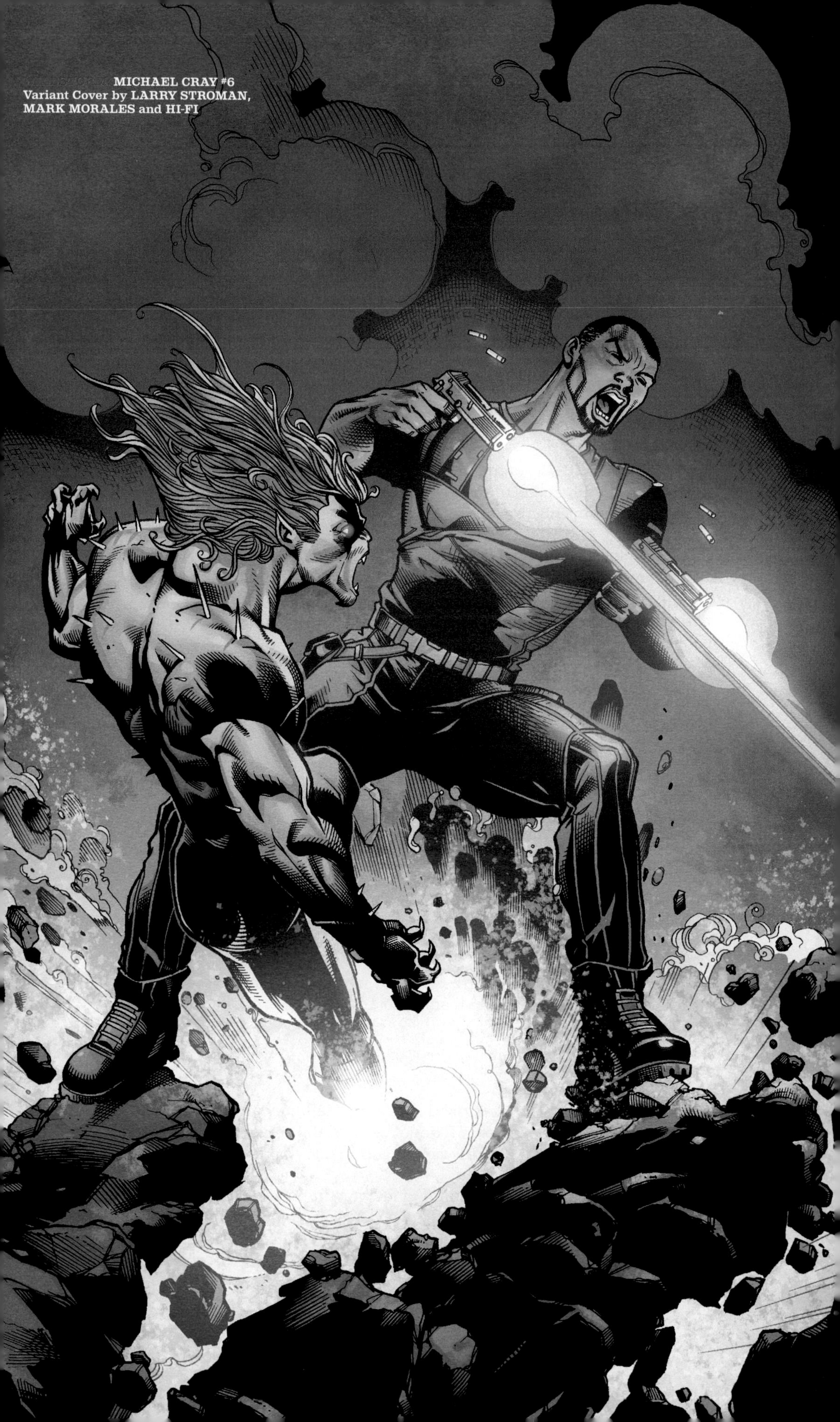

MICHAEL CRAY Series Proposal
By **Warren Ellis**

The best killer in the world has a brain tumour that's killing him. Except it's actually an alien organ growing in his head that is turning him into death. There. That's your first year of books. Have fun.

<u>WAIT, WHAT?</u>

Why MICHAEL CRAY as the first spin-off book? The answer relates both to comics and the needs of the WildStorm revival and the nature of DC Entertainment in this present time.

The first book should be a single-character book, to distinguish it from the multi-character, exploded structure of THE WILD STORM. It should be a straight-up action book, uncomplicated by continuity or the needs of superhero fiction. And, frankly, it should be something that'd make a good elevated-genre cable TV show. It's an emotionally and conceptually rich story about murdering a bunch of people. [And too ambiguous in its morality for network.]

ZEALOT was another option for this slot, but CRAY is the better fit: it's more direct, more focused, simpler in backstory and structure. Read issues 1-6 of THE WILD STORM now.

<u>PREMISE</u>

Is very simple. Michael Cray moves to the Bay Area to begin work for EPS, run by Christine Trelane, who is clearly the front for a mysterious benefactor. Cray's job is to eliminate high-value targets representing a clear and present danger to the future of the planet, in America. Because he's the best killer in the world, and has been killing people for years and years without detection. But he has a code. They don't die until he's sure they need to.

But. He's dying. He has an aggressive and inoperable brain tumour. He's trying to do good works and train up a small team to replace him and work by his code after he dies.

The problem: it's not a tumour.

At some point, Cray got parasitized by a bacterial mechanism that is building an alien organ inside his brain. The "effects" of the tumour are the mechanism reorganizing his brain to fit this new organ inside his head.

In issues 7-12, we get to understand what we glimpsed in THE WILD STORM, and what we will have continued to see without explanation in issues 1-6 here. The organ kills. The organ generates a field around Cray that simply shreds anything it encounters. He is becoming death.

SEASON 1 STRUCTURE

I don't particularly want to sit on the neck of you, the incoming writer. But I have a stunt I want to try. And since this is the bit I was hired for, you have to suffer. Sorry. The intent is to move at pulp-fiction speeds and embrace pulp-fiction formal structures while creating space for you to do something special with character and set pieces.

MICHAEL CRAY has a structure for issues 1-6. Each story has five parts:

1. Michael Cray is tasked with a kill.
2. We learn something new about Michael Cray's condition.
3. We learn about or spend time with Michael Cray's target.
4. Michael Cray prepares for the kill.
5. Michael Cray kills the victim.

Only THREE of these pieces appear per issue. The structure of the book is therefore:

ISSUE 1: 1 2 3
ISSUE 2: 4 5 1
ISSUE 3: 2 3 4
ISSUE 4: 5 1 2
ISSUE 5: 3 4 5

If we are, however, aiming for six-issue collections, then the sixth issue is always an OUTLIER, a single issue with a different structure. You find this sort of thing in TV shows like *House, M.D.*, which always had an episode, usually towards the end of a season, that threw out the usual individual episode structure and did something completely different. That's what we do here—the sixth issue is always random. Given the structure above, every issue is built differently, with its own kind of cliffhanger, and the sixth issue breaks the structure entirely.

Each of those pieces is charged with either plot or emotional interiority—therefore, each piece can serve as a cliffhanger if it lands at the end of an issue.

Focusing on three pieces per issue lets us do a number of things. We get to spend time with the villain of the piece, giving them some texture and a real sense of who they are and why they probably need to die. Or not! We advance the overarching plot—Cray's tumour—in careful steps that also let us spend some time with Cray in a non-action setting. Hit the three steps of an issue's structure and the reader has a reason to come back and gets told a significant chunk of story every time.

SEASON ONE [issues 1-6]: The best killer in the world has a brain tumour that's killing him.

THE VILLAINS/VICTIMS

The victims: are all DCU characters. Taking advantage of our parallel world situation, we use DC characters with a degree of name recognition as the targets. A corrupt corporate oligarch named Oliver Queen, perhaps, or a mad genius CSI called Barry Allen. You get the idea. All Michael Cray targets are DCU parallel-world alternates. [This, obviously, would not transfer to television—it's just an extra hook for the comic, not central to the value of the piece for adaptation.]

The assassinations: are the ones Cray accepts. He intends to use his time left in the world to make it a better place, and he can best achieve that by murdering the people who will make the world a worse place after he's gone.

Michael Cray is a black man in his mid-thirties. As a young man, he joined the Navy to see the world, and ended up as a Navy SEAL before being sheepdipped out of the service by IO, thereby becoming an IO strike asset.

Following the events of volume 1 of THE WILD STORM, and the diagnosis of his tumour, he's been stood down by IO. Who then tried to tidy up his contract by having him killed.

He is picked up again by EXECUTIVE PROTECTION SERVICES [EPS], run by a mysterious woman called CHRISTINE TRELANE. It's a sort of SpaceX/ Tesla for geopolitical engineering—a well-funded start-up for changing the direction of the world through security provisions. And also killing people.

What he doesn't know: EPS is a terrestrial front for the secret space programme SKYWATCH. The head of Skywatch, HENRY BENDIX, has decided they need to take more of a role in managing the homeworld. Which means killing some motherfuckers. Which means, for as long as Michael Cray is functional, EPS would like his help in making the world a better place. By killing some motherfuckers.

Dad: His father, **George Cray**, was a Black Panther circa 1970, and fathered Michael late in life, after a prison stretch. He's still alive, around 70. His mother is dead. George still fucks around like he's Picasso and combines art practice with political activism in the Bay. George was kind of horrified that Mike went into the Navy. George is a bohemian anti-government hedonist, obviously, but, after a while, we might start to see where Mike gets some of his cold ruthlessness from. Being back in proximity—and Mike knowing he may well be dying— leads them to see each other more, and for George to become a recurring character.

Christine Trelane: Your first note here is simple and direct. She's the only white member of the supporting cast. [As opposed to the villains/targets, who obviously come and go.] Do not be fucking shy about this. I don't want to see one more white person aside from Trelane.

Trelane has an agenda. She actually works for Skywatch—she runs their ground operation, and this is a side project. Essentially, it's a cover—Skywatch, due to treaties, cannot be seen to be directly outright murdering people. It's a spook operation, trying to get at the truth of what is actually happening on Earth [and whether or not the terrestrial power, IO, is illegally behind it all] without being seen to actually police IO or take direct action on Earth.

Trelane is friendly, perhaps even flirty with Cray. They acknowledge a mutual distrust, a mutual using of each other, and a mutual need. Each of them would probably kill the other if necessary. They'd feel a little bad about it, sure.

Team: Cray chooses three people from the EPS stable of operatives to take on and train into a team. None of these people are superhumans, by the way. Neither is Cray, apart from this weird thing that is happening to him. They just all have skills.

Hector Morales: The planner. One of those freak minds that gets groomed for the intelligence community when they're still at school and then gets burned out or turned weird by twenty-five. Technical, strategic. Twitchy. Probably sees kill-box geometries in his sleep.

Victoria Ngengi: Victoria's a hitter. Ex-military, could probably kill and eat any ten guys thrown at her. Probably found herself as personal security officer to some big general before she ended up beating the shit out of him and getting discharged.

Leon Carver: Investigator—I have an idea that he's ex-Secret Service, probably did something terrible and violent to someone who deserved it and got thrown out. Chilly detective. A sense of justice. Good at reading people, tends to favour intuition over evidence.

Together, they make one Michael Cray—but a better one, a more robust unit. If and when they learn to work with Cray and with each other.

Michael Cray's deal: He doesn't make a kill unless he's emotionally and intellectually invested in the positive result of that kill. Put another way, he's only ever killed people he believed should be killed.

This is obviously kind of problematic, gameable and nuts. But this is his code, and he is convinced of its utility. Murder as a positive form of creation. With IO, he was apparently under the impression that he was killing his way to a better world. And IO gave him that latitude because he was the best. But he was essentially working alone.

Now, he has the opportunity to build a team and train them in his credo. He can have a legacy.

BARRY ALLEN
Character Sketches
By **N. Steven Harris**

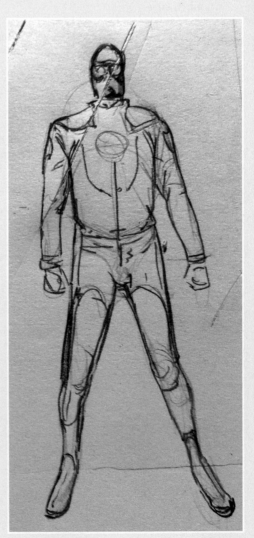